Engaging the Brain

4th Edition

Engaging the Brain

20 Unforgettable Strategies for Growing Dendrites and Accelerating Learning

4th Edition

Marcia L. Tate

CORWIN
A Sage Company

FOR INFORMATION:

Corwin

A SAGE Company

2455 Teller Road

Thousand Oaks, California 91320

(800) 233-9936

www.corwin.com

SAGE Publications Ltd.

1 Oliver's Yard

55 City Road

London EC1Y 1SP

United Kingdom

SAGE Publications India Pvt. Ltd.

Unit No 323-333, Third Floor, F-Block

International Trade Tower Nehru Place

New Delhi 110 019

India

SAGE Publications Asia-Pacific Pte. Ltd.

18 Cross Street #10-10/11/12

China Square Central

Singapore 048423

Vice President and
 Editorial Director: Monica Eckman

Senior Publisher: Jessica Allan

Senior Content
 Development Editor: Mia Rodriguez

Editorial Intern: Lex Nunez

Production Editor: Tori Mirsadjadi

Copy Editor: Michelle Ponce

Typesetter: C&M Digitals (P) Ltd.

Cover Designer: Candice Harman

Marketing Manager: Olivia Bartlett

Copyright © 2025 by Corwin Press, Inc.

All rights reserved. Except as permitted by U.S. copyright law, no part of this work may be reproduced or distributed in any form or by any means, or stored in a database or retrieval system, without permission in writing from the publisher.

When forms and sample documents appearing in this work are intended for reproduction, they will be marked as such. Reproduction of their use is authorized for educational use by educators, local school sites, and/or noncommercial or nonprofit entities that have purchased the book.

All third-party trademarks referenced or depicted herein are included solely for the purpose of illustration and are the property of their respective owners. Reference to these trademarks in no way indicates any relationship with, or endorsement by, the trademark owner.

Printed in the United States of America

ISBN 978-1-0719-3978-9

This book is printed on acid-free paper.

24 25 26 27 28 10 9 8 7 6 5 4 3 2 1

DISCLAIMER: This book may direct you to access third-party content via web links, QR codes, or other scannable technologies, which are provided for your reference by the author(s). Corwin makes no guarantee that such third-party content will be available for your use and encourages you to review the terms and conditions of such third-party content. Corwin takes no responsibility and assumes no liability for your use of any third-party content, nor does Corwin approve, sponsor, endorse, verify, or certify such third-party content.

Contents

ACKNOWLEDGMENTS	ix
ABOUT THE AUTHOR	xi
INTRODUCTION	1
SCENARIO I	1
SCENARIO II	1
BRAIN-COMPATIBLE INSTRUCTION	2
STRATEGY 1: BRAINSTORMING AND DISCUSSION	16
WHAT: DEFINING THE STRATEGY	17
WHY: THEORETICAL FRAMEWORK	18
HOW: INSTRUCTIONAL ACTIVITIES	19
ACTION PLAN	25
STRATEGY 2: DRAWING AND ARTWORK	26
WHAT: DEFINING THE STRATEGY	27
WHY: THEORETICAL FRAMEWORK	28
HOW: INSTRUCTIONAL ACTIVITIES	29
ACTION PLAN	33
STRATEGY 3: FIELD TRIPS	34
WHAT: DEFINING THE STRATEGY	35
WHY: THEORETICAL FRAMEWORK	36
HOW: INSTRUCTIONAL ACTIVITIES	37
ACTION PLAN	40

STRATEGY 4: GAMES — 42
- WHAT: DEFINING THE STRATEGY — 43
- WHY: THEORETICAL FRAMEWORK — 44
- HOW: INSTRUCTIONAL ACTIVITIES — 45
- ACTION PLAN — 52

STRATEGY 5: GRAPHIC ORGANIZERS, SEMANTIC MAPS, AND WORD WEBS — 54
- WHAT: DEFINING THE STRATEGY — 55
- WHY: THEORETICAL FRAMEWORK — 56
- HOW: INSTRUCTIONAL ACTIVITIES — 57
- ACTION PLAN — 68

STRATEGY 6: HUMOR — 70
- WHAT: DEFINING THE STRATEGY — 71
- WHY: THEORETICAL FRAMEWORK — 72
- HOW: INSTRUCTIONAL ACTIVITIES — 73
- ACTION PLAN — 78

STRATEGY 7: MANIPULATIVES, EXPERIMENTS, LABS, AND MODELS — 80
- WHAT: DEFINING THE STRATEGY — 81
- WHY: THEORETICAL FRAMEWORK — 82
- HOW: INSTRUCTIONAL ACTIVITIES — 83
- ACTION PLAN — 89

STRATEGY 8: METAPHORS, ANALOGIES, AND SIMILES — 90
- WHAT: DEFINING THE STRATEGY — 91
- WHY: THEORETICAL FRAMEWORK — 92
- HOW: INSTRUCTIONAL ACTIVITIES — 93
- ACTION PLAN — 98

STRATEGY 9: MNEMONIC DEVICES — 100
- WHAT: DEFINING THE STRATEGY — 101
- WHY: THEORETICAL FRAMEWORK — 102
- HOW: INSTRUCTIONAL ACTIVITIES — 103
- ACTION PLAN — 107

STRATEGY 10: MOVEMENT — 108
- WHAT: DEFINING THE STRATEGY — 109
- WHY: THEORETICAL FRAMEWORK — 110
- HOW: INSTRUCTIONAL ACTIVITIES — 111
- ACTION PLAN — 117

STRATEGY 11: MUSIC, RHYTHM, RHYME, AND RAP — 118
- WHAT: DEFINING THE STRATEGY — 119
- WHY: THEORETICAL FRAMEWORK — 121
- HOW: INSTRUCTIONAL ACTIVITIES — 122
- ACTION PLAN — 128

STRATEGY 12: PROJECT-BASED AND PROBLEM-BASED LEARNING — 132
- WHAT: DEFINING THE STRATEGY — 133
- WHY: THEORETICAL FRAMEWORK — 134
- HOW: INSTRUCTIONAL ACTIVITIES — 135
- ACTION PLAN — 140

STRATEGY 13: RECIPROCAL TEACHING AND COOPERATIVE LEARNING — 142
- WHAT: DEFINING THE STRATEGY — 143
- WHY: THEORETICAL FRAMEWORK — 144
- HOW: INSTRUCTIONAL ACTIVITIES — 145
- ACTION PLAN — 150

STRATEGY 14: ROLEPLAYS, DRAMA, PANTOMIMES, AND CHARADES — 152
- WHAT: DEFINING THE STRATEGY — 153
- WHY: THEORETICAL FRAMEWORK — 154
- HOW: INSTRUCTIONAL ACTIVITIES — 155
- ACTION PLAN — 159

STRATEGY 15: STORYTELLING — 160
- WHAT: DEFINING THE STRATEGY — 161
- WHY: THEORETICAL FRAMEWORK — 162
- HOW: INSTRUCTIONAL ACTIVITIES — 163
- ACTION PLAN — 168

STRATEGY 16: TECHNOLOGY — 170

- WHAT: DEFINING THE STRATEGY — 171
- WHY: THEORETICAL FRAMEWORK — 172
- HOW: INSTRUCTIONAL ACTIVITIES — 173
- ACTION PLAN — 178

STRATEGY 17: VISUALIZATION AND GUIDED IMAGERY — 180

- WHAT: DEFINING THE STRATEGY — 181
- WHY: THEORETICAL FRAMEWORK — 182
- HOW: INSTRUCTIONAL ACTIVITIES — 183
- ACTION PLAN — 187

STRATEGY 18: VISUALS — 188

- WHAT: DEFINING THE STRATEGY — 189
- WHY: THEORETICAL FRAMEWORK — 190
- HOW: INSTRUCTIONAL ACTIVITIES — 191
- ACTION PLAN — 194

STRATEGY 19: WORK STUDY AND APPRENTICESHIPS — 196

- WHAT: DEFINING THE STRATEGY — 197
- WHY: THEORETICAL FRAMEWORK — 198
- HOW: INSTRUCTIONAL ACTIVITIES — 199
- ACTION PLAN — 203

STRATEGY 20: WRITING AND JOURNALS — 204

- WHAT: DEFINING THE STRATEGY — 205
- WHY: THEORETICAL FRAMEWORK — 206
- HOW: INSTRUCTIONAL ACTIVITIES — 207
- ACTION PLAN — 212

RESOURCE A: BRAIN-COMPATIBLE LESSON PLANS — 213

RESOURCE B: GRAPHIC ORGANIZERS — 231

BIBLIOGRAPHY — 247

INDEX — 253

Acknowledgments

This book is dedicated to the countless educators who, despite an unprecedented pandemic, never stopped providing students with the exemplary instruction so necessary during the most challenging of circumstances. You continue to find ways to unwrap every student's inherent gifts and use brain-compatible strategies to engage students' brains.

I am especially grateful to Warren Phillips, distinguished Disney Teacher of the Year and USA Today Top Teacher, and Jacqueline Collins, 2021 National Business Teacher of the Year and a National Board Certified Teacher, for the activities contributed to Strategy 16: Technology.

I continue to be deeply grateful for family members and professional educators who have supported me through and assisted me with the writing of the best-selling *Worksheets Don't Grow Dendrites* series and subsequent books.

To my exceptional children—Jennifer, Jessica, and Christopher—and my nine grandchildren, as I have watched you grow and develop, I have realized that regardless of how you learn, there are brain-compatible strategies on the list of 20 that will address your learning styles and enable you, and other students just like you, to experience success.

To the associates who present for our company, *Developing Minds, Inc.*, you enable us to spread the word to more educators who would not otherwise be reached without your expertise.

To our administrative assistant, Carol Purviance, as you work with clients, your professionalism, organization, and technical expertise are obvious and help to make the company what it is.

All of you deserve my gratitude. I could not do what I do without you!

About the Author

Marcia L. Tate is the former executive director of professional development for the DeKalb County Schools in Decatur, Georgia. During her 30-year career with the district, she has been a classroom teacher, reading specialist, language arts coordinator, and staff development executive director. Marcia was named Staff Developer of the Year for the state of Georgia, and her department was selected to receive the Exemplary Program award for the state.

Marcia is currently an educational consultant and has presented her workshops to over 500,000 administrators, teachers, parents, and community leaders from all over the United States and the world, including Australia, Canada, Egypt, Hungary, Oman, New Zealand, Singapore, and Thailand. She is the author of the best-selling series *Worksheets Don't Grow Dendrites: 20 Instructional Strategies That Engage the Brain*, as well as *"Sit & Get" Won't Grow Dendrites: 20 Professional Learning Strategies That Engage the Adult Brain* (2nd ed.), *Preparing Children for Success in School and Life: 20 Ways to Increase Children's Brain Power*, and *Formative Assessment in a Brain-Compatible Classroom*. Her more recent books, *100 Brain-Friendly Lessons for Unforgettable Teaching and Learning (K-8)* and *(9-12)*, provide teachers with exemplary lessons replete with brain-compatible strategies. Marcia's latest book, *Healthy Teachers, Happy Classrooms*, enables educators to renew the passion inherent in the profession. Participants in her workshops call them some of the best ones they have ever attended, since Marcia models the 20 strategies in her books to engage her audiences.

She received her bachelor's degree in psychology and elementary education from Spelman College in Atlanta, her master's in remedial reading from the University of Michigan in Ann Arbor, and her specialist and doctorate degrees in educational leadership from Georgia State University and Clark Atlanta University, respectively. Spelman College awarded her the Apple Award for excellence in the field of education.

Marcia is married to Tyrone Tate and is the proud mother of three children: Jennifer, Jessica, and Christopher. If she had known how wonderful it would be to be a grandmother, Marcia would have had her nine grandchildren, Christian, Aidan, Maxwell, Aaron, Roman, Shiloh, Aya, Noah, and Alyssa, before she had her children. She and her husband own the company Developing Minds, Inc. and can be contacted by calling the company at (770) 918–5039, by e-mailing her at marciata@bellsouth.net, or by visiting her website at www.developingmindsinc.com.

Introduction

SCENARIO I

Mrs. Anderson teaches American History at Washington High School. The bell rings for class to begin, and only a few students are seated and ready. The others are hanging out in the hall socializing with friends, reluctant to come into the classroom. A frustrated Mrs. Anderson goes to the door and threatens students that any time lost in instruction due to their behavior will be made up in time spent in in-school suspension. Additional students take their seats within a few minutes, the roll is checked, and the lesson begins.

Today's lesson objective will be for students to analyze the meaning, importance, and relevance of the Bill of Rights. Students are instructed to open their textbooks to page 231 and silently read from page 231 to page 235. No purpose for reading is given. During this time devoted to silent reading, individual conversations break out, and Mrs. Anderson constantly reprimands students to be quiet so that others can concentrate. After approximately 15 minutes, she requests that certain students read selected passages from the text regarding the Bill of Rights. The content from these passages will be needed to answer the questions on the worksheet that follows. Students are then given the worksheet and allowed an additional twenty minutes to respond to the following:

- Write down a couple of sentences describing the Bill of Rights.
- Summarize the main idea of each amendment in a sentence or two.

SCENARIO II

Mr. Copeland teaches American History at McNair High School. He is standing at the door greeting each student as they enter his doorway. He refers to them as Mr and Ms. and calls them by their last name. The songs *Times, They Are a-Changing* by Bob Dylan and *Changes* by David Bowie are softly playing. From day one, Mr. Copeland taught them that if he could hear their voices over the music as they talked, then they were talking too loudly. Students are taught to look on the board for a riddle to be solved. Today's riddle is as follows: *Why was the broom late for school? Answer: It overswept.*

Mr. Copeland begins a whole class discussion regarding the specific protections for individuals that apply to students and those that apply to teachers.

They then discuss the limits that are placed on the authority of students and those of teachers. This leads to an introduction to the Bill of Rights.

Mr. Copeland has set up six learning stations. The class will be divided into six groups and will rotate through each station every few minutes. During their time in the learning station, they will have a copy of the Bill of Rights to refer to and will be asked to complete a graphic organizer with their group. Each station addresses a different amendment and has a different assignment. For example, the assignment for the Seventh Amendment is to explain the importance of having the right to a trial by jury. Following the station rotation, students work with their groups to either create a picture or diagram as a visual aid for teaching an amendment to the class or design a skit depicting an amendment being violated.

BRAIN-COMPATIBLE INSTRUCTION

The world has just fallen prey to an unexpected pandemic, and school systems worldwide have suffered severe consequences. The face-to-face teacher and student interactions that customarily occurred during instruction prior to COVID-19 were replaced with virtual offerings. In many cases where parents were not available to ensure that students were online, there were no guarantees that students were even paying attention. As things began to improve and a modicum of students returned to the schoolhouse, some teachers were challenged to offer a hybrid model where they were simultaneously teaching those students who sat in front of them in the classroom and the ones whose parents insisted that they remain at a distance. As a result, educators have been telling me that students have fallen behind, have experienced gaps in their learning, and need to make up ground as quickly as possible. It stands to reason that the best way to expedite learning would be to teach students' brains in ways that their brains learn best.

Thousands of years of history support one major concept. When students actively engage in experiences with content, they stand a much better chance of learning and remembering what we want them to know. Yet, with increased emphasis on *high-stakes testing*, teachers are still apt to spend the majority of time using worksheets and lectures to teach lower-level concepts that traditional methods can best assess.

Let's explore why brain research tells us that lectures and worksheets may not be the best way to accelerate learning for most students.

MEMORY PATHWAYS

There are two major memory pathways in the brain, as depicted in the graphic organizer below. One is called *Explicit Memory,* and the other is called *Implicit Memory.* For most people, *Explicit Memory* tends to be weak and more short term, while *Implicit Memory* tends to be stronger and more long term. An understanding of the function of these pathways provides justification as to how we ought to teach if learning is to be accelerated.

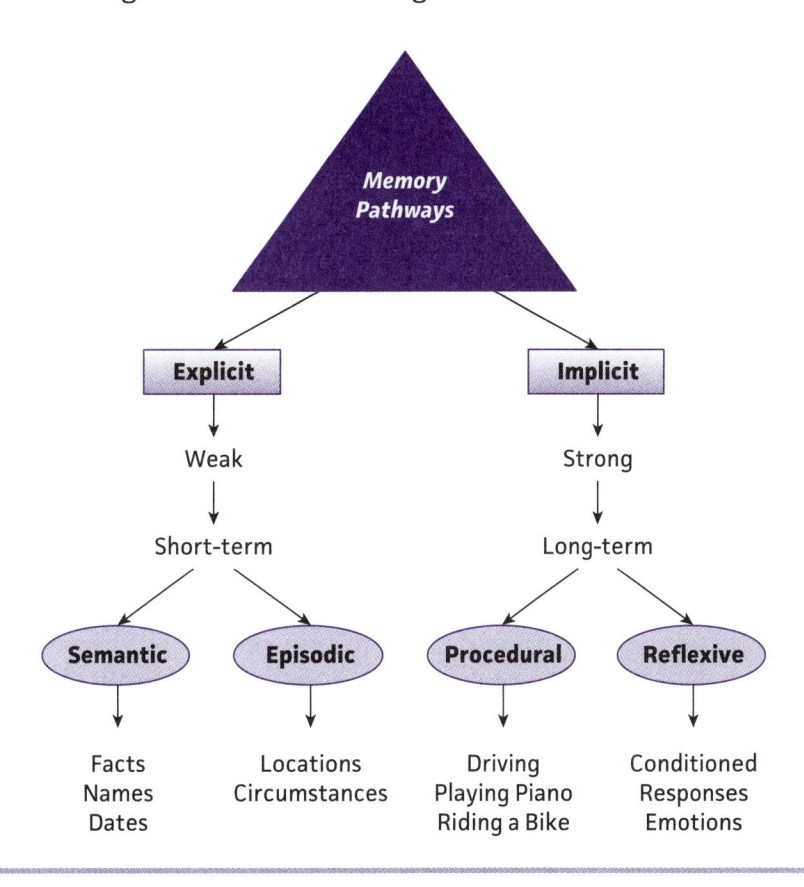

```
                    Memory
                    Pathways
                   /        \
              Explicit      Implicit
                 |             |
               Weak          Strong
                 |             |
            Short-term     Long-term
              /    \         /    \
       Semantic  Episodic  Procedural  Reflexive
          |         |          |          |
        Facts    Locations   Driving   Conditioned
        Names  Circumstances Playing Piano Responses
        Dates              Riding a Bike  Emotions
```

SEMANTIC MEMORY

One of the explicit memory pathways in the human brain is called *semantic memory*. It involves our capacity to recall words, facts, names, concepts, or numbers and is an essential part of understanding language. Without semantic memory, we would have trouble communicating since we would be unable to recall the names of everyday objects. Here is the problem! While the majority of content taught in traditional classrooms is explicit, that content is being forced into a weak semantic container. This is why students can cram for an exam and not remember much of anything once the exam has ended. It is also the reason that I never spend time in my workshops having participants stand and say their names to the entire class. If participants did not know the name of each participant before they got up, they would not know the names after they had sat down.

EPISODIC MEMORY

Another explicit memory system is *episodic memory*, which involves our conscious recollection of the condition, time, and place of previous experiences. Since it is still a weak memory system, it becomes the reason why the police do not consider eyewitness testimony as reliable.

Let me relate a true story to illustrate the difference between episodic and semantic memory and how they work together. Many years ago, I was instructing a group of high school teachers in Wiley, Texas. Since they would be with me for five days, I wanted a way to remember their names so that I could call them by name from day one. One teacher had a long, blonde ponytail extending from the top of her head. She stood and told me that her name was Jeannie. She then folded her arms and bowed her head the way Barbara Eden used to do whenever she granted a wish in the television show *I Dream of Jeannie*. I know that many of you will not even remember that show. It was easy for me to call her by name on that first day since I loved the show, and her connection to it helped to embed her name into my semantic memory.

On the second day, when class began, I could not find Jeannie. You see, she had taken down her ponytail, changed her clothes, and her location in the classroom. In other words, she had messed up my episodic memory. When I remembered her name, I also remembered her ponytail, what she wore, and where she sat in class. The two memory systems had worked together. Now, they were not in sync!

PROCEDURAL MEMORY

Good news! There is a stronger memory system in the brain called implicit memory; one of the types of this memory system is procedural. Procedural is a type of long-term memory involved when performing various actions or skills. In other words, it is the memory of how to put on our shoes, ride a bike, play the piano, or cook without a recipe. Therefore, anytime we can engage students in performing an action or skill, we stand a better chance of ensuring that the content ends up in long-term memory. One teacher related to me that her mother has dementia and can no longer recall the names of her children and grandchildren, which would be in her semantic memory. Since her mother is a pianist, she can still go to the piano and play the songs she has always played. Her ability to play is procedural.

REFLEXIVE MEMORY

A final type of memory system is called reflexive. This is one's memory for a conditioned response or an emotional connection to the content. For example, how many times would a person have to touch a hot stove before it dawns on their brain that it is hot? Usually, only once! The pain experienced would be a constant reminder not to touch the stove again.

Emotional connections also tend to correlate with long-term memories. Consider an emotional event that has happened in the United States, such as the Challenger disaster during which we lost seven astronauts, including teacher Christa McAuliffe; the tragic death of Martin Luther King Jr. or Princess Diana; or the attack by al-Qaeda on the Twin Towers on September 11, 2001. Even though these events are obviously negative, there is research to support that unless a student has a positive emotional connection either to the teacher or to the content itself, there is a real chance that the content may not be remembered. For example, if a student is in a teacher's classroom he cannot stand, he will not forget the experience of being in that teacher's room but will not be able to recall much of the content.

If teachers truly want to accelerate learning, they will find ways to place as much content as possible into the implicit memory systems of students so that they can recall content, not just for standardized, criterion-referenced, or teacher-made tests. However, they will still remember content long after the tests have ended.

BRAIN-COMPATIBLE INSTRUCTIONAL STRATEGIES

Learning-style theorists (Gardner, 1983; Marzano, 2007; Sternberg & Grigorenko, 2000) and educational consultants (Jensen, 2008, 2022; Sousa, 2011, 2022; Willis, 2006, 2007) have concluded that there are some instructional strategies that, by their very nature, result in long-term retention. Those strategies are addressed in numerous books about the brain but were not previously delineated in any one text. Now they are, and this is the text!

For more than 30 years, I have been studying the incredible functions of brain cells. Through my extensive reading, participation in workshops and courses with experts on the topic, and my observations of best practices in classrooms throughout the world, I have synthesized these instructional strategies into 20 methods for delivering instruction and accelerating learning. These strategies work for the three following reasons:

1. They increase academic achievement for *all* of the following students: students who are in elementary, middle, high school, and college; students who are in gifted classes, regular education classes, and special education classes; students for whom English is a second language; and students who are learning in all content areas across the curriculum.

2. They decrease behavior problems by minimizing the boredom factor in class since students are actively engaged and increasing the confidence factor in those students who would use their inadequacy as a cause for misbehavior.

3. They make teaching and learning fun for all grade levels so that even calculus students are just as excited about learning as kindergarten students on the first day of school.

The 20 strategies are as follows:

1. Brainstorming and discussion
2. Drawing and artwork
3. Field trips
4. Games

5. Graphic organizers, semantic maps, and word webs
6. Humor
7. Manipulatives, experiments, labs, and models
8. Metaphors, analogies, and similes
9. Mnemonic devices
10. Movement
11. Music, rhythm, rhyme, and rap
12. Project-based and problem-based learning
13. Reciprocal teaching and cooperative learning
14. Roleplays, drama, pantomimes, and charades
15. Storytelling
16. Technology
17. Visualization and guided imagery
18. Visuals
19. Work study and apprenticeships
20. Writing and journals

As millions of dollars are being spent in an effort to find cures for brain abnormalities such as Alzheimer's disease, dementia, and Parkinson's disease, more and more information is being gleaned about the brain. Teachers should be the first to avail themselves of this information since they are teaching students' brains every day. In fact, I tell teachers that the next time they complete a resumé, they need to include that they are not only *teachers but also gardeners*—better known as *dendrite growers*—because every time students learn something new in their classrooms, they grow a new brain cell, called a dendrite.

Refer to Table 0.1 for a correlation of these 20 strategies to Howard Gardner's Theory of Multiple Intelligences as well as to the four major learning modalities: (1) visual, (2) auditory, (3) kinesthetic, and (4) tactile. Each lesson incorporating multiple modalities increases students' test scores and stands a better chance of being remembered by students long after the teacher-made, criterion-referenced, or standardized tests are over. After all, isn't that why we teach—long-term retention?

The book you are about to read attempts to accomplish five major objectives:

1. Delineate the characteristics of a classroom that takes advantage of the way students' brains learn best

2. Review more than 200 pieces of research regarding the 20 brain-compatible strategies, as well as best practices in instruction regardless of the grade level or content area

3. Supply more than 200 examples of the application of the 20 strategies for teaching objectives at a variety of grade levels and in multiple cross-curricular areas

4. Provide time and space at the end of each chapter for the reader to reflect on specific Action Plans as they enable the reader to accelerate learning

5. Demonstrate how to plan and deliver unforgettable lessons by asking the five questions on the lesson plan template in the book's Resource section

The brain-compatible activities in each chapter are only samples of lessons that can be created when the strategies are incorporated from kindergarten to calculus. They are intended to get the reader's brain cells going as they think up a multitude of additional ways to deliver effective instruction to their students.

When you really examine the list of 20, you will find that they are used most frequently in the primary grades. It is when the strategies begin to disappear from the repertoire of teachers that students' academic achievement, confidence, and love for school also diminish. You may remember the book *Everything I Needed to Know I Learned in Kindergarten*. This also applies to teaching. If every teacher would teach the way a kindergarten teacher teaches, most students would learn. The content should change, but the way of delivering that content should not.

What if every teacher used the 20 strategies, including art, drama, music, and storytelling, to teach the academic subject areas of English, mathematics, science, and social studies? Would we not see gaps being closed, learning accelerated, and more students graduating at the end of high school? After all, *if students don't learn the way we teach them, then we must teach them the way they learn*. Here's an analogy. When you go fishing, do you use bait you like or bait the fish likes? There are 20 instructional strategies that brain research shows that your students will like and that you should be using as bait.

This book is the foundational text in a series of multiple cross-curricular bestsellers about *growing dendrites*. The books are as follows:

- *Worksheets Don't Grow Dendrites: 20 Instructional Strategies That Engage the Brain*, Third Edition

- *"Sit & Get" Won't Grow Dendrites: 20 Professional Learning Strategies That Engage the Adult Brain*, Second Edition

- *Reading and Language Arts Worksheets Don't Grow Dendrites: 20 Literacy Strategies That Engage the Brain*, Second Edition

- *Shouting Won't Grow Dendrites: 20 Techniques to Detour Around the Danger Zones*, Second Edition

- *Mathematics Worksheets Don't Grow Dendrites: 20 Numeracy Strategies That Engage the Brain, PreK–8*
- *Science Worksheets Don't Grow Dendrites: 20 Instructional Strategies That Engage the Brain*
- *Social Studies Worksheets Don't Grow Dendrites: 20 Instructional Strategies That Engage the Brain*

Two more recent books contain 100 lessons written by exemplary content specialists from across the country using the lesson plan template in this book's Resource section. Both books below contain 25 lessons in each of the four content areas of language arts/English, mathematics, science, and social studies.

- *100 Brain-Friendly Lessons for Unforgettable Teaching and Learning (K–8)*
- *100 Brain-Friendly Lessons for Unforgettable Teaching and Learning (9–12)*

The activities outlined in each chapter of this text are designed to be starting points for planning lessons intended to be brain compatible. They are in no way meant to be an exhaustive list of possibilities. The advantage of having activities that range from elementary through high school in the same book is that the reader can easily select activities that will meet the needs of students performing below, on, and above grade level and can, therefore, more easily differentiate instruction. You will also find that an activity designated for a specific grade range can be taken as is or easily adapted to fit the grade level the reader is teaching. Therefore, as you peruse this text, examine not only those activities in each content area that are age- or grade-appropriate but also look for ones at other grade levels that can easily meet your needs once you change the conceptual level of the material.

The Action Plan page at the end of each chapter enables readers to reflect on the activities described in the chapter that incorporate the strategy. Teachers can indicate which ones they are already using and commit to add others to their repertoire. The lesson planning section helps the reader synthesize the process of planning unforgettable lessons by asking and answering the five essential questions on the template.

CHARACTERISTICS OF A BRAIN-COMPATIBLE ENVIRONMENT

Teachers who use the brain-compatible instructional strategies addressed in the following chapters for lesson design and delivery deserve to have a classroom environment that is, likewise, brain compatible. Teachers who cannot create these environments for their students have students who may not be excelling at optimal levels. My observations in hundreds of classrooms and knowledge of brain-compatible instruction tell me that there are 10 characteristics of classrooms where students tend to excel. After you peruse the 10, your project will be to identify those characteristics that you are already very comfortable implementing and to identify two that you will work on for the next 21 days. Why 21 days? That is the minimum of how long it will take to make those two characteristics a habit in your daily instruction. You see, I have a theory. No matter how wonderful you are, you should be making specific plans to improve!

(1) A POSITIVE ENVIRONMENT

When you enter a brain-compatible classroom, you know it immediately! The teacher is standing at the door smiling, greeting students, asking them about their weekends or evenings, and complimenting them on some positive aspects of their lives. Did you know that the word *SMILE* is a mnemonic device that stands for *Show Me I'm Loved Everyday*? Students are not loitering in the hall but are entering class, excited about what they can expect in the day's lesson. As the class proceeds, the room has an obvious air of enthusiasm and optimism. The teacher is passionate about the subject matter, and students support each other in the learning and do not put one another down, as I see in so many classrooms. Students are confident that they can be successful and know that if a concept is not understood, the teacher and peers are there to assist and support them. Consult Strategy 4: Games and Strategy 6: Humor for specific activities to help create a positive environment.

(2) VISUALS

We live in a very visual world! With computers, video games, smartphones, television, and the like, students' brains absorb much information visually. At least 50% of students who walk into any classroom today will be predominately visual learners. Another 35% are likely to be kinesthetic, which is why they need to be moving, but we will discuss that under another characteristic. This means that if your primary method for delivering instruction is auditory, then *Houston, We Have a Problem!* Only 15% of the class is listening. Brain-compatible teachers accompany their lectures with images from the SMART board, video clips, virtual field trips, and so forth. They even ensure that those anchor charts and other visuals on the wall in the peripheral vision of students are content related.

Teachers often worry about taking down visuals from the walls before a test. I tell teachers, *Do not dismay!* If those visuals have been up long enough, your students can still visualize what was on the wall even if you remove them. Consult Strategy 17: Visualization and Guided Imagery and Strategy 18: Visuals for specific ways to engage the visual modalities of students.

(3) MUSIC

As students are assembling, brain-compatible teachers have soft, calming music playing, and students have learned from day one that if the teacher hears their voices over the music, they are talking too loudly! This music is used around 30% of the time but never while the teacher is delivering direct instruction. It can be distracting to many students to have music playing while your expectation is that students are giving you their undivided attention.

So when do these teachers play music? It may be when students are working together in cooperative groups, writing creatively, or solving math problems. The type of music used during these times should probably be instrumental with no lyrics, and the volume should be turned extremely low so as not to disturb students' thought processes. At other times, these teachers want high-energy, motivational music interwoven with the content or played during transition times or an engaging activity. Be sure that any music you use with students has appropriate lyrics for putting students' brains in a positive state. Consult Strategy 11: Music, Rhythm, Rhyme, and Rap for specific activities for infusing music into your classroom.

(4) RELEVANT LESSONS

What came first—school or brains? Of course, human beings had brains long before there was a formal place called school. Therefore, the purpose of the brain was never to make straight As or score high on a standardized or teacher-made test. The purpose of the brain is survival in the real world. Wouldn't it make sense that those things in real life that are crucial to man's survival are more easily remembered than those needed for tests in school?

I know that at some point in your teaching career, a student has asked you this question, *Why do we have to learn this?* When students cannot see the connection between what is being taught in school and their personal lives, they will often ask the question. Brain-compatible teachers attempt to take the objective they are teaching and relate it to students' personal lives. For example, rather than using the math problems in the book initially, these teachers create real-life problems and integrate the students' names into the problems so that they can actually see themselves solving them. Consult Strategy 12: Project-Based and Problem-Based Learning for specific activities for infusing relevant projects and problems into your instruction.

(5) RITUALS TAUGHT

A brain-compatible classroom is an active, engaging classroom but never a chaotic classroom. The teacher's routines, expectations, and procedures have been determined, taught, and practiced so often that they have become rituals that keep the classroom orderly and organized. In fact, effective classroom managers spend more time teaching those rituals than teaching their content at the beginning of the school year or term. When done well, the teacher can spend more time teaching the content for the remainder of the year.

Students must know how you expect them to begin and end class, when to talk and when to be quiet and listen, when to move and when to remain in their seats, or how to get into groups when cooperative learning is warranted. Chapter 14: Teach Your Rituals in the bestseller *Shouting Won't Grow Dendrites: 20 Techniques to Detour Around the Danger Zones* (2nd ed.) gives definitive suggestions for teaching and practicing those determined routines, expectations, and procedures.

(6) STUDENTS TALKING ABOUT CONTENT

The person doing the most talking about the content is growing the most dendrites, or brain cells, regarding the content. In many classrooms I observe in, that is the teacher. In a brain-compatible classroom, it should be the students. Making all students a part of the conversation helps ensure the content is understood and remembered. The teacher's job comes before the lesson—that of planning a lesson that can then be facilitated when it is taught. Some teachers have unrealistic expectations—that students will sit quietly for long periods and are even chastised for wanting to converse with their friends. Yet, we learn 70% to 90% of what we are capable of teaching to someone else. Strategy 1: Brainstorming and Discussion and Strategy 13: Reciprocal Teaching and Cooperative Learning, will provide teachers with multiple ways to engage students' brains as they process information.

(7) STUDENTS MOVING TO LEARN CONTENT

Students sit entirely too much! Brain-compatible teachers have students moving at certain points during the lesson, knowing that this behavior will give them some relief from sitting on the most uncomfortable piece of furniture known to man, the student desk. More importantly, movement correlates to procedural or long-term retention. Anything one learns while moving is hardwired into one of the strongest memory systems in the brain. If you have ever driven a stick shift, you will never forget how to do it—even if you have been driving an automatic for years. A Texas football coach once commented in a workshop that this research explains why football players who may not remember the content in class can remember every play on the field. Movement is probably my favorite strategy since it not only correlates with long-term retention but also makes teaching and learning so much fun! Consult Strategy 10: Movement and Strategy 14: Roleplays, Dramas, Pantomimes, and Charades for additional research to support the need to have students in motion.

(8) HIGH EXPECTATIONS

More than 50 years of research, beginning at Harvard University in the 1960s with the work of Dr. Robert Rosenthal and his famous 1968 study, *Pygmalion in the Classroom* with Lenore Jacobson, point to the fact that one gets what one expects. If teachers don't expect much from their students, they will not get much from those students. If the expectations are high and teachers give students the confidence to believe they can meet them, then exceptional things can happen. Instilling confidence in students should be a major part of the equation. A sports figure with the confidence to do well in a game has a much better chance of doing well than one who doesn't have such confidence. When the confidence in a game shifts from one team to another, that concept is known as a *momentum shift* and can often determine the game's outcome. We all have seen instances where one sports team was not as skilled as another and yet beat the more skilled team simply because they believed they could.

Brain-compatible teachers visualize every student in their class being successful! If a teacher cannot see that success, it is not likely to happen. One teacher told me that on the first day of class each year, she has every student write the word *can't* on a piece of paper. Then, she has students symbolically shred the paper and throw it in the trash. She then teaches students this motto: *Success comes in cans, not in can'ts.*

(9) HIGH CHALLENGE, LOW STRESS

A brain-compatible classroom is one where students are consistently challenged but have low levels of stress. There is no sense of accomplishment when people are successfully completing tasks that are too easy for them. If you don't believe that students want to be challenged, you have never watched them engage with video games that they have a difficult time abandoning. The creators of video games are smart and know how the brain reacts. Teachers would be wise to pay attention. Game makers have students start playing the game at an easy level where they can build up their confidence with appropriate responses. Then, as soon as the student is hooked, the difficulty level of the game increases. Students continue to play because they have the confidence that they can move to a more difficult level and still succeed. In addition, no image has ever appeared on a video game that pops up with the following message, *You have failed! Stop playing!* Students can continue perfecting their craft until they get it right. Then, they move on to the next, more difficult level. Brain-compatible classrooms are ones where students are consistently challenged, but the probability of failure is low.

(10) CONTENT TAUGHT IN CHUNKS WITH ACTIVITY

It may surprise you to know that even the adult brain can hold an average of only seven isolated bits of information simultaneously. This is why so much in the world comes in a series of seven. This concept will be addressed in more detail in the lesson planning section of this book. Effective teachers teach in small parts or chunks. They know that the brain can only hold a limited amount of information at one time, so they divide their lessons into meaningful bites or chunks and feed students one chunk at a time until the entire lesson is digested.

Here's a story to illustrate my point. I attended the wedding of one of my daughter's friends when the minister did not chunk the wedding vows appropriately. The bride and groom were expected to repeat the vows after the minister. However, the minister gave the bride too much to say in the first chunk. I turned to my husband and commented that unless the bride had memorized her vows, she would never be able to remember all she was given. Sure enough, when it was time for the bride to repeat the vows, she turned to the minister and asked, *Could you repeat that, please? I didn't get it all!* I really needed to give that minister some chunking lessons! Brain-compatible teachers divide the lesson into small parts and ensure that an activity is integrated into each part so that the brain has time to process the information contained in the chunk. Even your GPS knows that you can only hold one brief direction at a time and that you need that direction repeated if your trip is to be successful.

These are the 10 characteristics of a classroom that facilitates brain-compatible instruction. How many of them are already natural parts of your classroom? Which two will you work on for a minimum of the next 21 days?

The remainder of this book centers on delivering brain-compatible lessons within that context. Numerous teachers have told me that their instructional practice has been revolutionized since they began consciously incorporating more of the brain-compatible strategies (see Table 0.1 for a list of the 20 strategies). Turn the page and start your journey down a path that may help revolutionize your instructional practices or support the effectiveness of some of the practices you are currently using. We owe it to our students to accelerate their learning, to close gaps, and to increase academic achievement.

TABLE 0.1 • Comparison of Brain-Compatible Instructional Strategies to Learning Theory

BRAIN-COMPATIBLE STRATEGIES	MULTIPLE INTELLIGENCES	VISUAL, AUDITORY, KINESTHETIC, TACTILE (VAKT)
Brainstorming and discussion	Verbal-linguistic	Auditory
Drawing and artwork	Spatial	Kinesthetic/tactile
Field trips	Naturalist	Kinesthetic/tactile
Games	Interpersonal	Kinesthetic/tactile
Graphic organizers, semantic maps, and word webs	Logical-mathematical/spatial	Visual/tactile
Humor	Verbal-linguistic	Auditory
Manipulatives, experiments, labs, and models	Logical-mathematical	Tactile
Metaphors, analogies, and similes	Spatial	Visual/auditory
Mnemonic devices	Musical-rhythmic	Visual/auditory
Movement	Bodily-kinesthetic	Kinesthetic
Music, rhythm, rhyme, and rap	Musical-rhythmic	Auditory

(Continued)

(Continued)

BRAIN-COMPATIBLE STRATEGIES	MULTIPLE INTELLIGENCES	VISUAL, AUDITORY, KINESTHETIC, TACTILE (VAKT)
Project-based and problem-based learning	Logical-mathematical	Visual/tactile
Reciprocal teaching and cooperative learning	Verbal-linguistic	Auditory
Roleplays, drama, pantomimes, and charades	Bodily-kinesthetic	Kinesthetic
Storytelling	Verbal-linguistic	Auditory
Technology	Spatial	Visual/tactile
Visualization and guided imagery	Spatial	Visual
Visuals	Spatial	Visual
Work study and apprenticeships	Interpersonal	Kinesthetic
Writing and journals	Intrapersonal	Visual/tactile

Source: istock.com/kali9

Positive conversations trigger higher levels of a neurochemical brain cocktail consisting of dopamine, endorphins, and oxytocin (Balboa & Glaser, 2019).

STRATEGY 1

Brainstorming and Discussion

💡 WHAT: DEFINING THE STRATEGY

What is the main idea of this passage? Cite text evidence to support your answer.

What answer did you get for problem number eight? Defend your answer.

Did the science experiment support our hypothesis? Why, or why not?

Compare and contrast the American Revolution and the French Revolution.

What are the advantages and disadvantages of living in a technological society?

Participants in my workshops can be some of the chattiest people in the world. This fact is based on my over 40 years of teaching teachers and administrators. Yet, some of those same people who love to and should talk to one another in my classes will not let their students participate in that same behavior in their classrooms. Many students get in trouble for doing something that comes so naturally to the human brain—talking.

When people open their mouths to speak, they send more oxygen to the brain. If the brain is deprived of oxygen for three or more minutes, it can be declared dead. Those who were watching the Buffalo Bills football game will never forget when Damar Hamlin was knocked unconscious on the field. If medical professionals had not been close by, his brain would have suffered irreparable damage from a lack of oxygen. Fortunately, that did not happen! I have observed in some classrooms where students are breathing, but it is hard to tell. Their heads are on their desks! They are lethargic! Their brains are figuratively dead since the teacher is doing the majority of the talking.

Another benefit of talking is that it facilitates the growth of dendrites or brain cells. Having students discuss the answers to open-ended questions, express opinions, or brainstorm a variety of ideas is advantageous to the brain. According to Allen and Currie (2012), during discussion, students *can increase the amount of paper manipulated and stored into the filing cabinets of the brain, slowly forming a more complex outlook on the topic* (p. 41).

WHY: THEORETICAL FRAMEWORK

Five ways to organize discussions that literally run themselves include the following: (1) Video class discussions to ensure that you are not monopolizing the conversation; (2) Use a graphing tool (i.e., a spiderweb graph) to determine who is contributing and who is not; (3) Design a rubric to help define what a successful discussion looks like; (4) Assign students a coaching partner to track their contributions; and (5) Design good, open-ended questions that call for higher-order thinking and raise additional questions (Boryga, 2023).

Class discussions are beneficial with ESL students since they allow students to produce language in context, boost their confidence, practice specific content-area vocabulary, and enhance their critical thinking skills (Kialo Edu, 2023).

Brainstorming is one of the techniques a teacher can use to achieve positive transfer by assisting students in seeing the connection between what they already know and new learnings (Sousa, 2022).

Information is shared during conversations that trigger emotional and physical changes in the brain capable of opening one up or shutting one down (Balboa & Glaser, 2019).

Positive conversations trigger higher levels of a neurochemical brain cocktail (consisting of dopamine, endorphins, and oxytocin) that instills a sense of well-being (Balboa & Glaser, 2019).

Discussion strategies break complex concepts into digestible units, challenge students to analyze and synthesize information from a variety of perspectives, require students to participate even if only listening, engender confidence as students express their thoughts, and provide opportunities for immediate feedback (Ellis, 2023).

Having students dialogue with peers who have different perspectives is a civic engagement strategy used in social studies to help students prepare for becoming competent and responsible citizens (National Council for the Social Studies, 2010).

The quality and quantity of the questions that real-life scientists ask determine the progress of science in the real world (Berman, 2008).

> Students up to the age of 10 learn better when an academic discussion is directed by the teacher. Adolescents and adults benefit from discussions led by a cooperative group (Jensen, 2007).
>
> When a new math skill is viewed within the context of a problem, English language learners have opportunities to develop language skills through discussion (Coggins et al., 2007).
>
> The most widely known technique for stimulating creativity in the brain is probably the act of brainstorming, where all ideas are accepted, and there is a greater chance of reaching a workable solution (Gregory & Parry, 2006).
>
> Students with special needs benefit when the class works in groups of fewer than six and the teacher uses directed response questioning so that students have a chance to think aloud (Jensen, 2007).
>
> Teachers can guide students through very difficult solutions to mathematics problems by using a series of well-thought-out questions that address process rather than procedure (Posamentier & Jaye, 2006).

HOW: INSTRUCTIONAL ACTIVITIES

WHO: Elementary/Middle/High

WHEN: During a lesson

CONTENT AREA(S): Cross-curricular

- Give students a content-area question with more than one appropriate answer. Students brainstorm as many ideas as possible in a designated time while complying with the following **DOVE** guidelines:
    - *Defer* judgment when other students are contributing ideas.
    - *One* idea at a time is presented.
    - A *Variety* of ideas are encouraged.
    - *Energy* is directed to the task at hand.

WHO: Elementary/Middle/High

WHEN: Before a lesson

CONTENT AREA(S): Cross-curricular

- Stauffer's (1975) Directed Reading Thinking Activity (DR-TA) has stood the test of time with narrative and informational texts. Have students orally predict from a picture, a story title, or a chapter what the text will be about. Have them read a segment of text to confirm those predictions. Then, have them make another oral prediction from the new text they read. The sequence of predicting, validating, and predicting again continues until the end of the passage or text (Tate, 2014a).

WHO: Elementary/Middle/High

WHEN: During a lesson

CONTENT AREA(S): Cross-curricular

- Use the process of close reading described below to help students comprehend complex texts. These steps can be implemented with the whole class and may take more than one or two days to complete.
  - Following little or no prereading discussion, introduce the text to students.
  - *First Reading*—Have students read the entire text by themselves without assistance. If time is at a premium, this step can be done for homework.
  - *Second Reading*—Provide a fluent model by reading the entire text aloud. Stop periodically to discuss vocabulary, the historical or social context of the passage, or a complicated sentence structure. Do not explain the text's characters, ideas, or specific events. Have students discuss the text.
  - Formulate questions students can only answer from the text and pose them to the class. Students should not be able to rely on personal experiences to answer the questions.
  - *Third Reading*—Have students read the text and locate evidence to answer the text-dependent questions.
  - When appropriate, have students use other brain-compatible strategies, such as drawing, roleplay, or graphic organizers, to improve comprehension of the text. Subsequent chapters of this book will address these strategies.
  - Have students develop one concise sentence to answer each of the text-dependent questions.
  - Have students provide an analysis of the text orally or in writing, including text-based evidence to support their analysis (McLaughlin & Overturf, 2013).

WHO: Elementary/Middle/High

WHEN: During a lesson

CONTENT AREA(S): Cross-curricular

- When writing quality questions that can be used during discussion, Walsh and Sattes (2005) delineate the following five criteria for assessing those questions:
  - There should be a purpose in asking the question.
  - Each question should be clearly focused on the content.

- Each question should engage students at multiple cognitive levels.
- Each question should be concise and clear.
- No question should be asked merely by chance.

WHO: Elementary/Middle/High

WHEN: During or after a lesson

CONTENT AREA(S): Cross-curricular

- When asking questions in class or creating teacher-made tests, provide opportunities for all students to be successful by asking both knowledge or short-answer questions as well as those that enable students to use their reasoning, critical thinking, and creative-thinking skills. Refer to the circles in Figure 1.1 to ensure that students have opportunities to answer questions at all levels of the revised Bloom's taxonomy, particularly those above the *Remembering* level.

FIGURE 1.1 • Bloom's Taxonomy (Revised)

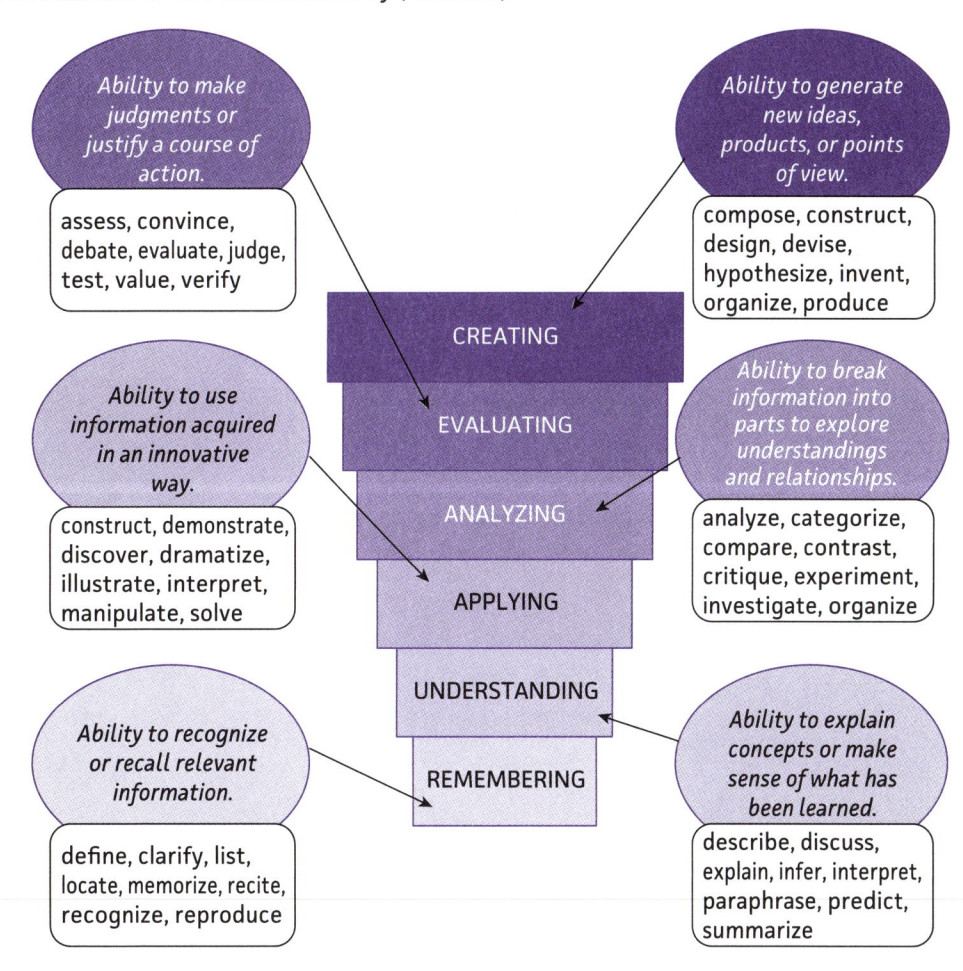

Ability to make judgments or justify a course of action.
assess, convince, debate, evaluate, judge, test, value, verify

Ability to generate new ideas, products, or points of view.
compose, construct, design, devise, hypothesize, invent, organize, produce

Ability to use information acquired in an innovative way.
construct, demonstrate, discover, dramatize, illustrate, interpret, manipulate, solve

Ability to break information into parts to explore understandings and relationships.
analyze, categorize, compare, contrast, critique, experiment, investigate, organize

Ability to recognize or recall relevant information.
define, clarify, list, locate, memorize, recite, recognize, reproduce

Ability to explain concepts or make sense of what has been learned.
describe, discuss, explain, infer, interpret, paraphrase, predict, summarize

CREATING
EVALUATING
ANALYZING
APPLYING
UNDERSTANDING
REMEMBERING

WHO:	Elementary/Middle/High
WHEN:	During or after a lesson
CONTENT AREA(S):	Cross-curricular

- A different taxonomy is the SOLO pyramid in Figure 1.2. SOLO is a mnemonic device for *Structure of Observed Learning Outcomes* since it encourages students to think about where they are currently performing with their learning and what they need to do to make progress. The five main stages are as follows:
    - **Pre-structural**—*I am not sure about . . .*
    - **Uni-structural**—*I have one relevant idea about . . .*
    - **Multi-structural**—*I have several ideas about . . .*
    - **Relational**—*I have several ideas about . . .* or *I can link them to the big picture . . .*
    - **Extended Abstract**—*I have several ideas about . . . , I can link them to the big picture, and I can look at these ideas in a new and different way.*

FIGURE 1.2 ● SOLO Taxonomy

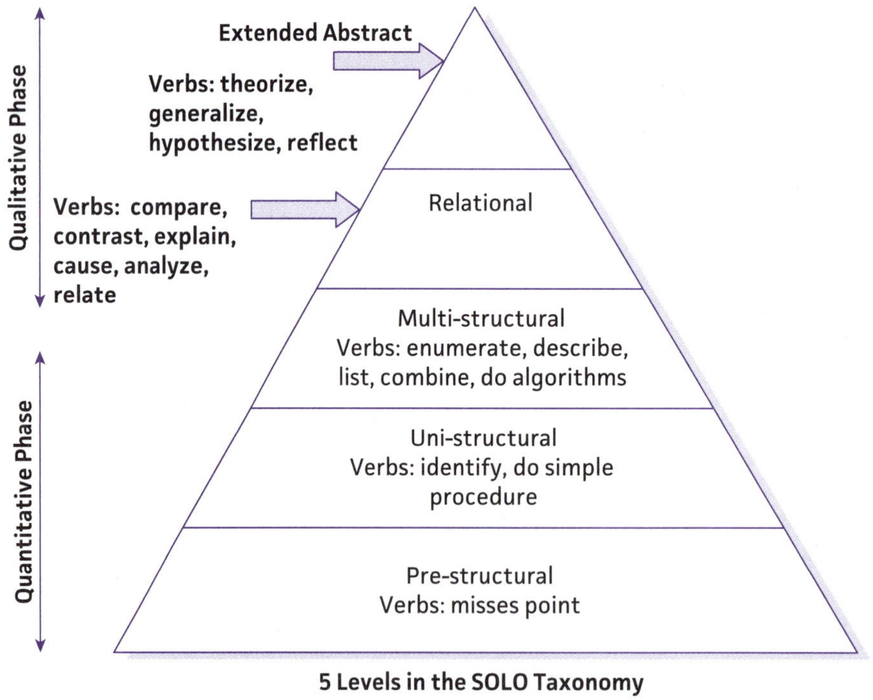

Qualitative Phase
Quantitative Phase
Extended Abstract
Verbs: theorize, generalize, hypothesize, reflect
Verbs: compare, contrast, explain, cause, analyze, relate
Relational
Multi-structural
Verbs: enumerate, describe, list, combine, do algorithms
Uni-structural
Verbs: identify, do simple procedure
Pre-structural
Verbs: misses point
5 Levels in the SOLO Taxonomy

Source: Adapted from Biggs and Collis, 1982.

WHO:	Elementary/Middle/High
WHEN:	During or after a lesson
CONTENT AREA(S):	Cross-curricular

- During cooperative group discussions or as students create original questions for content-area assessments following a unit of study, have them use the verbs in Figure 1.1. These verbs will help to ensure that questions representing various levels of thought are created.

WHO: Elementary/Middle/High

WHEN: During or after a lesson

CONTENT AREA(S): Cross-curricular

- According to Bellanca et al. (2012), there are seven rigorous proficiencies in the area of thinking that students need to master. Each of the proficiencies has three explicit-thinking skills that can be taught from kindergarten through Grade 12 and across all curricular areas. They are as follows:
  - **Critical Thinking**—Analyze, Evaluate, Problem Solve
  - **Creative Thinking**—Generate, Associate, Hypothesize
  - **Complex Thinking**—Clarify, Interpret, Determine
  - **Comprehensive Thinking**—Understand, Infer, Compare
  - **Collaborative Thinking**—Explain, Develop, Decide
  - **Communicative Thinking**—Reason, Connect, Represent
  - **Cognitive Transfer of Thinking**—Synthesize, Generalize, Apply

WHO: Elementary/Middle/High

WHEN: During a lesson

CONTENT AREA(S): Cross-curricular

- Have students work with peers in *families* of four to six. During the lesson, stop periodically and have families discuss answers to questions related to what is being taught. For example, in math class, students could compare their answers to the homework assignment, and when answers differ, they could engage in a discussion to reach a consensus on the correct answer. Have students stay together with their families long enough to build relationships and then change the composition of the families.

WHO: Elementary/Middle/High

WHEN: During a lesson

CONTENT AREA(S): Cross-curricular

- During discussions, sentence starters similar to the ones listed below are particularly effective for English language learners because they enable all students to take an active part (Coggins et al., 2007):
  - I realize that . . .
  - I agree with _____ that _____.

- o I would like to add to _____'s idea.
- o I don't understand what _____ meant when she said _____.

WHO: Elementary/Middle/High

WHEN: During a lesson

CONTENT AREA(S): Cross-curricular

- Use the **think, pair, share** technique with students. Pose a question or discussion topic to the class. Have them *think* of an individual answer. Then, have them *pair* with a peer and *share* their answer. Then, call on both volunteers and nonvolunteers to respond to the entire class. Always allow students to debrief with a peer before calling on them as a nonvolunteer.

WHO: Elementary/Middle/High

WHEN: During a lesson

CONTENT AREA(S): Cross-curricular

- Present a controversial issue to the class, such as, *Are we controlling technology, or is technology controlling us?* Divide the class in half, and have them research and prepare a debate for one side of the issue or another. Then, role-play the debate by having students take turns serving on opposing teams and orally presenting their arguments to the class. You can judge which side was more convincing at the culmination of the debate.

WHO: Middle/High

WHEN: During or after a lesson

CONTENT AREA(S): Cross-curricular

- Have students participate in a *Socratic Seminar*. Arrange the class so that students are sitting in two concentric circles. The inner circle speaks first and is given 15 minutes to discuss a couple of analysis questions regarding content previously read. Students in the outer circle are asked to listen carefully and record their thoughts or feedback in a shared Google doc. Then, the roles are reversed, and the protocol is repeated (Tate, 2020a).

Action Plan for Incorporating BRAINSTORMING and DISCUSSION

WHAT ARE MY PLANS FOR INCORPORATING MORE *BRAINSTORMING* AND *DISCUSSION* INTO MY LESSONS TO ACCELERATE LEARNING?

RECOMMENDATIONS	ALREADY DOING	PLANNING TO DO
Have students brainstorm ideas according to *DOVE* guidelines.		
Use the *Directed Reading Thinking* activity to assist students in predicting what the text will be about.		
Engage students in the process of *close reading* to comprehend text.		
Use the Walsh and Sattes criteria for assessing your discussion questions.		
Ask discussion questions at all levels of *Bloom's* taxonomy.		
Use the *SOLO* taxonomy to assist students in evaluating their progress.		
Have students use the verbs in *Bloom's* taxonomy to create original questions.		
Engage students in the seven rigorous proficiencies for thinking.		
During a lesson, stop and have students discuss an answer to a question with their peers or families.		
During discussions, incorporate sentence starters to enable all students to participate.		
Have students use the *think, pair, share* technique with a partner.		
Have students debate a controversial issue.		
Have students participate in a *Socratic Seminar*.		
Goals and Notes:		

Source: istock.com/SDI Productions

Drawing simultaneously taps into the linguistic, kinesthetic, and visual areas of the brain (Fernandes et al., 2018).

STRATEGY 2

Drawing and Artwork

💡 WHAT: DEFINING THE STRATEGY

Most little children love to draw. My seven-year-old granddaughter, Aya, is no exception. In fact, for Christmas, she only wanted Santa to bring her an art kit replete with markers, colored pencils, and paints to make her creative drawings beautiful. Yet, when I teach and tell my adult participants that we are getting ready to draw, you should hear the groans and negative comments. *Draw! Are you kidding? I can't draw!* In every instance, once they find out what they are to draw, they all do quite well! What happens to our belief in our ability to create artistic exploits from childhood to adulthood? I guess it is called *life* and an inability to retain the confidence we once enjoyed regarding our artistic pursuits.

A person's ability to draw and design serves them well in the real world. Artists, architects, and interior designers are paid well to use their unique skills to transform the visual-spatial world around them. Yet, in traditional classrooms, these talents are often perceived as interfering with instruction. I have seen students engaged in off-task behavior, drawing imaginative cars, tennis shoes, superheroes, or celebrities of far greater interest than the boring lessons being taught in the front of the room.

Drawing, a fundamental form of visual expression, is a cross-curricular strategy that would serve many students well in comprehending and retaining content. For more than 90 years, researchers (Dewey, 1934; Fraser, 2013; Prystay, 2004) have written about the positive relationship between thinking in art and thinking across the curriculum. Yet, when school budgets become tight, the art program is one of the first thought to be expendable. Educators need to think again! Why? Read on!

WHY: THEORETICAL FRAMEWORK

Drawing improves hand-eye coordination, boosts our ability to solve problems, increases the brain's ability to increase attention span while focusing on a single task, and helps students understand the content areas of writing and math (Okuha, 2023).

According to the American Art Therapy Association, art therapy can help children share their feelings without words and can be very helpful when working with students who use nonverbal communication, students with autism spectrum disorder, or students with attention deficit disorder (Mayo Clinic Press Editors, 2023).

Some research-based benefits of drawing include the following: (1) lowering cortisol, or stress, levels in the brain; (2) increasing self-esteem; (3) signaling the brain to increase blood flow toward the prefrontal cortex; (4) sharpening focus and enhancing memory; and (5) increasing visual-spatial thinking (Gaviola, 2022).

Drawing simultaneously taps into the linguistic, kinesthetic, and visual areas of the brain enabling students to process information in three different ways (Fernandes et al., 2018).

Painting and drawing promote a child's cognitive development and coordination and fine motor skills, as well as assist in developing their personality, creativity, and emotions (Maria, 2018).

A recent study shows that drawing is superior to reading or writing and increases recall by nearly double since a person is forced to process information visually, semantically, and kinesthetically (Terada, 2019).

The visual imagery children acquire when drawing is crucial for helping them to understand other curricular subjects such as math and geography (Fraser, 2013).

Putting ideas on paper through diagrams and sketches helps external memory and lessens the burden experienced when problem solving or remembering ideas (Busche, 2013).

Drawing a nonlinguistic representation or image during instruction is a literacy strategy that can enable students to understand written sources (National Council for the Social Studies, 2010).

When useful, teachers should encourage students to draw pictures in mathematics, which can help them gain more insight by representing abstract concepts graphically (Posamentier & Jaye, 2006).

"If a picture is worth a thousand words, perhaps drawing and visualizing can help science students enhance their learning potential" (National Science Teachers Association [NSTA], 2006, p. 20).

Math books in Singapore teach students to draw models in an effort to visualize math problems prior to solving them (Prystay, 2004).

Different areas of the brain, including the amygdala and the thalamus, are activated when people are involved in art activities (Jensen, 2001).

HOW: INSTRUCTIONAL ACTIVITIES

WHO: Elementary/Middle/High

WHEN: During or after a lesson

CONTENT AREA(S): Cross-curricular

- Allow students to create a personal Pictionary by illustrating assigned content-area vocabulary words. Each page of the Pictionary consists of an assigned word written in color, a drawing that depicts the meaning of the word, and an original sentence using the word in the appropriate context. For example, in science, students could draw and describe the following forms of mechanical weathering: frost weathering, exfoliation, thermal expansion, crystal growth, tree roots, and abrasion.

WHO: Elementary/Middle/High

WHEN: After a lesson

CONTENT AREA(S): Cross-curricular

- To reinforce the concept of main idea or theme, have students design a book jacket or cover that depicts their understanding of the major idea of a book or story previously read. For example, following the teaching of the significance of Martin Luther King Jr. Day, have students create a book about the life of Dr. Martin Luther King Jr.

WHO: Elementary/Middle/High

WHEN: During or after a lesson

CONTENT AREA(S): Cross-curricular

- Have students design a poster that illustrates the major details of a specific concept or unit of study. For example, in science, students could draw the *wee beasties* (microorganisms) they find when looking through a projecting microscope. In social studies, students could draw a picture depicting a particular location's climate, topography, and natural resources.

WHO: Elementary/Middle/High

WHEN: During a lesson

CONTENT AREA(S): Language Arts/ Social Studies

- Provide a sheet of 8 x 10 construction paper folded into thirds. Once students have selected a city of interest, have them use the information from the graphic organizer to create a brochure. Provide colored markers and pencils for students to create vivid illustrations. The brochure should be created according to the following guidelines:

Outer Flap—Title, illustration, and student's name

Inner Left Flap—Introduction to the brochure

Middle—Fact, three supporting details, illustration

Right—Fact, three supporting details, illustration

Back Right—Fact, supporting details, illustration

Back Middle—References

Back Right—Illustration of the outline of the city

WHO:	Elementary/Middle/High
WHEN:	During a lesson
CONTENT AREA(S):	Social Studies

- Have students select a particular culture or social group and make a collage, either by drawing or by collecting pictures, of the culture's commonly held values, beliefs, traditions, and behaviors. As students display their collages, assist them in comparing cultures and determining similarities and differences (Tate, 2012, p. 26).

WHO:	Elementary/Middle/High
WHEN:	During a lesson
CONTENT AREA(S):	Mathematics

- Give students a math word problem to read, and then have them draw a series of pictures illustrating their understanding of what is happening in each step of the problem. Have them use the pictures to assist them in writing the numerical symbols for the word problem. For example, using a straightedge and a compass, students could draw three equilateral triangles where the first and second triangles share a common side and the second and third triangles share a common side. Students could write the precise list of steps required to accomplish this construction in their journals.

WHO:	Elementary/Middle/High
WHEN:	After a lesson
CONTENT AREA(S):	Science

- Have students draw and label the particular parts or processes of the human body, that is, the heart, lungs, digestive process, and so forth. Have students work in groups and use modeling clay to identify, create, and label essential parts of the human heart. Follow with a discussion on how the heart pumps blood throughout the body.

WHO: Elementary/Middle/High

WHEN: After a lesson

CONTENT AREA(S): Social Studies

- When students come into class, have a piece of butcher paper on one wall and markers available. Tell students that they will design a class mural today based on details they remember from yesterday's class, such as one thing they remember about the Harlem Renaissance. Have them draw on their spot on the mural and be prepared to explain to the class what they drew and why. Then, allow students to view one another's pictures, which should help them recall information.

WHO: Elementary/Middle/High

WHEN: After a lesson

CONTENT AREA(S): Science

- On a single sheet of paper, have students create a foldable booklet. An example of such a booklet can be seen at www.pocketmod.com. On the booklet's pages, have students describe and draw (in rank order) the following: electron, proton, neutron, nucleus, atom, and molecule. This activity will rank order by size and reinforce structure at the nanoscale (Tate & Phillips, 2011).

WHO: Elementary/Middle/High

WHEN: After a lesson

CONTENT AREA(S): Mathematics

- Have students make drawings that illustrate mathematical terms that have already been taught. These could include such terms as fractions, decimals, perpendicular lines, parallel lines, isosceles triangle, rhombus, radius, chord, and so forth.

WHO: Elementary/Middle/High

WHEN: During a lesson

CONTENT AREA(S): Music

- Give students paper with the bass and treble clef lines and spaces already drawn in. Have them draw in the notes to represent a simple or complicated piece of music. Assist them in connecting the musical notation to the actual notes played on a keyboard or other musical instrument.

WHO:	Elementary/Middle/High
WHEN:	During a lesson
CONTENT AREA(S):	Social Studies

- Have students choose one of the regions of Africa or another location and create a postcard representing their selected region. Have them draw the area on the front of the postcard. On the back of the card, have them write a note to a friend or family member explaining the following: temperature, precipitation patterns, vegetation, and examples of wildlife.

WHO:	Elementary/Middle/High
WHEN:	After a lesson
CONTENT AREA(S):	Social Studies

- To assist students in recalling information regarding a person or group of people, have them draw a stick person symbol. Have them attach notes about the person or group in eight areas to the appropriate spot on the figure: ideas to the brain, hopes or vision to the eyes, words to the mouth, actions to the hands, feelings to the heart, movement to the feet, weaknesses to the Achilles tendon, and strengths to the arm muscle (Sousa, 2006).

WHO:	Elementary/Middle/High
WHEN:	During a lesson
CONTENT AREA(S):	Language Arts

- Have students create a visual representation connected to a character they selected from a previously read story. They should accompany their drawing with a paragraph full of descriptive language concerning the character. Students should combine what they know from the text itself with their own inferences, which will assist them in shaping their visual creation.

Action Plan for Incorporating DRAVING and ARTWORK

WHAT ARE MY PLANS FOR INCORPORATING MORE *DRAWING* AND *ARTWORK* INTO MY LESSONS TO ACCELERATE LEARNING?

RECOMMENDATIONS	ALREADY DOING	PLANNING TO DO
Have students create a personal Pictionary of content-area vocabulary words.		
Have students design a book jacket or cover depicting a story's main idea.		
Ask students to design a poster illustrating a concept's main idea and details.		
Have students create an original brochure regarding a city of interest.		
Ask students to make a collage regarding a particular culture.		
Have math students draw pictures illustrating their understanding of a word problem.		
Ask students to draw and label the parts or processes of the human body.		
Assist students in designing a class mural as a review of a previous lesson.		
Have students create a foldable booklet related to the content.		
Ask math students to make drawings of terms previously taught.		
Have music students draw in the notes on a piece of music.		
Ask students to create a postcard representing one of the world's regions.		
Have students draw a stick symbol and attach information regarding a person or group to different parts of the symbol.		
Ask students to create a visual representation of a book character.		
Goals and Notes:		

Strategy 2 • Drawing and Artwork   33

Source: istock.com/SolStock

Field trips, a form of experiential learning, enable students to acquire new knowledge through firsthand experience (Bouchrika, 2024).

STRATEGY 3

Field Trips

💡 WHAT: DEFINING THE STRATEGY

Several years ago, I was invited to present for the Honolulu Association for Supervision and Curriculum Development. My husband and I went one week earlier than the day I was to present so that we could enjoy the scenic beauty and historical significance of our 50th state. I will never forget spending one of those days at Pearl Harbor. We were there with several high school classes who experienced the same emotional impact on this field trip as we did. After a tour of the grounds and a video recalling the horrific attack on December 7, 1941, we were transported by boat to the *U.S.S. Arizona* Memorial. All of us tourists, including the students, disembarked the boat and realized that we were now standing over the remains of almost 1,000 servicemen whose bodies were still buried beneath the water since the ship was never raised after it was bombed. It was such a spiritual experience that no one said a word. Students did not even have to be told not to talk. They just didn't! As I read the names of each serviceman engraved on the wall, I shuddered with the thought that all of these brave men had given their lives in service to our country. We were later told that there was so much camaraderie on that ship that many survivors of that day asked that their ashes be brought back to the water upon their deaths and deposited into the ocean with their fellow seamen.

The purpose of the brain is not to make good grades or to score high on standardized tests. The brain has but one purpose: survival in the real world. Students can read about Pearl Harbor, research it on the Internet, or view a video, but none of those things can serve as substitutes for the field trip the students and I took on that day. Due to the Covid-19 pandemic, for a time, students had to rely on virtual field trips as their only means of experiencing life outside of the four walls of the classroom. Even now, virtual field trips enable students to visit places that would be inaccessible or cost prohibitive. Is it any wonder that the places you and your students travel to in the real world are long remembered? This would make the strategy of field trips one of the most unforgettable!

WHY: THEORETICAL FRAMEWORK

Field trips are a form of experiential learning that enables students to acquire new knowledge through interaction and experience firsthand the concepts they are encountering in textbooks (Bouchrika, 2024).

Field trips provide a great deal of information that teachers can refer to as they lecture, adding more context to what students have already experienced (Kelly, 2019).

Field trip excursions hold more than enough educational value to remain a part of the curriculum since they provide a means for hands-on learning, improve students' observational skills, enable them to develop an affinity for culture and art, and engage students in their studies (Bouchrika, 2024).

Field trips, such as those to interactive science museums, enable lessons to be presented in a variety of modalities (Explorable Places, n.d.)

Virtual field trips can eliminate financial concerns, are less challenging to student safety or logistics, and are less time consuming, enabling teachers to conduct follow-up within the class period (Bouchrika, 2024).

Field trips that immerse students in art, history, or community service engender students who develop more empathy with other members of society, even those of different eras (Greene & Kisida, 2013).

Researchers at the University of Arkansas found that when students take field trips to cultural institutions, their critical-thinking skills, levels of tolerance, and historical empathy improve (Greene & Kisida, 2013).

Field trips to live performances of plays enhance students' tolerance, literary knowledge, and empathy for what other people think and feel (University of Arkansas, 2014).

In a large-scale study of 11,000 students at more than 120 schools, research suggested that students retained a large amount of information from field trips taken and actually improved their critical-thinking skills. This was particularly the case with students from high-poverty schools (Greene & Kisida, 2013).

Since the field trip provides a real experience that makes content more relevant, it is a valuable and time-honored part of the social studies curriculum (Melber & Hunter, 2010).

Aristotle and Socrates, two of the world's greatest teachers, used field trips thousands of years ago, as tools of instruction (Krepel & Duvall, 1981).

HOW: INSTRUCTIONAL ACTIVITIES

WHO: Elementary/Middle/High

WHEN: Before or during a lesson

CONTENT AREA(S): Cross-curricular

- For a change of scenery, convene class outside the classroom on the school grounds. Allowing students to absorb the vitamin D and other positive effects of sunlight and the beauty of nature calms students' brains and puts the mind in a good state for learning. Conducting a class discussion while sitting under a tree can add a whole new dimension to instruction.

WHO: Elementary/Middle/High

WHEN: After a lesson

CONTENT AREA(S): Cross-curricular

- Once students have completed an exemplary original story or poem, have them participate in a publishing party where they share their work with an authentic audience. If possible, high school students could take a field trip to a nearby elementary school to share their stories during story time, or students could share their creative efforts with a lower grade level within the building.

WHO: Elementary

WHEN: During a lesson

CONTENT AREA(S): Mathematics

- Field trips do not have to cost money. Use the school and the community for your field trip. Ask students to look for patterns in their environment, such as in the stars and stripes on the American flag, the clothing of classmates, the bricks in the school building, or the leaves on the trees. Point out the obvious way that objects, shapes, and colors are patterned in the real world.

WHO: Elementary/Middle/High

WHEN: After a lesson

CONTENT AREA(S): Mathematics

- Following lessons on the concepts of angles, circles, rays, lines, line segments, and intersecting and parallel lines, take the class outside and have them identify these items on the sports fields or in the outside environment. Have students measure these fields. Following this field trip, lead students in a discussion of how geometry affects the design of sports fields (Tate, 2009).

WHO: Elementary/Middle

WHEN: Before a lesson

CONTENT AREA(S): Science

- Before a unit of study on the solar system, have students visit a planetarium where they see replicas of what they will be studying, including the stars, planets, constellations, and so on.

WHO: Elementary/Middle/High

WHEN: During a lesson

CONTENT AREA(S): Social Studies

- Plan and take a field trip to a natural history or other type of museum to view exhibits and artifacts related to a unit of study. Visit the museum in advance, and plan a scavenger hunt so students can search for predetermined items and find the answers to prearranged questions.

WHO: Elementary/Middle

WHEN: During a lesson

CONTENT AREA(S): Science

- To beautify the campus and learn about gardening, have students research, design, and plant a garden, butterfly garden, or water garden. Bulbs can be planted in the design of the school's initials or logo. The more familiar and scientific names of the plants can be labeled. Have students plan and conduct tours for other classrooms visiting the garden (Tate & Phillips, 2011).

WHO: Elementary/Middle/High

WHEN: During a lesson

CONTENT AREA(S): Cross-curricular

- Often, the classroom does not provide enough space for movement and games. Take the class outside, and engage them in purposeful movement to reinforce a content objective or to play a game that requires more space than four walls will allow.

WHO: Middle/High

WHEN: During a lesson

CONTENT AREA(S): Mathematics

- Have students walk around their community and create math problems from their environment based on what they discover as they walk around the neighborhood. Have them accompany their problems with photographs, videos, or recordings essential for others to solve the problem.

WHO: Elementary/Middle/High

WHEN: During a lesson

CONTENT AREA(S): Cross-curricular

- Thanks to virtual field trips, have students experience what it is like to visit locations of interest around the globe and never leave the classroom. Go online to websites, and access virtual field trips that pertain to a concept being taught.

WHO: Elementary/Middle/High

WHEN: After a lesson

CONTENT AREA(S): Social Studies

- Have students emulate the work of an ethnographer by observing and describing one area of the school, including the entrance to the building, the front office, the principal's office, the cafeteria, the halls when students are changing classes, and the media center. Have students, like the social scientist, gather data, select and interpret the relevant data, and reflect on the findings as well as the process of collection. Then, have them describe what they have observed for a specific audience, such as students who will attend the school, a visitor from another country, or any other target audience they select (Melber & Hunter, 2010).

Action Plan for Incorporating FIELD TRIPS

WHAT ARE MY PLANS FOR INCORPORATING MORE *FIELD TRIPS* INTO MY LESSONS TO ACCELERATE LEARNING?

RECOMMENDATIONS	ALREADY DOING	PLANNING TO DO
Convene class on the school grounds but outside of the classroom.		
Have students take a field trip to share their original exemplary story or poem with an authentic audience at another school or for another grade level.		
Have math students look for patterns in their school environment.		
Have math students recognize geometric shapes previously taught by identifying them on the sports fields of the school grounds.		
Take science students to a planetarium to view concepts related to the solar system.		
Have social studies students visit a natural history museum to view exhibits related to a unit of study.		
Have students research, design, and plant a garden on school grounds.		
Take students outside for purposeful movement or to play a game related to a taught concept.		
Have math students walk around the neighborhood, creating problems for others to solve.		
Go online to access virtual field trips related to the content being studied.		
Have social studies students emulate the work of an ethnographer by observing and writing about an area of the school.		
Goals and Notes:		

Source: istock.com/SDI Productions

Gaming and simulations assist students in developing alternative learning strategies and aid in problem solving (Hattie, 2023).

STRATEGY 4

Games

💡 WHAT: DEFINING THE STRATEGY

One of the games I love to play with teachers is called a *People Search*. This is a perfect game for you to play with students. Students have to find answers to 12 short, unfinished statements in a 4 × 3 grid drawn on a piece of paper. The statements should reflect content that you would like for students to review. Students can supply only one answer for themselves. Then, they must get the remaining 11 answers from 11 different classmates. Students get up and move around the room to fast-paced music, finding peers who can answer correctly and place their initials inside each block. Here is the catch. One student can provide only one answer for another, so students have to talk to at least 11 additional students in class when looking for answers. Remember that you know the answers to all these but can provide only one answer for each student with your initials. That student can now pass your answer to other students with their initials. Be sure to give different students different answers so that the correct answers are being passed. The winner is the first student to get back to you with 12 different initials, including their own, and all correct answers. Review the answers to all statements with the entire class by tossing a ball to nonvolunteers.

As I travel around the United States presenting, I realize that the fun has gone out of teaching and learning in many classrooms. With increased emphasis on standardized and criterion-referenced testing, benchmarks, and accountability, school is just not fun anymore! In the name of increased academic achievement, many school systems are even removing recess time from the students' school day. Fortunately, other school systems are doing just the opposite. They are even recommending that students take their more difficult subjects immediately after taking physical education. As I taught in Singapore, where students have some of the highest math scores in the world, I noticed that students were spending time learning math and then, just as importantly, stopping math instruction for recess.

While preschool children love to play games, it is also one of the 12 principles that keep people living beyond the age of 80 (Tate, 2022). There is even a pertinent saying: *You don't stop playing because you grow old. You grow old because you stop playing.* That would lead one to believe that games are beneficial throughout one's life and that elementary, middle, and high school students would benefit from spirited interaction in the pleasurable strategy of game playing. Not only is the strategy motivating, but it can also put students' brains in a positive state. When students hear their teacher say, *Let's play a game!,* the stress level decreases, and the content retention rate increases. Boys, especially, are naturally motivated when a review is turned into a competition.

WHY: THEORETICAL FRAMEWORK

The most practical use of gaming and simulations is to teach the consolidation of information since these techniques are much more enjoyable than drill and practice (Hattie, 2023).

When selecting a good learning game, Louisa Rosenheck of MIT suggests (1) providing players with a choice in the way they play the game or determine their goals in the game; (2) sparking students' curiosity so that they ask questions about how things work; and (3) determining an engaging and satisfying level of challenge (Boudreau, 2021).

Using games during instruction can foster social and emotional learning, increase participation, and encourage students to take risks (Nguyen, 2021).

Gaming and simulations can assist students in developing alternative learning strategies and can aid in problem solving and critical and trial-and-error thinking (Hattie, 2023).

Games can provide a fun and interactive way for students to promote problem solving and critical thinking skills while engaging with cross-curricular content (Lane, 2023).

A good game puts the learning first, allows students to solve problems on their own, and encourages students to collaborate and reflect to connect the game with the real world (Boudreau, 2021).

Especially for students who have trouble focusing or who have not found their niche in learning, gameplay can provide a more engaging, collaborative classroom as students learn to link content with low-stakes competition (Nguyen, 2021).

Gaming and simulations enable learners to see goals, can provide immediate feedback on performance, and can lead to positive reputations among peers (Hattie, 2023).

All ages can benefit from play since it improves brain function and relationships, relieves stress, and boosts creativity (Robinson et al., 2021).

Having students develop a game to test one another on their knowledge of the content not only results in fun but also forces students to rehearse and comprehend the concepts taught (Sousa, 2011).

> When students develop a game's content as well as play the game, the amount of time they are exposed to and involved with the content is doubled (Allen, 2008).
>
> Games are not only perfect for raising the level of *feel-good amines* in the brain, but, in the correct amounts, games can also increase cognition and working memory (Jensen, 2007, p. 4).
>
> Students not only learn more when playing a game, but their participation in class and their motivation for learning math increases (Posamentier & Jaye, 2006).
>
> The need for survival, belonging and love, power, freedom, and fun are the five critical needs that must be satisfied if people are to be effectively motivated (Glasser, 1999).

HOW: INSTRUCTIONAL ACTIVITIES

WHO: Elementary/Middle/High

WHEN: After a lesson

CONTENT AREA(S): Cross-curricular

- Buy a generic game board, such as Candy Land, or have students work in cooperative groups to construct an original game board according to the following guidelines: The game must provide at least 30 spaces, including *begin* and *end* spaces, two *move ahead* spaces, and two *go back* spaces. Have students make game question cards appropriate to whatever content needs to be reviewed with an accompanying answer key. Each group of students uses another group's game board and questions. Each group reviews content by rolling a number generator (die), moving the rolled number of spaces, selecting a card, and answering the designated question on the card. The student moves the rolled number of spaces if the answer is correct. If the answer is incorrect, the student stays put. The first student in each group to get to the end of the game board wins.

WHO: Elementary/Middle

WHEN: After a lesson

CONTENT AREA(S): Mathematics

- Following a lesson on factors, have students play the game SWITCH. Place a number on the SMART board, such as 36. Ask students to consider all of the factors of 36. Call out another number, such as 6. If the second number (6) is a factor of the pictured number (36), then students are given the count of five to switch seats with another student in class. If a student is not in another student's seat by the count of five, that student is considered out of the game. If the second number is not a factor of the original number, then all students must remain seated. If students get up when they shouldn't, they are also out of the game. Give students several examples of numbers that are factors and not factors of the given number. Then, change to another given number. I played this game with a group of fifth-graders, and we were laughing so hard we could hardly finish the game. Let me tell you one that always gets students out. The original number is 36. The second number is 13. Many students get up since they think 13 is a factor of 36. It is not! If you are not teaching factors, change the content of SWITCH to a concept you are teaching that has positive and negative examples.

WHO: Elementary/Middle

WHEN: After a lesson

CONTENT AREA(S): Cross-curricular

- Have students make 15 matched pairs of content-area vocabulary words and their definitions. Have them write each word on one index card and the accompanying definition on another card. Have them spread the word and definition cards out face down in random order. Students work in pairs, taking turns matching each word to its appropriate definition. One match entitles the student to another try. The student with the most matches at the end of the game wins.

WHO: Elementary/Middle

WHEN: During or after a lesson

CONTENT AREA(S): Mathematics

- Have students work in pairs to become more automatic with addition facts. Give each pair a deck of cards. Have students deal the deck equally between the two of them. Have each student hold their half deck in their hand with the cards face down. Have them turn the top cards up simultaneously and add the value of the two cards together. For example, if one student turns over a 7 and another a 3, the first student to say 10 gets both cards. Jacks are worth 11 points, queens are worth 12 points, and kings are worth 13 points. Aces can be worth either 1 point or 14 points. The winner is the first student to take all the cards or the one with the most cards when the time is up. You may want to pair students with similar abilities together.

WHO: Elementary/Middle/High

WHEN: After a lesson

CONTENT AREA(S): Cross-curricular

- Write each content-area vocabulary word on a different index card. Have students play *Charades* by taking turns coming to the front of the room, selecting a word card, and acting out the word's definition. The student cannot speak or write but must use gestures to act out the word. The first student in class to guess the word gets a point. The student with the most points at the end of the game is the winner.

WHO: Elementary/Middle/High

WHEN: After a lesson

CONTENT AREA(S): Cross-curricular

- Play *Jeopardy* with the class by dividing them into three heterogeneous teams. Each team selects a team captain who gives the answers to the emcee and a scribe who keeps track of the points for the team and writes down the *Jeopardy* answer during the bonus round. Select key points from the chapter or unit of study and turn them into answers for the board. Five answers are placed into five columns of $100 increments, with the easiest answers worth $100 and the most difficult worth $500. Teams then compete against one another by taking turns selecting an answer and providing the appropriate question. If the answer is correct, the points are added to the score. If the answers are incorrect, the points are subtracted. Include two *daily doubles* to make the game more interesting. Play continues according to the rules of the television show until all of the answers have been selected. Any team with money can wager any or all of it during the *bonus round*. The bonus question should be one of the most difficult ones. The team with the most money at the end of the game wins. A computerized version of *Jeopardy* is available.

WHO: Elementary/Middle/High

WHEN: After a lesson

CONTENT AREA(S): Cross-curricular

- Play *Wheel of Fortune* with the class by selecting a content-area vocabulary word previously taught. Place one line on the board for each letter in the chosen word. Have students take turns guessing alphabet letters that may be in the word. If the letter is in the word, write it on the correct line. If it is not, place the letter in a column off to the side. The first student to guess the word wins a point.

Adaptation: Have students work in pairs to select a word and have their partner guess it. The student in each pair who guesses their word in the shortest time is the winner.

WHO: Middle/High

WHEN: During a lesson

CONTENT AREA(S): Cross-curricular

- Have students play the Loop game by writing statements and questions similar to the following on index cards and passing them out randomly to students in the class. Students then stand and read the answer if they have the card that answers another student's question.
    - **I have a right triangle.** Who has a triangle with all sides congruent?
    - **I have an equilateral triangle.** Who has the number of degrees in each of its angles?
    - **I have 60 degrees.** Who has the segment of a triangle from a vertex to the midpoint of the opposite side?
    - **I have a median.** Who has a triangle with each angle less than 90 degrees?
    - **I have an acute triangle.** Who has a triangle with at least two congruent sides?
    - **I have an isosceles triangle.** Who has an equation whose graph is a line?
    - **I have a linear equation.** Who has the name of the side opposite the right angle in a right triangle?
    - **I have the hypotenuse.** Who has an equation for the area of a circle?
    - **I have a = πr².** Who has an equation that states that two ratios are equal?
    - **I have proportion.** Who has a quadrilateral with four congruent sides?

Students can write additional questions and answers to form the basis of the remaining cards for playing this game. You should have as many cards as students in class (Bulla, 1996). This game can also be adapted to any content area by changing the answers and the questions.

Adaptation: This game can be made more fun by recording the time it takes to get through one cycle and then repeating the cycle two more times in an effort to beat the time. The repetition of hearing the answers more than once is good for students' brains.

WHO: Elementary/Middle/High

WHEN: During a lesson

CONTENT AREA(S): Cross-curricular

- Provide students with a bingo sheet containing 25 blank spaces. Have students write previously taught, content-area vocabulary words randomly in any space on their cards. Then, have students take turns randomly pulling from a bag and reading the definition of a designated word. Have students cover or mark out each word as the definition is read. The first student to cover five words in a row, horizontally, vertically, or diagonally, shouts out, "Bingo!" However, to win, the student must orally define the five words that comprise the Bingo. If the student cannot supply the definitions, play continues until a subsequent student wins.

Adaptation: Have students randomly write answers to math problems in the 25 blank spaces. Have students randomly pull and read math problems from the bag as students cover the correct answers.

WHO: Elementary/Middle/High

WHEN: During a lesson

CONTENT AREA(S): Language Arts/History

- Have students play the Who Am I? game by providing written clues regarding a famous literary or historical figure already studied. Have students take turns standing and reading their clues aloud as class members try to guess the identity of the figure. Any student who is the first to guess wins a point. If no one can identify the figure, then the student providing the clues gets the point.

WHO: Elementary/Middle/High

WHEN: After a lesson

CONTENT AREA(S): Cross-curricular

- Have students compete in pairs and take turns being the first to get their partners to guess a designated vocabulary word by providing them with a one-word synonym or clue for the word. No gestures are allowed. Bring two pairs of students to the front of the class, and show one person in each pair the same word. One pair begins. If the word is missed, the play reverts to the other pair. The point value starts at 10 and decreases by one each time the word is not guessed. If the word has not been guessed by the time the point value gets to five, tell the word. Bring up two new pairs of students, and a new word is given. This game is patterned after the television game show *Password*.

WHO: Elementary/Middle/High

WHEN: During a lesson

CONTENT AREA(S): Cross-curricular

- During a class discussion, when a question is asked, toss a Nerf or any other soft ball to the student who is to respond. The student gets one point for catching the ball and two points for answering the question correctly. If the student is correct, they can randomly pick the student to answer the next question and randomly toss the ball to that student. If the student answers incorrectly, they must throw the ball back to you so that you can select the next student. Be sure to ask the entire class the question before choosing someone to catch the ball and answer the question.

   WHO: Elementary/Middle/High

   WHEN: After a lesson

   CONTENT AREA(S): Cross-curricular

- Following a unit of study and before a test, have students work in heterogeneous groups to write 10 questions regarding the content at varying difficulty levels with four possible answer choices. Each question is assigned a monetary difficulty level in $100 increments, ranging from $100 to $1,000. Have them also write three additional difficult questions worth $5,000, $25,000, and $100,000, respectively. Have student groups compete to earn money for their team by answering another team's questions. This game is adapted from the television game show *Who Wants to Be a Millionaire?*

   WHO: Elementary/Middle/High

   WHEN: During a lesson

   CONTENT AREA(S): Cross-curricular

- Encourage students to review appropriate content-area vocabulary by playing *Pictionary*. Divide the class into two heterogeneous teams. Students from each team take turns coming to the front of the room, pulling a vocabulary word from a box, and drawing a picture on the SMART board that will get their team members to say the word before time is called. No words may be spoken. If the team succeeds in guessing the word within a specific time limit (such as 15 seconds), the team gets one point. The winner is the team with the most points when all words have been used.

   WHO: Elementary/Middle/High

   WHEN: During a lesson

   CONTENT AREA(S): Cross-curricular

- Download *Game Show TV Theme Music* on *YouTube* or *Spotify* so you have the music accompanying many of the games you will play with your class. Themes from the following game shows are included:

Wheel of Fortune, Jeopardy, Password, Family Feud, The Price Is Right, and many more.

WHO: Elementary/Middle

WHEN: During a lesson

CONTENT AREA(S): Cross-curricular

- Consult the series *Engage the Brain Games* for a plethora of additional game ideas across the curriculum. Books for kindergarten through Grade 5 are cross-curricula, including games in the content areas of language arts, math, science, social studies, music, and physical education. There is a separate book in language arts, mathematics, science, and social studies for Grades 6 through 8. Consult the Corwin website at www.corwin.com for information on this series.

Action Plan for Incorporating GAMES

WHAT ARE MY PLANS FOR INCORPORATING MORE *GAMES* INTO MY LESSONS TO ACCELERATE LEARNING?		
RECOMMENDATIONS	**ALREADY DOING**	**PLANNING TO DO**
Have students construct an original game board with content-related question cards.		
Have math students play the game SWITCH to identify the factors of a number.		
Have students match content-area vocabulary words to their definitions.		
Have math students practice adding facts by adding the numbers on two cards together.		
Play Charades by having students act out the definition of a vocabulary word.		
Play *Jeopardy* by having students provide content-area questions to answers on the gameboard.		
Play *Wheel of Fortune* by having students guess the letters in a content-area word.		
Play the Loop game by having one student answer another's question.		
Play BINGO by matching words with their definitions.		
Play Who Am I? by identifying a character based on clues provided.		
Play *Password* by getting students to guess a content-area word based on a one-word clue.		
Toss a soft ball as students respond to questions.		
Have students play *Who Wants to Be a Millionaire?* by writing and answering questions at varying difficulty levels.		
Have students guess vocabulary words based on pictures drawn by their peers.		
Download *Game Show TV Theme Music* to provide music to accompany the games played.		
Consult the *Engage the Brain Games* series for additional ideas.		
Goals and Notes:		

52　Engaging the Brain

Source: istock.com/JasonDoiy

Graphic organizers provide the structure that enables information to move from short-term into long-term memory (Marlett, 2019).

STRATEGY 5

Graphic Organizers, Semantic Maps, and Word Webs

WHAT: DEFINING THE STRATEGY

When I teach the course accompanying this book, there is a section called *Five Facts About Neurons*. Participants experience the five actions that should characterize every brain-based classroom since when teachers practice these, neurons grow, and learning is accelerated for students. By the way, I use those same five elements in the workshop to accelerate the participants' learning. This part is accompanied by the graphic organizer or mind map in Figure 5.1, which the participants fill in as I teach. The main ideas, or five elements, are in boxes and capital letters. Underneath each main idea are details on why these actions work so well. It would be very difficult to teach this section without the assistance of this graphic organizer.

FIGURE 5.1 • Neuron: The Memory Cell

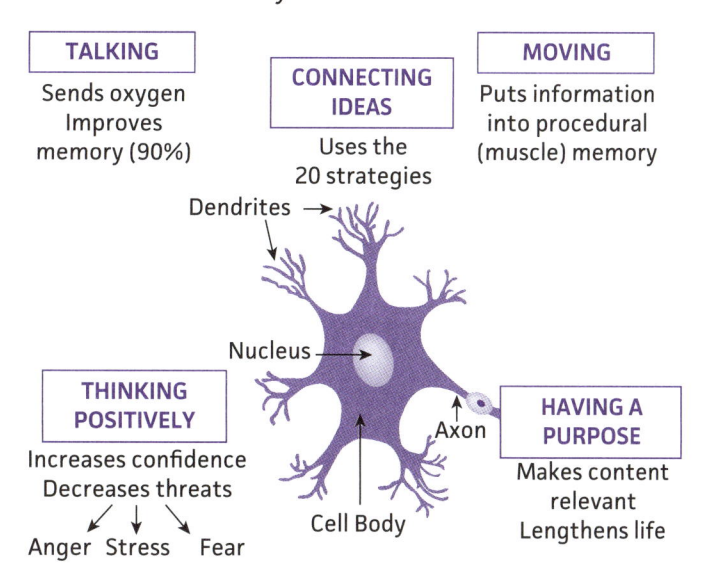

TALKING
Sends oxygen
Improves memory (90%)

CONNECTING IDEAS
Uses the 20 strategies

MOVING
Puts information into procedural (muscle) memory

Dendrites
Nucleus

THINKING POSITIVELY
Increases confidence
Decreases threats
Anger Stress Fear

Axon
Cell Body

HAVING A PURPOSE
Makes content relevant
Lengthens life

55

Whether referred to as concept, mind, semantic maps, or word webs, graphic organizers are one of the best friends of a teacher who desires to facilitate students' comprehension. Graphic organizers address both the left and the right hemispheres of students' brains so they benefit all. The students strong in the left hemisphere can supply the verbiage, and the right-hemisphere students have the option of showing what they know pictorially. Having students draw the organizer along with you as you explain the major concepts and details facilitates memory.

WHY: THEORETICAL FRAMEWORK

During sessions where students help co-develop concept maps, there can be discussions about capturing main ideas, noting interrelationships, and identifying themes, especially for those students who do not possess organizing and synthesizing skills (Hattie, 2023).

Story maps, a form of graphic organizers, can be very useful for readers who are having difficulty classifying the main idea and supporting details in a piece of writing (Sousa, 2022).

Graphic organizers provide the structure that enables information to move from short-term into long-term memory and can make concrete visual representations from more abstract concepts (Marlett, 2019).

A Venn diagram shows the similarities and differences between two concepts and can ascertain whether two concepts are too similar to be taught in the same lesson (Sousa, 2022).

The powerful, visual, learning tool of a graphic organizer can make complex concepts simple, assist with problem solving, or be useful in brainstorming ideas or planning research (Cox, 2020).

The use of graphic organizers is more critical now than ever since they can show students how to make new information more meaningful and manageable and help students connect new skills and concepts with their prior knowledge (Marlett, 2019).

Graphic organizers, as a preorganization strategy, assist students who receive special education services in getting their main ideas in order before they start the writing process (Sousa, 2016).

Graphic organizers are very effective with students who have learning disabilities and those who are English language learners (Konrad et al., 2011; Sheriff & Boon, 2014).

When visual patterns are shown through graphic representations, a 49-percentile point gain can be achieved (Tileston & Darling, 2009).

When students write study notes, if they include graphics that correspond to the symbols on a class mind map, their memory of the notes will be facilitated (Allen & Scozzi, 2012).

Graphic organizers make abstract ideas more visible and concrete and can make connections between a student's prior knowledge, what they are learning today, and what they can apply to future learning (Burke, 2009).

Flow charts, continuums, matrices, Venn diagrams, concept maps, and problem-solution charts are all types of graphic representations that can be used by mathematics teachers because they can be quickly understood and can provide structure for synthesizing new information (Posamentier & Jaye, 2006).

"Graphic organizers make thinking and learning visible" (Fogarty, 2009, p. 112).

Graphic organizers represent a form of *nonlinguistic representation* and are one of the most popular ways teachers can have students represent the knowledge that they have experienced (Marzano, 2007, p. 52).

According to the Institute for the Advancement of Research in Education (IARE), 29 scientifically based research studies support the use of graphic organizers for improving student achievement across all grade levels, content areas, and with diverse student populations (Institute for the Advancement of Research in Education [IARE], 2003).

HOW: INSTRUCTIONAL ACTIVITIES

WHO: Elementary/Middle/High

WHEN: Before and after a lesson

CONTENT AREA(S): All

- To access students' prior knowledge and summarize content after a lesson is taught, have students complete a K-W-L graphic organizer as shown in Figure 5.2. Have students discuss or brainstorm (1) what they already *know* about a concept or unit of study, (2) what they *wonder about* related to the concept, and (3) what they have learned following instruction.

FIGURE 5.2 • KWL Chart

KWL Chart

Name: _____

Date: _____

Topic: _____

KNOW	WONDER	LEARNED
Before reading, write what you think you already know about this topic.	Before or during your research, write down questions you might have about this topic.	After finishing your reading, write what you learned about this topic.

Source: Reprinted from Tate (2020b)

WHO: Elementary/Middle/High

WHEN: During a lesson

CONTENT AREA(S): Cross-curricular

- Because the brain thinks in chunks or connections, have students increase their knowledge of vocabulary by using a word web. As new vocabulary is introduced, have students complete the word web in Figure 5.3 by brainstorming additional synonyms for the new word. Students can keep their word webs in a notebook for review and add synonyms throughout the year. Encourage them to add these words to their speaking and writing vocabularies as well.

FIGURE 5.3 • Word Web

Vocabulary Word Web

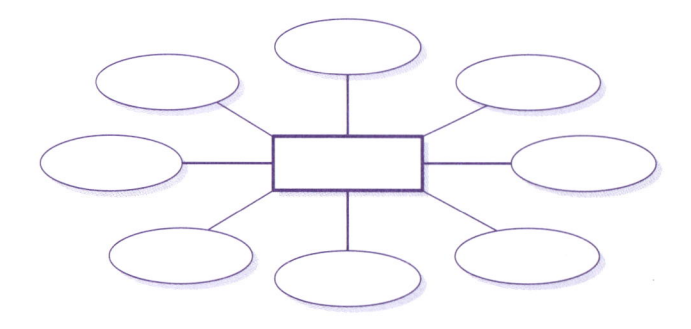

WHO:	Elementary/Middle/High
WHEN:	During or after a lesson
CONTENT AREA(S):	Cross-curricular

- Have students work individually or with a partner to complete the *Frayer Model* in Figure 5.4. After reading a selection from any content area, have students take a key concept and complete the four squares by defining the concept, stating key characteristics, and providing examples and non-examples of the concept.

FIGURE 5.4 • Frayer Model

Frayer Model

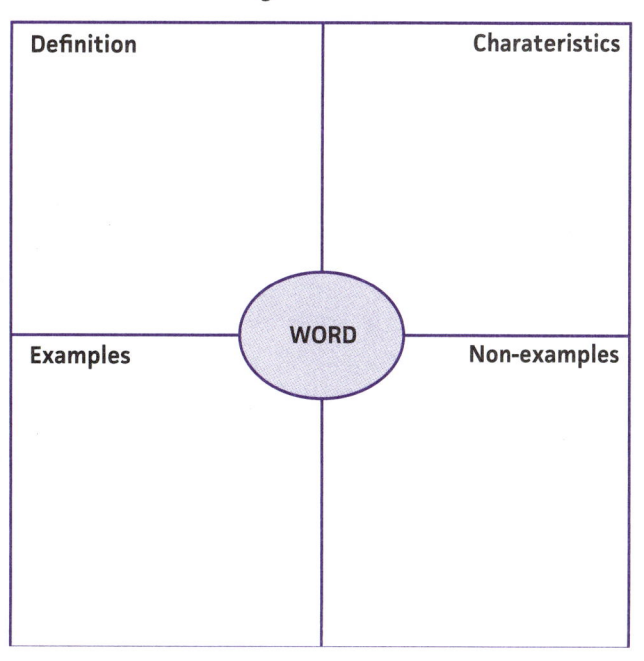

Definition	Charateristics
Examples	Non-examples

(WORD in center)

Source: Reprinted from Tate (2020b)

WHO:	Elementary/Middle/High
WHEN:	After a lesson
CONTENT AREA(S):	Cross-curricular

- After reading a story or novel where problems exist that must be resolved, have students complete a story frame as shown in Figure 5.5 to demonstrate their understanding of the story's plot.

FIGURE 5.5 • Story Map

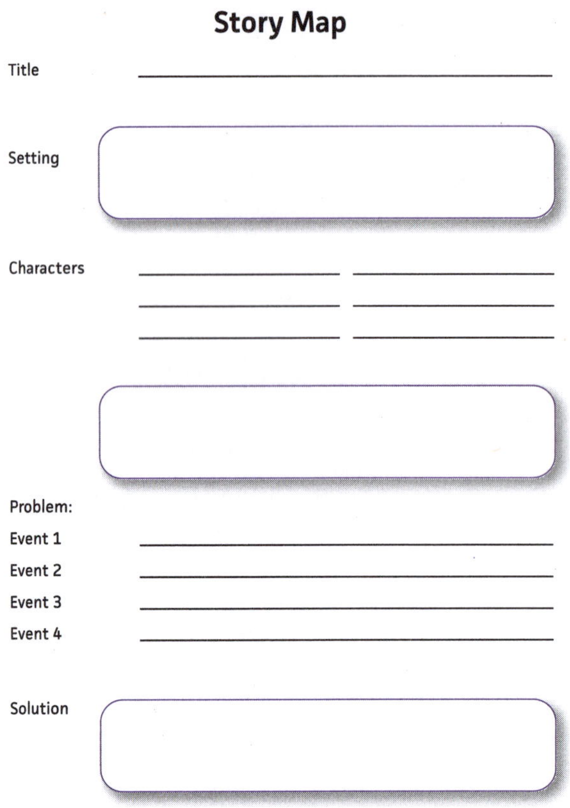

Story Map

Title _____

Setting

Characters _____ _____
_____ _____
_____ _____

Problem:
Event 1 _____
Event 2 _____
Event 3 _____
Event 4 _____

Solution

WHO: Elementary/Middle/High

WHEN: During a lesson

CONTENT AREA(S): Cross-curricular

- To help students identify the main idea and details in narrative or content-area texts, use the simile that a main idea and details are like a tabletop and legs. Draw a table with legs like the one shown in Figure 5.6, and have students write the main idea on the top of the table and one supporting detail on each leg.

FIGURE 5.6 • Tabletop Main Idea Organizer

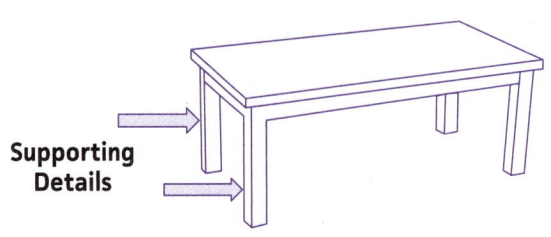

Main Idea Organizer

Main Idea

Supporting Details

---

60 • Engaging the Brain

WHO: Elementary/Middle/High

WHEN: During or after a lesson

CONTENT AREA(S): Cross-curricular

- Use the *Character Traits* graphic organizer in Figure 5.7 to distinguish at least two character traits in either narrative or informational texts. Students should refer to at least two events in the text that support the designated character trait.

FIGURE 5.7 • Character Traits Graphic Organizer

Character Traits

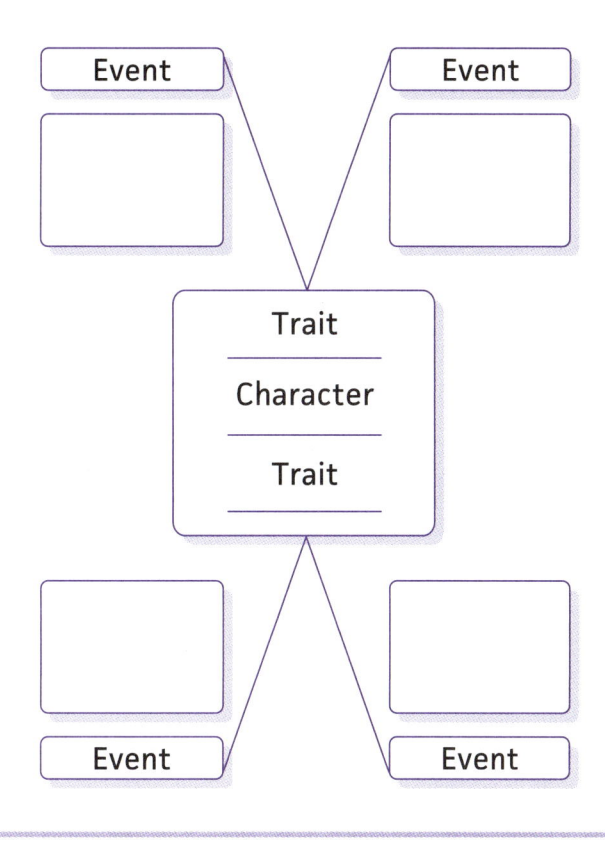

```
  [Event]              [Event]
   ┌──┐                 ┌──┐
   │  │                 │  │
   └──┘                 └──┘
        \             /
         ┌───────────┐
         │   Trait   │
         │ Character │
         │   Trait   │
         └───────────┘
        /             \
   ┌──┐                 ┌──┐
   │  │                 │  │
   └──┘                 └──┘
  [Event]              [Event]
```

Source: Reprinted from Tate (2020a)

WHO: Elementary/Middle/High

WHEN: During or after a lesson

CONTENT AREA(S): Cross-curricular

- Have students use the *Biography Research* graphic organizer in Figure 5.8 to capture their thoughts related to a historical figure they are researching. This map can also be used across the curriculum whenever a real or fictional character is studied.

FIGURE 5.8 • Biography Research Graphic Organizer

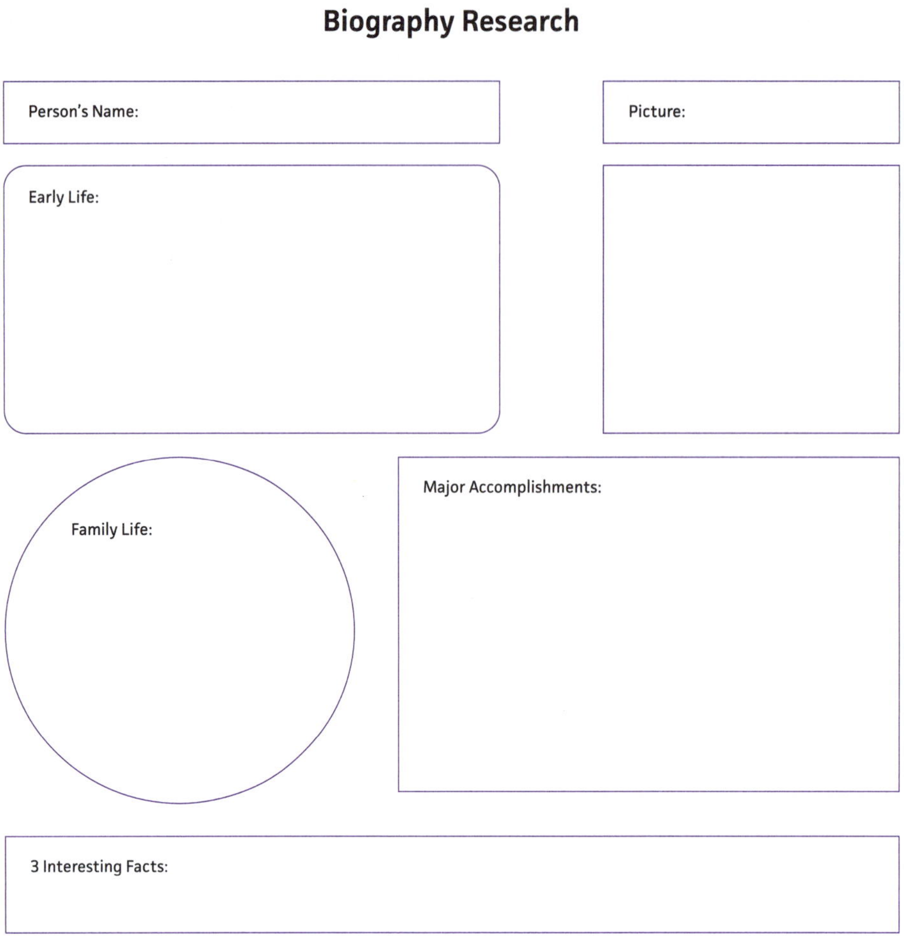

Biography Research

| Person's Name: | Picture: |

Early Life:

Family Life:

Major Accomplishments:

3 Interesting Facts:

Source: Reprinted from Tate (2020a)

WHO: Elementary/Middle/High

WHEN: During a lesson

CONTENT AREA(S): Cross-curricular

- Using the graphic organizer in Figure 5.9, have students complete the 5Ws and 1 H Template chart to ask and answer *what, who, when, where, why,* and *how* questions regarding either narrative or informational texts. Students should go into the text and look for specific text-dependent answers (Tate, 2020b).

FIGURE 5.9 • 5 Ws and 1 H Template

5 Ws and 1 H

Topic:

	Data
What	
Who	
When	
Where	
Why	
How	

Source: Reprinted from Tate (2020b)

WHO: Elementary/Middle/High

WHEN: During a lesson

CONTENT AREA(S): Cross-curricular

- Have students use one or more of the visual organizers shown in Figures 5.10, 5.11, 5.12, 5.13, and 5.14 to assist them in understanding the basic formats of text structure (Strong et al., 2002).

FIGURE 5.10 • Cause/Effect Organizer

Cause/Effect Organizer

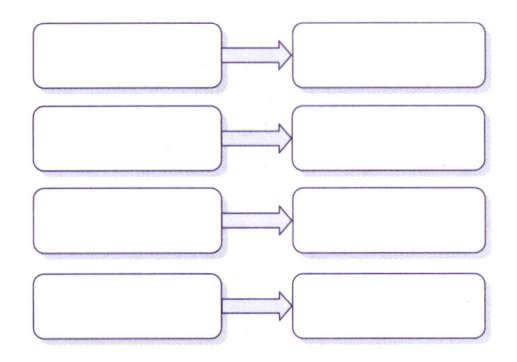

FIGURE 5.11 • Comparison Organizer

Comparison Organizer

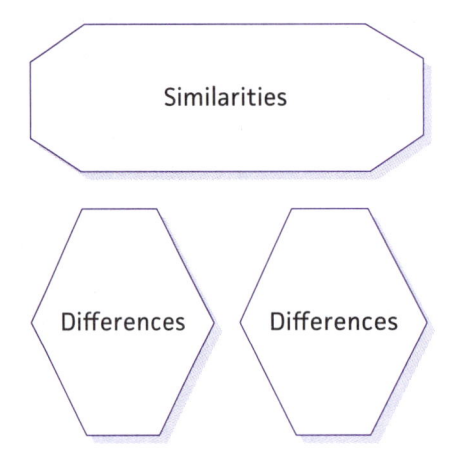

Similarities

Differences   Differences

FIGURE 5.12 • Cycle Organizer

Cycle Organizer

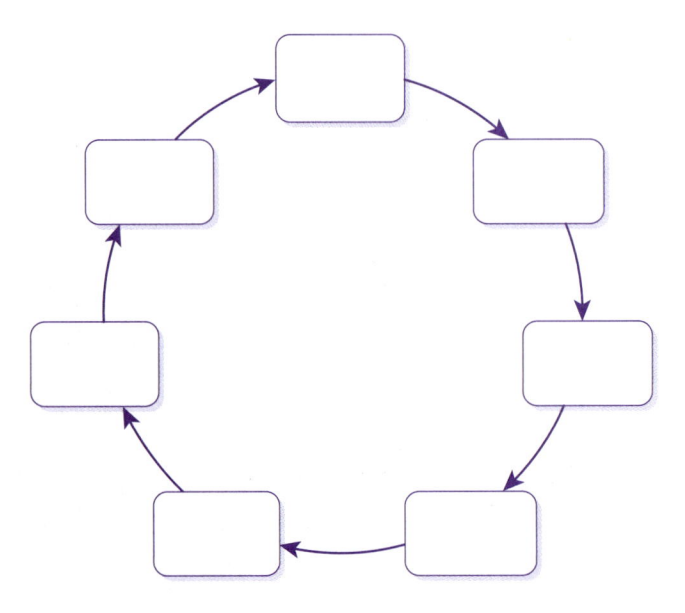

64 • Engaging the Brain

FIGURE 5.13 • Sequence Organizer

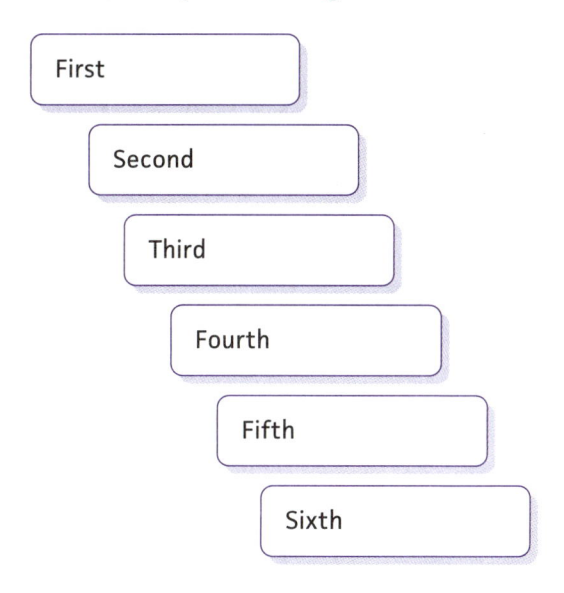

Sequence Organizer

- First
- Second
- Third
- Fourth
- Fifth
- Sixth

FIGURE 5.14 • Topic Description Organizer

Topic Description Organizer

Strategy 5 • Graphic Organizers, Semantic Maps, and Word Webs 65

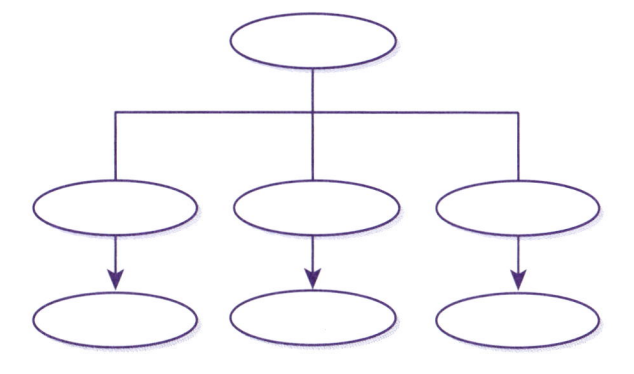

FIGURE 5.15 • Compare and Contrast Chart

Compare and Contrast Chart

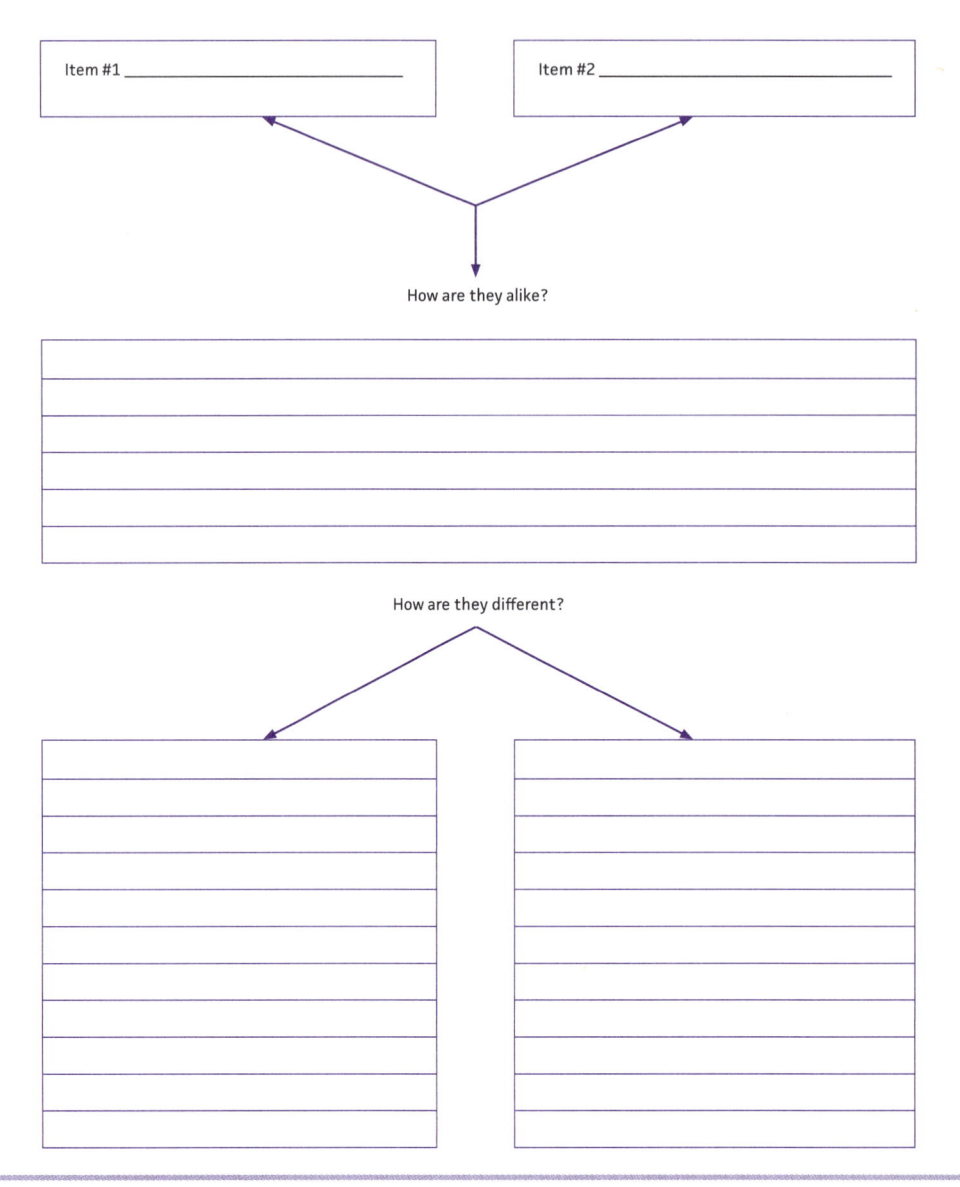

Item #1 _____

Item #2 _____

How are they alike?

How are they different?

Source: Reprinted from Tate (2020a)

WHO: Elementary/Middle/High

WHEN: Before, during, or after a lesson

CONTENT AREA(S): Cross-curricular

- While lecturing or discussing informational text with students, complete a semantic, concept, or mind map on the board as a visual of how the major concepts are related to one another. Have students copy the map in their notes as you explain each part. See the sample format in Figure 5.16.

FIGURE 5.16

Mind Map

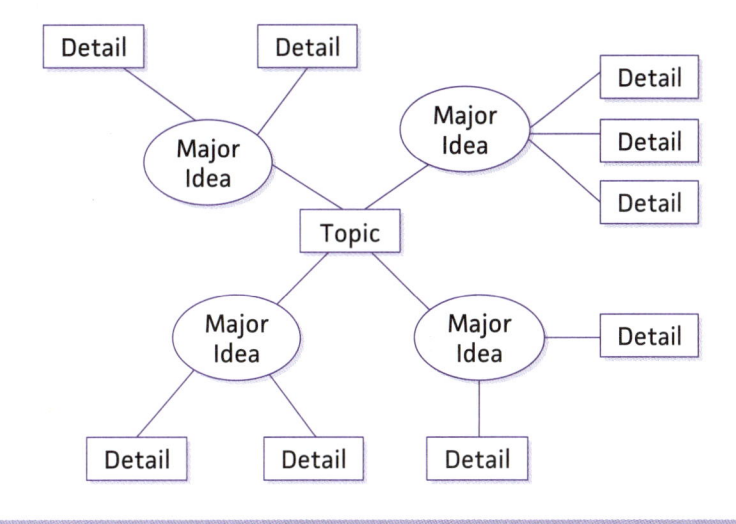

```
        Detail    Detail                    Detail
           \      /                   ┌───── Detail
         (Major Idea)      (Major Idea)────── Detail
              \           /           └───── Detail
               \         /
                [ Topic ]
               /         \
         (Major Idea)      (Major Idea)────── Detail
          /      \              |
       Detail   Detail        Detail
```

WHO: Elementary/Middle/High

WHEN: After a lesson

CONCEPT AREA(S): Cross-curricular

- Once you have demonstrated how to do so, encourage students to create their own semantic, concept, or mind maps regarding a unit of study. This technique alone will enhance comprehension because these mind maps can be reviewed before testing to facilitate long-term retention.

WHO: Elementary/Middle

WHEN: Before, during, and after a lesson

CONCEPT AREA(S): Cross-curricular

- Refer to the series *Engage the Brain: Graphic Organizers and Other Visual Strategies* to find additional graphic organizers in the content areas of language arts, math, science, and social studies. Grades K–5 have all content areas contained in the same book. Grades 6–8 have separate books for each of the four content areas. Consult the Corwin website at www.corwin.com for information on this series.

Action Plan for Incorporating GRAPHIC ORGANIZERS, SEMANTIC MAPS, and WORD WEBS

WHAT ARE MY PLANS FOR INCORPORATING MORE *GRAPHIC ORGANIZERS*, *SEMANTIC MAPS*, AND *WORD WEBS* INTO MY LESSON TO ACCELERATE LEARNING?

RECOMMENDATIONS	ALREADY DOING	PLANNING TO DO
Have students complete the K-W-L graphic organizer to summarize content.		
Have students complete a word web to increase their vocabulary.		
Have students use the *Frayer Model* to increase their knowledge of vocabulary concepts.		
Have students complete a story map to demonstrate their understanding of a story's plot.		
Use a tabletop and legs as a simile to help students understand the main idea and details of texts.		
Use the Character Traits Organizer to help students identify at least two traits of a character in narrative or informational texts.		
Have students use the *Biography Research* organizer to organize their thoughts regarding a person they are researching.		
Have students complete the *5Ws and 1 H chart to* answer *what, who, when, where, why,* and *how* questions regarding texts.		
Have students use a number of different visual organizers to understand the format of text structure.		
Complete a concept map on the board while lecturing to show how major concepts are related to one another.		
Encourage students to create their own concept map regarding a unit of study.		
Refer to the series *Engage the Brain: Graphic Organizers and Other Visual Strategies* to find additional organizers.		
Goals and Notes:		

Source: istock.com/Goodboy Picture Company

Laughter releases dopamine, a positive neurotransmitter in the brain, which stimulates long-term memory (Previte, 2019).

STRATEGY 6

Humor

💡 WHAT: DEFINING THE STRATEGY

By the time students reach middle or high school, several will consider themselves class clowns. Take advantage of these positive characteristics by allowing these students to bring in jokes to be shared with the class. I personally like riddles better than jokes since you often have to think at high levels to solve them. Following are a few content-specific riddles that can be used with the class. Be sure to try and guess the answer before it is revealed.

What is the difference between a cat and a comma? Answer: A cat has claws at the end of its paws. A comma is a pause at the end of a clause. (English)

What did the number zero say to the number eight? Answer: Nice belt (Math)

What is a snake's favorite subject? Answer: HISStory (Social Studies)

Why did the football coach go to the bank? Answer: To get his quarterback. (Physical Education)

Here is an additional riddle a teacher told me recently. I laughed hysterically!

Where do you go when you've been in a peek-a-boo accident? Answer: The ICU

These are riddles I tell in my workshops. If these riddles made you laugh or even smile, it put your brain in a more positive state. Research (Allen, 2008; Jensen, 2007) tells us that jokes, riddles, celebrations, and other forms of positive interaction not only create a positive learning environment but may also facilitate the learning itself. According to Jensen (2007), having laughter breaks in class increases the flow of positive neurotransmitters, which are necessary for alertness and memory.

Did you know that the brain does not know the difference between real laughter and fake laughter? You can use fake or forced laughter, and it will have the same positive effect on the brain. That is why there are more than 1,800 laughing clubs in India alone. Laughter is still the best medicine, even in the classroom.

Please do not confuse the use of humor in the classroom with sarcasm, which has the exact opposite effect on the brains of students. The literal definition of sarcasm is "a tearing of the flesh," aptly named because remarks directed to students that demean, tease, or deride can, at minimum, hinder or incapacitate higher-level thinking (Jensen, 1995).

WHY: THEORETICAL FRAMEWORK

Incorporating humor into lessons creates a more positive and relaxed environment that supports increased collaboration and creativity, along with boosting student engagement and retention (Yussif, 2023).

School psychologist Rosemarie Foote states that humor puts students' brains in an optimal state for learning by increasing their motivation, helping the learning stick, and creating space for the divergent ideas of other classmates (Bailey, 2023).

Psychological, sociological, and educational benefits of humor include the following: gaining students' attention, creating a climate in which students bond with one another, increasing students' retention and recall of content, improving their mental attitudes, and lowering their stress levels as well as lessening the incidence of discipline problems (Sousa, 2022).

Laughter is contagious and helps to build relationships. It also releases dopamine, a positive neurotransmitter in the brain, which stimulates long-term memory and enables the brain to become more focused and alert (Previte, 2019).

Forced, or fake, laughter practiced during yoga, can lower blood pressure, improve heart rate, and strengthen the immune system (Manohar, 2020).

Laughter can make it easier to cope when situations become difficult and can enable people to connect with one another (Mayo Clinic Staff, 2019).

International Teacher Magazine, a Consilium Education publication, includes the following in its eight reasons to use humor in the classroom: holds students' attention yet helps them relax, makes facts and data easier to understand, can assist in gaining control following a disturbance, helps to maintain relationships, and can serve as a tool to build resilience when a setback occurs (Consilium Education, 2020).

Since laughter enables teachers to take their work seriously and themselves lightly, the mental attitudes of both teachers and students are improved (Sousa, 2017).

It is possible for learning to be both rigorous and enjoyable (Cooper & Garner, 2012).

Kinesthetic actions in the form of cheers can send more oxygen and glucose to the brain, resulting in the laughter that can raise endorphin levels (Gregory & Chapman, 2013).

Older adolescents are more apt to understand the subtleties of humor, satire, or irony since their language skills are more highly developed than those of younger students (Feinstein, 2004).

What we learn with pleasure, we never forget (Allen, 2008, p. 99).

HOW: INSTRUCTIONAL ACTIVITIES

WHO: Elementary/Middle/High

WHEN: Before a lesson

CONTENT AREA(S): Cross-curricular

- Have teachers in a grade level or a department form a laughing club. Since the brain does not know the difference between real laughter and fake laughter, these clubs appear to work. The laughing club can meet before school long enough for a teacher to share a joke or riddle with the members. Teachers can take turns bringing the jokes for the week. Everyone gets his or her day off to a positive start that can carry over into instruction.

WHO: Elementary/Middle/High

WHEN: Before a lesson

CONTENT AREA(S): Cross-curricular

- To create an environment conducive to optimal learning, place humorous signs around the room. For example, one sign could say, *Knowledge given away here, free. Bring your own container* (Burgess, 2000, p. 20). Another sign could be *The longer you sit, the dumber you get!* (Tate, 2014b) or *Success comes in cans, not in can'ts!* (Tate, 2014b).

WHO: Elementary/Middle/High

WHEN: Before a lesson

CONTENT AREA(S): Cross-curricular

- As you stand at the door to greet your class daily, SMILE! SMILE is a mnemonic device that stands for <u>S</u>how <u>M</u>e <u>I</u>'m <u>L</u>oved <u>E</u>veryday! Many students come in under threat or high stress, and just a smiling teacher can help to change the state of their brains from negative to positive. After all, the brain learns best when it is not in high stress! On those days that you don't feel like smiling, get a *Smile on a Stick!* Go to www.smileonastick.com and purchase a smile connected to a stick. Put the smile up to your mouth as you greet students. The smiles come in several varieties and are good for a hearty laugh from your students!

WHO: Elementary/Middle/High

WHEN: Before a lesson

CONTENT AREA(S): Cross-curricular

Strategy 6 • Humor 73

- Don't take yourself or your students too seriously. Most students love a teacher who can make fun of himself. One high school teacher related to me how much his students love him, mostly due to his sense of humor. For example, when he teaches about plate tectonics, a shifting of the earth's plates, he tells students that there is a place in Africa where the plates collide. It is called Djibouti (jih-BOOT-ee). He told me that by the time they get through discussing the cracks in Djibouti, everybody remembers. If you don't get that joke, think about it a little longer! Remember to laugh with your students but not at them!

WHO: Elementary (Primary Grades)

WHEN: Before, during, or after a lesson

CONTENT AREA(S): Cross-curricular

- The brains of some primary students are not developed enough to understand the subtleties of a joke. However, they enjoy riddles. I actually like riddles better than jokes for the brain. Students have to think at high cognitive levels to solve a riddle. Find some riddles that would be appropriate for this age level. Here are a few to get you started:

  Why did the turtle cross the road? Answer: *To get to the Shell Station*

  Why don't the circus lions eat the circus clowns? Answer: *Because they taste funny*

  What did one strawberry say to another strawberry? Answer: *If you weren't so fresh we wouldn't be in this jam* (Tate, 2014a).

WHO: Middle/High

WHEN: Before, during, or after a lesson

CONTENT AREA(S): Cross-curricular

- Almost every middle and high school classroom has a class clown. Use that student to your advantage. Have them bring in jokes or riddles to tell the class. Make sure you approve of each joke before it is shared. Either before class, during the last few minutes, or at appropriate times during the period, have the class clown tell a joke. The entire class will laugh, putting each brain in a positive state for learning. The job of the class clown can rotate to other volunteers in the class each week until every student who wants a turn has had one. One high school teacher shared with me that since she started sharing a riddle to be solved at the beginning of each class period, students are showing up on time!

WHO: Elementary/Middle/High

WHEN: During a lesson

CONTENT AREA(S): Cross-curricular

- As you teach, locate or create and incorporate cartoons, riddles, and jokes that reinforce concepts you are teaching into the delivery of instruction.

WHO: Middle/High

WHEN: After a lesson

CONTENT AREA(S): Cross-curricular

- Have students create original jokes or riddles regarding a concept previously taught. The creation of jokes not only reinforces students' conceptual understanding but also encourages students to use their higher-level thinking skills. One math student created this original riddle. *Why did the fraction 1/5 go to the psychiatrist?* Answer: *He was just too tense (2/10).* Another student thought up this original riddle: *Why do you never want to say 288 in front of anyone?* Answer: *It is just too (two) gross!*

WHO: Middle/High

WHEN: Before or during a lesson

CONTENT AREA(S): Cross-curricular

- Have students bring in riddles to share with the class. Read over each riddle, and place the ones you approve in a *riddle box*. At the beginning of class or periodically throughout the period, stop and read a riddle from the box. Give points to the first student who can come up with the answer. The student who brought in the riddle is not allowed to guess but gets points for bringing in the riddle and extra points if no student can come up with the answer in an allotted time.

WHO: Elementary/Middle/High

WHEN: During or after a lesson

CONTENT AREA(S): Cross-curricular

- Use humorous ways to randomly involve students in lessons. When students are working in cooperative groups and it is time to select a spokesperson for the group, have students point into the air. Then, on the count of three, have them point to the person in their group they want to be the spokesperson. The student with the most fingers pointing at him or her becomes the spokesperson. This activity always gets a hearty laugh!

WHO: Elementary/Middle/High

WHEN: Before a lesson

CONTENT AREA(S): Cross-curricular

- Select students to fulfill a variety of roles in cooperative groups according to humorous categories such as the following:
  - Students wearing red (or any other color)
  - Students wearing contacts or glasses
  - Students with the longest/shortest hair (The hair does not have to be theirs.)
  - Students wearing the most jewelry, such as rings or earrings
  - Students who have the most brothers, sisters, or pets
  - Students who live closest to or farthest from school

WHO: Middle/High

WHEN: After a lesson

CONTENT AREA(S): Mathematics

- The National Council of Teachers of Math (NCTM) learned the power of humor over 50 years ago. They published a book in 1970 called *Mathematics and Humor*, where every joke, riddle, or pun taught a math concept. If you can retrieve a copy of this book, you will have a rich resource for incorporating humor into your math instruction. The cartoon in Figure 6.1 depicts an example.

FIGURE 6.1 • Example of Mathematics Humor

WHO: Middle/High

WHEN: During a lesson

CONTENT AREA(S): Cross-curricular

- Locate editorial or other cartoons that emphasize cross-curricular concepts already taught. Display them in class, and have students use their higher-level thinking skills to explain the concept displayed in the cartoon. For older students, you may want to display the cartoon omitting the caption, and have students work individually or in groups to create their own captions. You would be surprised how your students' original captions may be superior to the ones provided in the cartoons.

WHO: Elementary/Middle/High

WHEN: During a lesson

CONTENT AREA(S): Cross-curricular

- Provide positive feedback for appropriate student responses in humorous ways, such as providing applause with a plastic hand clapper, sending positive energy with a *positive energy stick* (magic wand), or blowing a paper horn.

WHO: Elementary/Middle/High

WHEN: During a lesson

CONTENT AREA(S): Cross-curricular

- Have students support and celebrate appropriate answers given by peers. These might include, but are not limited to, clapping, high-fives, thumbs-up, or any of the following affirmations:
    - *Fantastic! Fantastic!* Student place their hands on either side of their faces and fan their faces as they say, *Fantastic! Fantastic!*
    - *Seal of Approval!* Students extend their arms, turn their palms outward, clapping, and make a noise like a seal.
    - *WOW!* Students make a W by sticking up the three middle fingers of the right hand and the three middle fingers of the left hand and placing them on either side of the mouth which is formed in an O.
    - *Microwave* Have students take their little finger and wave at a peer.

Consult Chapter 16, "Celebrate Good Times, Come On!," of the book *Shouting Won't Grow Dendrites: 20 Techniques to Detour Around the Danger Zones* (2nd ed.) for more than 30 additional ways to celebrate student success in the classroom (Tate, 2014b).

WHO: Elementary/Middle/High

WHEN: After a lesson

CONTENT AREA(S): Cross-curricular

- Play games with students to review content prior to a test. Consult Strategy 4 (Games) for numerous examples of involving students in a fun class with lots of laughter.

Action Plan for Incorporating HUMOR

WHAT ARE MY PLANS FOR INCORPORATING MORE *HUMOR* INTO MY LESSONS TO ACCELERATE LEARNING?

RECOMMENDATIONS	ALREADY DOING	PLANNING TO DO
Join a laughing club to get each day off to a positive start.		
Place humorous signs as visuals around the classroom.		
SMILE as you greet your class daily.		
Use humor to make fun of yourself.		
Use riddles with primary students.		
Assign class clowns to share jokes and riddles with the class.		
Incorporate cartoons, riddles, and jokes into the delivery of instruction.		
Have students create jokes or riddles regarding the content taught.		
Have students bring in riddles and place them in a riddle box.		
Use humorous ways to involve students in a lesson.		
Select students for cooperative groups in a variety of humorous ways.		
Check out *NCTM's Mathematics and Humor* book.		
Infuse appropriate editorial cartoons into lessons.		
Provide positive feedback for appropriate student responses.		
Use affirmations to support correct student answers.		
Play games with students to review content.		
Goals and Notes:		

Engaging the Brain

Source: istock.com/SerrNovik

Hands-on learning represents the fast track to building neural pathways in the brain (ALI Staff, 2023).

STRATEGY 7

Manipulatives, Experiments, Labs, and Models

💡 WHAT: DEFINING THE STRATEGY

When I was growing up, there was an oddity called a Rubik's Cube. The object of the challenge was to get each side of the cube turned to the same color. No matter how hard I tried, I couldn't do it! The only way I could get all cube sections on one side turned to the same color was to peel off the stickers and stick them back on in the appropriate place. Those of you who are familiar with the Rubik's Cube know that this would be considered cheating. Oh well! I know you recall those tests where you had to identify an object that had been rotated to a different position. I could not recognize that either! In fact, when what Howard Gardner calls visual-spatial intelligence was being handed out, I do not think I was in the room. Yet, according to brain consultant Sousa (2022), students must realize that they must discover and order real-world relationships.

The use of the hands and brain activity are so complicated and interconnected that no one theory explains it (Jensen, 2001). I cannot explain it either! I know that some students need to have their hands involved before their brains can comprehend. My son, Christopher, was one of those students. He had difficulty paying attention in class when his teachers lectured for the majority of the period. However, this was the same child who, as a teenager, could spend hours in his room constructing a moving Ferris wheel out of K'nex blocks or who excelled in a summer hands-on science camp sponsored by the Georgia Institute of Technology. When anything we bought needed to be assembled, we would give it to Chris, who would put it together without even referring to the directions. He just instinctively knew how to do it! Chris's gift of his hands has been passed down to one of his sons, twelve-year-old Maxwell, who will stay up all night constructing the complicated Lego models his grandmother, yours truly, buys for him.

These students, like my son and grandson, usually excel with hands-on strategies, such as using manipulatives or graphing calculators, conducting experiments, or constructing models, and teachers would do well to incorporate this strategy into their repertoire.

WHY: THEORETICAL FRAMEWORK

There are three major themes from the meta-analyses related to manipulatives in math: (1) The effects appear to be greatest with lower-ability students; (2) Aids can be provided for all to reduce the cognitive load, that is, using calculators during problem solving; and (3) High levels of quality feedback from teachers to students and from students to teachers should be provided. (Hattie, 2023).

Hands-on learning represents the fast track to building neural pathways in the brain and can make challenging subjects easier and more exciting for visual, auditory, and kinesthetic learners (ALI Staff, 2023).

Hands-on learning has the following benefits for the brain: (1) By engaging both the left and right sides of the brain, better connections occur, and more relevant information is stored; (2) Curiosity and creativity are stimulated along with critical thinking and reasoning skills; and (3) Since learning is more fun and meaningful, intrinsic motivation and engagement are boosted (Chanchal, 2023).

Each student having their own set of manipulatives increases hands-on-time resulting in much greater learning; time spent on harder-to-measure skills is increased; the motor planning piece of executive function in the brain is utilized; and self-efficacy from having more autonomy is built (Jacobs, 2022).

Some of the benefits of hands-on learning include fostering critical thinking, innovation, and problem solving; intrinsically motivating students, which increases learning and retention; and understanding the real-world implications of the content (Valid Education, 2022).

Manipulatives enable teachers to teach complex subjects in an easy, student-focused manner, assist students in seeing the reasons behind the solutions they derive, and offer an engaging way to enable students to arrive at solutions to math problems while comprehending the strategy behind the process (Singh, 2022).

Hands-on learning engages both the left and right hemispheres and increases activity in sensory and motor-related parts of the brain, thereby creating better connections and storing more relevant information (Ms. Miriam, 2021).

Students' understanding of mathematical ideas is broadened when concrete representations are used (Coggins et al., 2007).

Manipulatives are valuable resources for assisting even high school students in accelerating their mathematical ability (Burns, 1996).

When learning is active and hands-on, the formation of neural connections is facilitated and information is much more readily remembered than information learned from an abstract viewpoint, where the teacher is doing the work while the students watch (Gregory & Parry, 2006).

Because concrete materials assist English language learners in focusing on new concepts and vocabulary at the same time, they are a crucial part of the instruction in fluency with mathematics (Coggins et al., 2007).

When students use manipulatives over a long period, they make gains in verbalizing their thinking, discussing ideas, taking ownership, and gaining confidence in independently finding answers to problems (Sebesta & Martin, 2004).

Students in the early grades should be allowed to use manipulatives for as long as the students feel they are needed (Checkley, 1999).

HOW: INSTRUCTIONAL ACTIVITIES

WHO:	Elementary
WHEN:	During a lesson
CONTENT AREA(S):	Mathematics

- Pass out attribute blocks to groups of students. Give them directions to follow. For example, ask students to place a red shape with four sides *below* a blue shape with three sides. Demonstrate. Have students place a red shape *above* their heads or a green six-sided shape *in* their chairs. Repeat with several different shapes in a variety of configurations.

WHO:	Elementary/Middle
WHEN:	During a lesson
CONTENT AREA(S):	Social Studies

- Group students into groups of three to four. Give each group eight Styrofoam cups. Explain to the groups that they are to create a "stack" using these cups and pictures/images provided from top to bottom, with the bottom cup being themselves and the top being the solar system. Provide students with images of the solar system, Earth, North America, the United States, your state, your city, a picture of your school, and a picture of the group (or outline symbol). These can be downloaded from clip art. Have students cut and paste one picture on each cup and then "stack" the cups in the order indicated.

WHO:	Elementary
WHEN:	During a lesson
CONTENT AREA(S):	Cross-curricular

- Have students practice spelling or content-area vocabulary words in a number of tactile ways, including the following: writing the words in the air; writing them in rice, grits, or in shaving cream spread on the desk (a side benefit of this activity is that you end up with a clean desk when the activity ends); forming the words with clay or other pliable materials; or using magnetic alphabet letters to build the words.

WHO:	Elementary
WHEN:	During a lesson
CONTENT AREA(S):	Mathematics

- Give students pieces of construction paper cut in the shape of pizza slices. Some students have two slices, some four slices, and some have eight slices, all of which form a whole pizza. Have students assemble the slices of their pizzas and then compare the sizes of their pieces with other classmates. Ask them to make assumptions regarding the sizes of the slices, becoming familiar with terms such as halves, thirds, fourths, and eighths.

Adaptation: Instead of a pizza, give students a hamburger with all of the condiments cut out of round circles. The burger is on brown construction paper and is divided into halves; the cheese on top is on yellow paper and is in thirds, the red tomato is in fourths, the green pickle is in fifths, and the white onion is in sixths. The hamburger is set between two buns, enabling students to see that although each part of the hamburger is in different fractional pieces, each piece adds to the whole circle.

WHO: Elementary

WHEN: During a lesson

CONTENT AREA(S): Language Arts

Write the *Commonly Used Prefixes/Suffixes* and base words on the appropriate colored index cards as shown in the Figure 7.1. Cut them apart and put them in three separate small zip lock bags. Have students work in groups of four to build words using either a red and white index card or a white and blue index card. When students create a new word, have them write it on a sheet of paper. See how many words students can make! This activity also works well with compound words.

FIGURE 7.1 • Index Cards

RED INDEX CARDS	
Prefix	Meaning
re-	Again
dis-	Not, opposite of
un-	Not
pre-	Before
im-	Not, opposite of
non-	Not
mis-	Wrong, bad

WHITE INDEX CARDS
Base Words
Able
Learn
Happy
Like
Agree
Kind
Read
Paint
Lead

BLUE INDEX CARDS	
Suffix	Meaning
-ful	Full
-less	Without
-ly	Characteristic of
-y	Like

Source: Reprinted from Tate (2020a)

WHO:	Elementary/Middle/High
WHEN:	During a lesson
CONTENT AREA(S):	Cross-curricular

- Have students respond with manipulatives when answering questions in class. These response items can be in the form of index cards, discarded copy paper, or a dry-erase board that can be erased with a sock that students bring from home. Have students write down short answers to selected questions asked in class. The objective of this activity is to have all students respond simultaneously and immediately assess students' understanding and retention (Tate, 2012).

WHO:	Elementary/Middle/High
WHEN:	During a lesson
CONTENT AREA(S):	Science

- Place students in groups of four or five. Discuss paper airplanes and research designs, and have each group make several airplanes out of single sheets of paper. Have a paper airplane flying contest. Create contest rules, such as the farthest flight, curviest flight, most spins, and so on. Have students color and decorate their entries. Then, help them formulate and write hypotheses using vocabulary as planes from each group are tested.

WHO:	Elementary/Middle/High
WHEN:	During a lesson
CONTENT AREA(S):	Mathematics

- Have students use manipulatives, such as Unifix cubes, tiles, blocks, tangram pieces, Cuisenaire rods, miniature clocks, or geoboards, during mathematics instruction to display their understanding of a particular concept taught.

WHO:	Elementary/Middle/High
WHEN:	During a lesson
CONTENT AREA(S):	Science

- Design a laboratory experiment for students, and allow them to follow specific directions to complete the experiment, demonstrating their understanding of a science concept being taught. For example, Warren Phillips conducts this experiment while teaching his science workshop. Get an entire roll of Mentos and a two-liter bottle of diet cola. Unwrap the whole roll of Mentos and position them directly over the mouth of the diet cola bottle so that all candies can drop into the bottle simultaneously. CO_2 will release the soda about 10 feet in the air. Have students come up and try varying numbers of Mentos, measuring eruption heights and times. This experiment should be done outdoors. Be sure that students have goggles and a lab apron (Tate & Phillips, 2011).

WHO: Elementary/Middle/High

WHEN: During a lesson

CONTENT AREA(S): Language Arts

- Give students small Post-it notes. As they locate text evidence to support an author's point of view or make inferences, have students put the Post-it notes on specific references in the book to be easily located during small-group or whole-class discussion.

WHO: Elementary/Middle/High

WHEN: After a lesson

CONTENT AREA(S): Cross-curricular

- Have students construct models that show their understanding of a concept previously taught. For example, have students build a model of the solar system that shows the planets in order from the sun—from Mercury to Neptune, or have students construct a model of a home to scale with all of the necessary rooms and fixtures.

WHO: Elementary/Middle/High

WHEN: During a lesson

CONTENT AREA(S): Cross-curricular

- Have students use their hands to show agreement or disagreement with an answer or level of understanding for an answer by doing one of the following:
  - Thumbs-up if you agree
  - Thumbs-down if you disagree
  - Five fingers if you completely understand
  - One finger if you don't understand
  - Pat head if you understand
  - Scratch your head if you don't understand

WHO: Elementary/Middle/High

WHEN: Before and after a lesson

CONTENT AREA(S): Cross-curricular

- Engage students in the Sort and Report activity according to the following guidelines: (1) Pick a topic that is about to be studied, and list words and phrases connected to it on a piece of paper. (2) Have students work with a partner or in groups to cut the words and phrases apart to use as manipulatives. (3) Have students discuss the words and concepts and put them into categories the group labels. (4) Have students make predictions as to what the topic will be about based on the concepts and categories. (5) Then, have students read the passage or chapter and revisit the categories. (6) If necessary, have students re-sort the categories based on what they have read. (7) Have student groups create a final sort and explain why they sorted the categories as they did (Perez, 2008).

Action Plan for Incorporating
MANIPULATIVES, EXPERIMENTS, LABS, *and* MODELS

WHAT ARE MY PLANS FOR INCORPORATING MORE *MANIPULATIVES, EXPERIMENTS, LABS,* AND *MODELS* INTO MY LESSONS TO ACCELERATE LEARNING?

RECOMMENDATIONS	ALREADY DOING	PLANNING TO DO
Have math students use attribute blocks when solving problems.		
Have social studies students place cups to indicate their world from self to solar system.		
Have students practice spelling vocabulary in tactile ways.		
Use pizza slices to have students understand fractions.		
Have students make words by combining prefixes and suffixes with base words.		
Ask students to show responses using manipulatives.		
Conduct a paper airplane flying contest to test formulas and hypotheses.		
Use manipulatives, that is, Unifix cubes, Cuisenaire rods, and geoboards, during instruction to clarify concepts.		
Have students replicate a laboratory experiment.		
Give students Post-it notes to point out specific references in texts.		
Have students construct models to show their understanding.		
Have students show their levels of understanding with their hands.		
Engage students in the Sort and Report activity.		
Goals and Notes:		

Source: istock.com/SDI Productions

The meaning of abstract material is conveyed as well and as rapidly as literal language with the use of metaphors (Sousa, 2022).

STRATEGY 8

Metaphors, Analogies, and Similes

WHAT: DEFINING THE STRATEGY

When I teach the workshop accompanying this book, I use the strategy of metaphor to acquaint participants with the brain functions of neurons and dendrites. As each participant stands, I ask them to raise their dominant arms with their fingers outstretched and the palms of their hands facing away from them. Then I tell them that their dominant arm is a metaphor for a neuron and that we are born with approximately one hundred billion of them. I have them tap the palm of their dominant hand with the other hand since this represents the cell body of the neuron, and their fingers become connections at the end of each neuron, known as dendrites. Participants are surprised to know that every neuron can have up to 6,000 dendrites and that every time a student learns something new, their brain grows a new dendrite. I tell teachers they should list themselves as dendrite growers on their next resume. Then, they are told to rub their arm. I identify the arm as the neuron's axon and tell them that dendrites do not choose to talk to one another but instead talk to the axon of another neuron. But they are reminded that dendrites and axons don't touch since the message has to cross over an area called the synapse. The fun part is when they are told to take their dendrites and talk to the axon of another person without touching them. This activity always gets the audience laughing. We conclude with the understanding that repetition enables messages to cross the synapse faster, and I stress the importance of teaching and reviewing a concept multiple times. There have been participants I have not seen for years who still remember the parts and functions of a neuron due to the power of movement and the strategy of metaphor.

Of all 20 strategies, this one is probably one of the most effective. Because the brain is a *meaning-maker,* it *constantly searches* for connections and patterns. Students can understand many new and complicated concepts when those concepts are compared to dissimilar ones that the students already know and understand.

WHY: THEORETICAL FRAMEWORK

Metaphors, analogies, and similes are very useful in helping the brain make the transfer connection between abstract application of knowledge and skills to new situations (Sousa, 2022).

Studies suggest that both hemispheres of the brain are engaged when people process and understand metaphors (Chatterjee, 2021).

Metaphors are effective since they help us express our ideas in pictures that are vivid and very memorable and enable us to understand and internalize concepts at a more creative and effective level (Science World, 2016).

According to Orson Scott Card, "metaphors have a way of holding the most truth in the least space" (Science World, 2016).

"Metaphors can convey the meaning of abstract material as well and as rapidly as literal language" (Sousa, 2022, p. 134).

Metaphors stretch the brain's imagination, enrich our thinking, and activate the regions of the brain that are associated with tactile experiences (ScienceDaily, 2019).

Metaphors are both literary and psychological techniques since they take a hard to understand, abstract idea and compare it to a simple, concrete idea that is well understood (Burkley, 2017).

The hardware for making metaphors may be inborn, the software is earned and learned through living (Popova, 2015).

Students would probably learn better if teachers used *metaphorical truth*, which is communicated by comparing two things but whose meaning goes beyond what is communicated by the actual words of the metaphor (Scott & Marzano, 2014, p. 90).

While metaphors convey meaning of content and skills as rapidly as literal language, they are customarily more rich in imagery (Sousa, 2011).

Creating metaphors and creating analogies are two of the four types of tasks students should use to identify similarities and help them develop knowledge (Marzano, 2007).

When students connect what they are learning in mathematics with other content areas, math is viewed as more useful and interesting than when math is taught as a separate subject (Posamentier & Jaye, 2006).

HOW: INSTRUCTIONAL ACTIVITIES

WHO: Elementary

WHEN: During a lesson

CONTENT AREA(S): Language Arts

- Have fun asking students to compare and contrast the treatment of the plot in two different children's books. Examples could include the following: *Cinderella* by RH Disney and *Cinder-Elly* by Frances Minters; *Mufaro's Beautiful Daughters* by John Steptoe and *The Gospel Cinderella* by Joyce Carol Thomas; *Little Red Riding Hood* by James Marshall and *Honestly, Red Riding Hood Was Rotten* by Trisha Speed Shaskan; and *The Three Little Pigs* by Stephen Kellogg and *The Three Little Wolves and the Big Bad Pig* by Eugene Trivizas. Discuss how the plots are analogous to one another and how they are different.

(Tate, 2020a)

WHO: Elementary

WHEN: During a lesson

CONTENT AREA(S): Cross-curricular

- To introduce the concept of *simile*, read aloud the book *I'm as Quick as a Cricket* by Audrey Wood. Read it the first few times simply for enjoyment. Then, have students think of ways they are like animals. Help them write a story using the following pattern: *I'm as* _____ *as a* _____. Compile their stories into a class book.

WHO: Elementary/Middle/High

WHEN: During a lesson

CONTENT AREA(S): Cross-curricular

- Have students fill out the following graphic organizer to write an *I Am* poem expressing the blueprint for their lives. Once they have filled out the organizer, have them put the lines together in any order to compose an original poem to be shared with classmates. Students may add other similes and metaphors that are not listed.

SIMILES (I AM . . .)	METAPHORS
Like (a type of weather)	I am (a type of musical instrument)
Like (an animal)	I am (an insect)
Like (a type of food)	I am (a season of the year)
Like (a place)	I am (an article of clothing)
Like (a favorite song)	I am (a time of day)
Like (a color)	I am (a type of vehicle)

Source: Reprinted from Tate (2020b)

WHO: Elementary

WHEN: During a lesson

CONTENT AREA(S): Mathematics

- Assist students in understanding that certain operations in math are analogous to other operations. Help them to see that addition and subtraction are simply inverse operations, as are multiplication and division. Show them that multiplication is simply a faster form of addition. Because the brain constantly searches for connections, consistently demonstrating these relationships to students should help them better understand and apply these concepts.

WHO: Elementary/Middle/High

WHEN: During a lesson

CONTENT AREA(S): Cross-curricular

- Regardless of the content area, students should engage in Glynn's TWA (teaching with analogies) approach by using the following procedure:
    - Introduce the concept to be learned.
    - Review a familiar but similar concept through the use of analogy.
    - Identify the features of both the new and known concepts.
    - Explain what both concepts have in common.
    - Explain how the new concept is different from the known. (At this point, the analogy breaks down.)
    - Draw conclusions regarding the major ideas that students need to remember about the new concept (Metsala & Glynn, 1996).

WHO: Elementary/Middle/High

WHEN: During a lesson

CONTENT AREA(S): Language Arts

- Select a theme, such as *prejudice* or *growing up*, and have students compare and contrast several different stories, examining their approach to the particular theme. Have students cite text evidence that shows the similarities and differences in the treatment of the themes in two or more texts.

WHO: Elementary/Middle/High

WHEN: During a lesson

CONTENT AREA(S): Cross-curricular

- Whenever possible, introduce a new or difficult concept by comparing it to a concept that students already know and understand, particularly one they will experience in the real world. For example, when teaching math students the meaning of logarithms, remind them that the Richter Scale for measuring the intensity of earthquakes is a logarithmic scale. When teaching equations, tell students that equations are like balanced scales. Since both sides must always be equal, the same operation must be performed on both sides.

WHO: Elementary/Middle/High

WHEN: During a lesson

CONTENT AREA(S): Cross-curricular

- To assist students in comprehending the relationship between two concepts in any content area, have them create analogies. Give them the pattern a : b :: c : d (a is to b as c is to d) to show how two sets of ideas or concepts are related. For example, Shakespeare : *Hamlet* :: Charles

Dickens : A *Christmas Carol* or Eli Whitney : the cotton gin :: Thomas Edison : the light bulb. Once they get the hang of it, students can then create their own analogies, leaving a blank line for other students to complete.

WHO: Elementary/Middle/High

WHEN: After a lesson

CONTENT AREA(S): Music

- Assist students in seeing the analogous relationship between types of notes in music and fractions in math. For example, in 4/4 time, it takes two half notes, four quarter notes, and eight eighth notes to make a whole note. Similarly, it takes, 2/2, 4/4, and 8/8 to also make a whole. Have students write musical notation to symbolize fractional parts.

WHO: Elementary/Middle/High

WHEN: During or after a lesson

CONTENT AREA(S): Cross-curricular

- Have students pretend to be detectives and look for metaphors, analogies, and similes in narrative and expository texts. Post a list of the examples students find, and periodically ask students to explain the relationships that exist between the two concepts. Add to the list throughout the year.

WHO: Elementary/Middle/High

WHEN: During a lesson

CONTENT AREA(S): Language Arts

- As students write, have them create metaphors that improve the quality of their writing and symbolize their understanding of the relationship between two unrelated concepts. Have them explain the relationship to a partner. For example, students could write the following: *My life is a roller coaster. I have my ups and downs.*

WHO: Elementary/Middle/High

WHEN: During a lesson

CONTENT AREA(S): Cross-curricular

- To encourage creative thinking, have students complete a cloze sentence such as the following: If _____ were a _____, it would be _____ because _____. For example, *If the brain were a piece of technology, it would be a computer because it has a great deal of memory*.

WHO: Elementary/Middle/High

WHEN: During a lesson

CONTENT AREA(S): Social Studies

- To understand that history repeats itself, help students connect current events to similar events that happened in the past. For example, students could compare a more current recession with the Great Depression that occurred years earlier. Have them use a Venn diagram to compare and contrast how the two periods are alike and how they are different.

Action Plan for Incorporating METAPHORS, ANALOGIES, and SIMILES

WHAT ARE MY PLANS FOR INCORPORATING MORE *METAPHORS, ANALOGIES,* AND *SIMILES* INTO MY LESSONS TO ACCELERATE LEARNING?

RECOMMENDATIONS	ALREADY DOING	PLANNING TO DO
Have students compare and contrast the plot in two different children's stories.		
Ask students to complete the simile pattern: *I'm as ___ as a ___.*		
Have students use the graphic organizer to compose an original simile and metaphor poem.		
Have math students comprehend how some operations are analogous to others.		
Engage students in Glynn's TWA (teaching with analogies) approach.		
Have students compare and contrast the approach of different stories to a theme.		
Introduce a new concept by comparing it to a known concept.		
Ask students to create analogies to show how concepts are related.		
Assist math students in seeing the analogous relationships between notes in music and fractions in math.		
Have students compile a list of the metaphors, analogies, and similes they encounter in texts.		
To improve the quality of students' writing, have them create appropriate metaphors.		
Encourage creative thinking with the cloze sentence provided.		
Assist social studies students with connecting current and past events.		
Goals and Notes:		

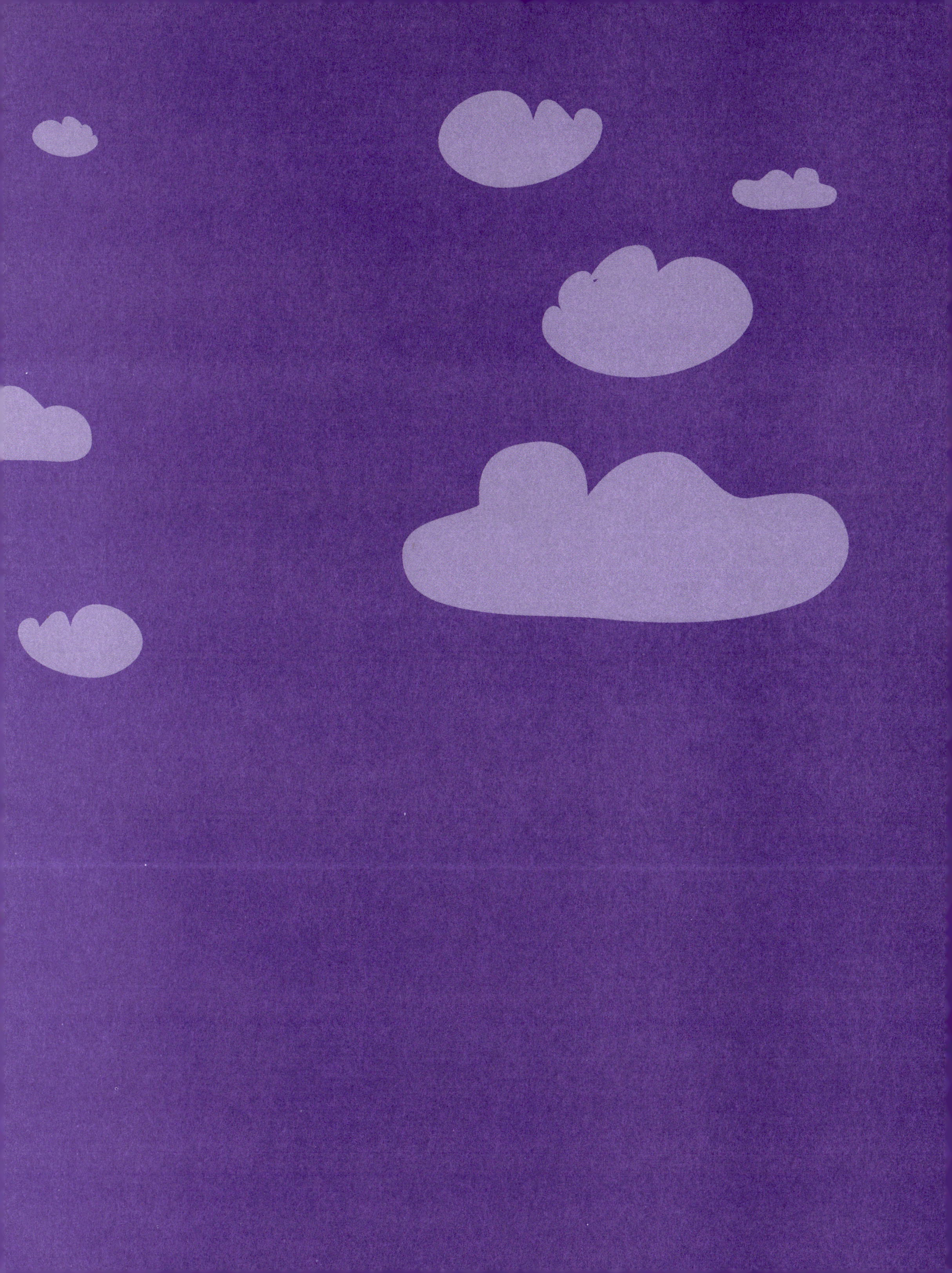

Source: istock.com/pixdeluxe

Mnemonics, a form of chunking, enables people to take smaller pieces of information and combine them into more memorable wholes (Cherry, 2022).

STRATEGY 9

Mnemonic Devices

💡 WHAT: DEFINING THE STRATEGY

IVAN CAPP: Interjection, Verb, Adjective, Noun, Conjunction, Adverb, Pronoun, Preposition (Language Arts)

HOMES: Huron, Ontario, Michigan, Erie, Superior (Social Studies)

ROY G. BIV: colors of the spectrum (Art)

PEMDAS: Please excuse my dear Aunt Sally. (Mathematics)

In Poland, Men Are Tall. Interphase, prophase, metaphase, anaphase, telophase (Science)

Elephants Go Break Dancing Friday: EGBDF (Music)

LOL: Laughing Out Loud (Social Media)

OMG: Oh! My God! (Social Media)

Social Media is replete with mnemonic devices. These are acronyms and acrostics and can assist the messenger in shortening the message, which appears to be the goal of most social media junkies. Acronyms are words where the first letter in the word stands for the content to be remembered. For example, *IVAN CAPP* helps students remember the eight parts of speech; *HOMES*, the Great Lakes; and *ROY G. BIV*, the seven spectrum colors. Acrostics, on the other hand, are sentences where the first letter in each word in the sentence begins with the same letter as the concept to be remembered. For example, Please Excuse My Dear Aunt Sally actually helps students recall the order of operations in math (Parentheses, Exponents, Multiply, Divide, Add, Subtract); *In Poland Men Are Tall*, the stages of cell division in mitosis; and Elephants Go Break Dancing Friday represents the notes on the lines of the treble clef, *EGBDF*.

101

Mnemonic devices are practical tools for remembering and transmitting large amounts of information. In fact, the word itself derives from the Greek word *mnema*, which means memory. Mnemonic devices used in the real world to help the public remember include *AI*, *RSVP*, *FBI*, and *NFL*.

WHY: THEORETICAL FRAMEWORK

Mnemonics is a form of chunking that enables people to take smaller pieces of information and combine them into more memorable and meaningful wholes (Cherry, 2022).

Ordinary people can greatly improve their memory with mnemonics, very useful devices for remembering unrelated patterns, rules, or basic information (Sousa, 2022).

Mnemonic devices, which are often illogical, arbitrary, or nonsensical, work because they associate easy-to-remember clues with unfamiliar or complex data (Kelly, 2020).

Mnemonic devices not only help students encode information into short-term memory, they also assist them in retrieving information from long-term memory (Suraj, 2018).

Mnemonics enable students to associate new knowledge with knowledge that already exists and gives a framework for more easily organizing and recalling that information (Gepp, 2022).

Mnemonic devices are valuable memory tricks that help students remember factual information or steps in a procedure (Sousa, 2016).

Adolescents find mnemonic devices more meaningful when they can personally create them (Feinstein, 2009).

Since students' brains have difficulty holding information that is not meaningful or does not have a *hook*, acrostics and acronyms help to provide that hook (Sprenger, 2008).

Acronyms turn a recall task into an "aided recall task" because students are remembering chunks of information rather than a great deal of information at one time (Allen, 2008, p. 16).

Learning is increased two- to three-fold when people rely on mnemonic devices rather than their regular learning habits (Markowitz & Jensen, 2007).

Mnemonic devices should be used only after students have had an opportunity to thoroughly process the information, even if their understanding is incomplete (Marzano, 2007).

Mathematics instruction is more relevant and cohesive when mnemonics are used to link abstract symbols with concrete associations (Bender, 2005).

HOW: INSTRUCTIONAL ACTIVITIES

WHO: Elementary/Middle/High

WHEN: During a lesson

CONTENT AREA(S): Language Arts

- Discuss the formula for writing informational texts with students. Place the formula on an anchor chart as a visual for students to reference when writing.

  I Introduction
  N Name three facts
  F Facts require supporting details
  O Offer a conclusion

  (Tate, 2020a)

WHO: Elementary/Middle/High

WHEN: During a lesson

CONTENT AREA(S): Language Arts

- Before making inferences or drawing conclusions about a character in a story, have students use the mnemonic device FLATS to organize evidence from the text regarding the character. Have them go back to the text and look for the desired information.

  F Feelings
  L Looks
  A Actions
  T Thoughts
  S Statements

  (Tate, 2020a)

WHO: Elementary/Middle/High

WHEN: During a lesson

CONTENT AREA(S): Cross-curricular

- To assist students in recalling previously taught and thoroughly processed content, create acronyms and acrostics to help them remember. Teach these mnemonic devices and use them consistently during instruction so students hear them multiple times and can use them to recall content during and after tests. For example, to remember the five states that border Virginia, a social studies teacher could give students the acrostic *Kiss Me With No Teeth!* Which stands for Kentucky, Maryland, West Virginia, North Carolina, and Tennessee (Tate, 2012).

WHO: Elementary/Middle/High

WHEN: During a lesson

CONTENT AREA(S): Cross-curricular

- Have students create their own acrostics to assist them in remembering content. For example, one teacher had students make original acrostics to remember the order of operations in math. Students will best recall what they choose to create, especially if the mnemonic devices are humorous or novel. For example, instead of the customary *Please Excuse My Dear Aunt Sally* (**P**arentheses, **E**xponents, **M**ultiply, **D**ivide, **A**dd, **S**ubtract), one student created the following original acrostic: *Please End My Day At School.*

WHO: Elementary/Middle/High

WHEN: During a lesson

CONTENT AREA(S): Mathematics

- To help eliminate the threat in the brain when some students lack confidence in their ability to succeed in your math class, teach them the acronym that Connie Moore of Los Angeles, California, uses: MATH, which stands for **M**ath **A**in't **T**hat **H**ard! I know the word "ain't" is not grammatically correct, but this acronym is too good to overlook. If you use the 20 strategies as you teach, you can watch this acronym come true.

WHO: Elementary/Middle/High

WHEN: During a lesson

CONTENT AREA(S): Science

- Have students remember the acrostic *Never Does Eating Some Chocolate-Covered Goodies Really Ruin Meals* to recall the 10 systems of the human body (in no particular order). They are **n**ervous, **d**igestive, **e**xcretory, **s**keletal, **c**irculatory, **c**overing, **g**land, **r**espiratory, **r**eproductive, and **m**uscular (Tate & Phillips, 2011). Medical doctors have told me that using mnemonic devices to remember parts of the human body aided them in getting through medical school.

WHO: Elementary/Middle/High

WHEN: During a lesson

CONTENT AREA(S): Cross-curricular

- Have students use the Acrostics Topics activity to recall important information about a subject being studied. Divide students into groups of four to six. Give each group a large piece of chart paper with a topic written horizontally down the left-hand side. This topic becomes an acronym that each group will use to list facts about the subject. The following example could be used in a social studies classroom:

    C Came to America for religious freedom

    O On long trips in boats

    L Loyalists agreed with the British King.

    O Often, people farmed and hunted.

    N No taxation without representation

    I If you wanted independence, you were a patriot.

    E Even the kids helped with chores, such as cooking or fishing.

    S Some took the Native Americans' land.

    Ask groups to share their finished products with the class. If groups cannot come up with a fact that begins with the designated letter, have them use information in their textbooks or from the Internet. Watch the creativity of your students blossom (Green & Casale-Giannola, 2011)!

    WHO: Elementary/Middle/High

    WHEN: During a lesson

    CONTENT AREA(S): Language Arts

- Writing to convey information and writing to argue or persuade readers are the two types of writing required for incoming college students (ACT Inc., 2009). The acronym DEFENDS provides students with a structure for finishing initial and final drafts of argumentative writing:

    Decide on a specific position.

    Examine your own reasons for this position.

    Form a list of points explaining each reason.

    Expose a position in the first sentence of the written task.

    Note each reason and associated points.

    Drive home position in the last sentence.

    Search for and correct any errors (Collier, 2010, p. 207).

    WHO: Elementary/Middle/High

    WHEN: During a lesson

    CONTENT AREA(S): Cross-curricular

- Mnemonic devices are used in the real world consistently to help the public remember content that would be otherwise difficult to recall.

Have students look for examples of mnemonic devices in the real world, such as SCUBA, CIA, or SIDS, and bring their list to class. Post a list of real-life examples, and see how many the class can come up with in a combined list.

WHO: Elementary/Middle/High

WHEN: During a lesson

CONTENT AREA(S): Mathematics

- To help students comprehend the text of a word problem, use the SQRQCQ strategy, which serves as a mnemonic device:

  Survey: Obtain a general understanding of the problem by reading it quickly.

  Question: Find out what information is required in the problem.

  Read: Reread the problem to find information that is relevant to solving the problem.

  Question: Ask what operations must be performed and in which order to solve the problem.

  Complete: Do the computations necessary to get a solution.

  Question: Ask whether the answer is reasonable and the process complete.

WHO: Elementary/Middle/High

WHEN: During a lesson

CONTENT AREA(S): Mathematics, Science

- Have students remember the following acrostic to help them recall the prefixes for units of the metric system, from large to small: *Kids Have Dropped Over Dead Converting Metrics,* which stands for kilo, hecto, deka, ones unit, deci, centi, milli.

WHO: High

WHEN: During a lesson

CONTENT AREA(S): Mathematics

- Have students remember the acrostic, *Some Old Hen Caught Another Hen Taking Oats Away,* to help them remember the following formulas:

$$\text{Sine} = \frac{\text{Opposite}}{\text{Hypotenuse}}$$

$$\text{Cosine} = \frac{\text{Adjacent}}{\text{Hypotenuse}}$$

$$\text{Tangent} = \frac{\text{Opposite}}{\text{Adjacent}}$$

Another high school teacher told me he uses a similar acrostic, but his is as follows: *Some Old Hippie Caught Another Hippie Tripping On Acid.*

Action Plan for Incorporating MNEMONIC DEVICES

WHAT ARE MY PLANS FOR INCORPORATING MORE *MNEMONIC DEVICES* INTO MY LESSONS TO ACCELERATE LEARNING?		
RECOMMENDATIONS	ALREADY DOING	PLANNING TO DO
Have students use the acronym INFO when writing informational texts.		
Teach students to use the acronym FLATS when organizing evidence regarding a character.		
Create acronyms and acrostics as you teach to assist students in remembering content.		
Have students create their own acronyms and acrostics to remember content.		
Teach students the acronym MATH to increase their confidence.		
Have science students use an acrostic to recall the 10 systems of the human body.		
Use the Acrostics Topics activity to help students recall pertinent information about a cross-curricular topic.		
Provide the acronym DEFENDS to assist students with their argumentative writing.		
Have students look for real-life examples of mnemonic devices.		
Have students use the SQRQCR strategy to comprehend the text of a math word problem.		
Give students an acrostic to help them remember prefixes for units of the metric system in order.		
Give students acrostics to help them remember math formulas.		
Goals and Notes:		

Source: istock.com/Prostock-Studio

The same parts of the brain that coordinate movement also coordinate the flow of thoughts (Sousa, 2022).

STRATEGY 10

Movement

💡 WHAT: DEFINING THE STRATEGY

One of my favorite language arts activities is the *Living Sentence*. Here is how it works. Create a sentence that has in it all of the language arts concepts that you have previously taught. For example, if you have taught the terms subject, predicate, prepositional phrase, and so on, then those elements should be included in the sentence. A sample sentence might be **My dog, Bailey, runs out of the house whenever I open the front door**. Using a dark marker, write each word in the sentence in large letters on a separate piece of paper and pass the pieces out randomly to students. Then, have students with papers walk to the front of the room, form a line, and turn their words around so that everyone in the class can see them. Be sure that the students are mixed up and not standing in the correct order of the sentence. Have a volunteer come to the front of the room and move the students around to form a sentence. Here is the catch! They must complete the sentence before the theme from *The Price Is Right* is over. Once the student has completed all moves, the remainder of the class must tell if the sentence is in the correct order. Once the sentence is correct, the fun begins! The sentence is *living*; therefore, you can have the sentence do whatever you want. For example, have the subject take one step forward, the complete predicate turns around in a circle to the right, the prepositional phrase sticks out its tongue, and so on. In other words, we are diagramming a live sentence!

Students love this activity and never forget what they learned while doing it. Why? When students move while learning, they put information into *procedural* or *muscle* memory. Procedural memory is one of the strongest memory systems in the brain and the reason that one seldom forgets how to drive a car, ride a bicycle, play the piano, or type on a keyboard. One teacher related to me that her mother has Alzheimer's disease and no longer recognizes her or her children. She stated, however, that her mother still remembers how to play the piano and can still play songs that she always has!

In many traditional classrooms, students sit for long periods in uncomfortable desks, and if they get up, they are chastised for being out of their seats. One teacher told me that we spend the first three years of our children's lives teaching them to walk and talk and the next 15 telling them to *Sit down!* and *Shut up!* Rather than having students watching you as you move around the classroom, have them up and moving along with you. Not only does it strengthen memory and decrease behavior problems, but it also makes teaching and learning so much fun!

WHY: THEORETICAL FRAMEWORK

The same parts of the brain (the cerebellum, motor cortex, and midbrain) that coordinate movement also coordinate the flow of thoughts, resulting in complex problems often being solved just by taking a walk (Sousa, 2022).

While boosting focus, motivation, concentration, and engagement, research is also showing that movement is increasing academic achievement, especially in the areas of recall, memory, and problem solving (Hardy, 2022).

"Physical activity, especially aerobic exercise, greatly increases the number of new neurons that are produced in the hippocampus, the structure highly involved in declarative memory" (Jensen, 2022, p. 161).

While health experts are recommending that the body get 10,000 steps (or 60 minutes of physical activity) per day, most students take fewer than 5,000 during a non-P.E. school day (Pantuosco-Hensch, 2019).

Physical activity increases the brain's blood flow and the oxygen needed for fuel, thereby significantly enhancing cognitive performance (Sousa, 2022).

Research studies show that students who are physically active within the hour before learning are better able to retrieve long-term memories than those who are not (Pontifex et al., 2016).

Studies indicate that physical activity not only increases the capillaries in the brain that transport blood but also increases the blood's oxygen, which is needed as fuel for the brain. Both enhance cognitive performance (Sousa, 2022).

Students of color perform better academically when there is physical activity at school (Basch, 2011).

When students get up and move, they recirculate the blood that pools in their seats and feet when sitting for more than 20 minutes; 15% of this recirculated blood goes to the brain within a minute (Sousa & Tomlinson, 2011).

Physical performance is probably the only known cognitive activity that uses 100% of the brain (Jensen, 2008).

Regular exercise increases the levels of brain-derived neurotrophic factor (BDNF), which keeps existing neurons healthy, helps them communicate with neighboring neurons, and facilitates the growth of new neurons (Sousa, 2012).

Movement not only assists with reading, gets blood and glucose to the brain, changes the state or mood of the brain, and provides lots of fun during learning, but it also assists with our strongest memory system—procedural memory (Sprenger, 2007b)

Having students work quietly at their desks eliminates up to 40% of kinesthetic learners who have to be moving to learn (Hattie, 2009).

Repeat a movement often enough, and that movement becomes a permanent memory (Sprenger, 2007a).

HOW: INSTRUCTIONAL ACTIVITIES

WHO: Elementary

WHEN: Before, during, or after a lesson

CONTENT AREA(S): Mathematics

- Have students walk around the room using fly swatters as they read word walls and anchor charts. Have them swat and name the words that they recognize. Students could work with a partner if the teacher is otherwise occupied. (Tate, 2020a).

WHO: Elementary

WHEN: During a lesson

CONTENT AREA(S): Language Arts

- To recognize the phonemes in three-letter words, have students stand and touch the parts of their bodies corresponding to the separate phonemes in a word. For example, for the word *cat*, the students would give the *k* sound for the *c* and touch their shoulders, the short *a* sound for the *a* and put their hands on their waists, and the *t sound* for the *t* and touch their knees. Every phoneme you want students to pronounce in a word should be associated with the corresponding body part.

WHO:	Elementary
WHEN:	During a lesson
CONTENT AREA(S):	Mathematics

- Have the entire class skip-count aloud by 2s, 3s, 5s, 10s, 20s, and so on. Add movement by having them clap or take turns jumping rope while skip counting.

WHO:	Elementary/Middle/High
WHEN:	Before a lesson
CONTENT AREA(S):	Cross-curricular

- Have students draw the appointment clock (see Figure 10.1) on their paper. Put on fast-paced music and have students move around the classroom making appointments with four students in class, one appointment for 12 o'clock, a different student for 3 o'clock, a different one for 6 o'clock, and a final student for 9 o'clock. Have them write each student's name on the corresponding line. Then, as you teach lessons throughout the day or week, have students keep their appointments by standing and discussing content with one another or reteaching a concept previously taught.

FIGURE 10.1 • Appointment Clock

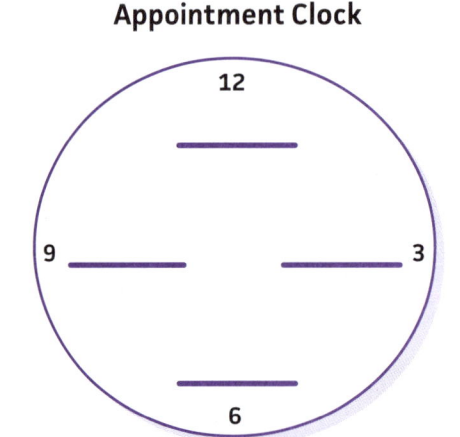

Appointment Clock

Adaptation: Students can also make appointments using the following a seasonal appointment clock, a timeline in social studies, or quadrants in mathematics (see Figures 10.2 and 10.3).

112 • Engaging the Brain

FIGURE 10.2 • Seasonal Appointment Clock

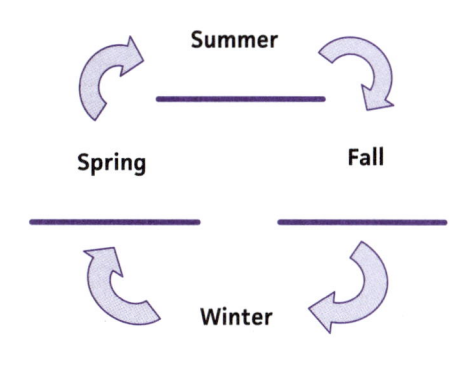

Seasonal Dates

Summer

Spring   Fall

Winter

FIGURE 10.3 • Appointment Timeline

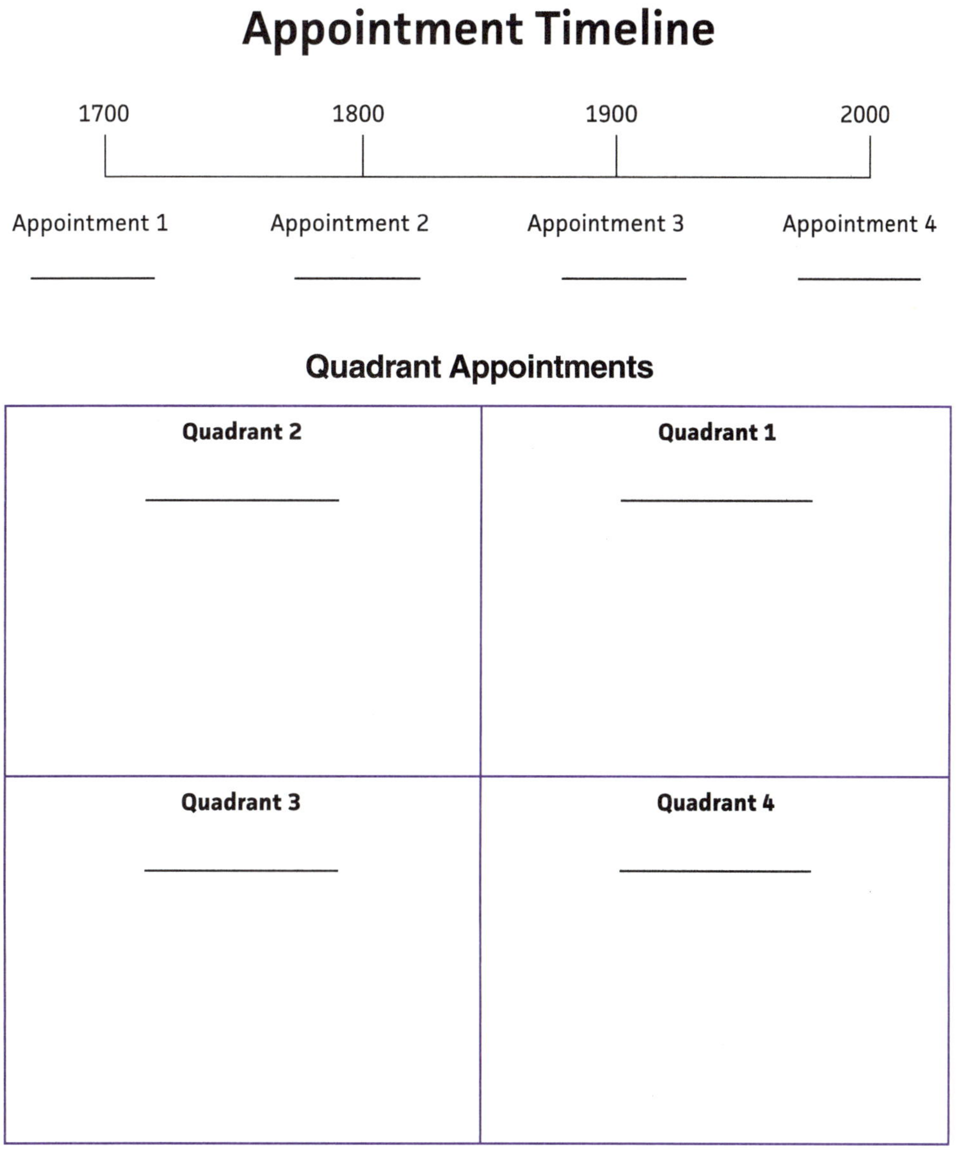

Appointment Timeline

1700   1800   1900   2000

Appointment 1   Appointment 2   Appointment 3   Appointment 4
_____   _____   _____   _____

Quadrant Appointments

Quadrant 2	Quadrant 1
_____	_____
Quadrant 3	**Quadrant 4**
_____	_____

Strategy 10 • Movement   113

WHO: Elementary/Middle/High

WHEN: During a lesson

CONTENT AREA(S): Cross-curricular

- Rather than having students always raise their hand if they agree with an answer provided by a classmate, have them stand if they agree and remain seated if they disagree. Standing provides more blood and oxygen throughout the body and keeps students more alert.

WHO: Elementary/Middle/High

WHEN: During a lesson

CONTENT AREA(S): Cross-curricular

- When discussing content with their families (or students seated near them) for one or two minutes, have students stand and talk rather than remain seated.

WHO: Elementary/Middle/High

WHEN: During a lesson

CONTENT AREA(S): Cross-curricular

- Have students take turns standing and reading short passages aloud in a choral response. Because students are reading together, those students who may be struggling can still participate and will hear the passage read correctly by others. Make this activity more fun by having students read while standing on one foot, in a whisper, holding their paper in the air, without taking a breath, and so forth.

WHO: Elementary/Middle

WHEN: During a lesson

CONTENT AREA(S): Language Arts

- To help students distinguish between two concepts, use the *Sit/Stand* technique. For example, use the following activity to help students with the difference between common and proper nouns. Compile a list containing common and proper nouns taken from content previously taught in class. Read each word aloud. Have students stand when a proper noun is called, since proper nouns are extremely important, and remain seated when a common noun is called, since common nouns are not as important. This activity could be adapted to any concept with positive and negative examples.

WHO:	Elementary/Middle/High
WHEN:	After a lesson
CONTENT AREA(S):	Cross-curricular

- Following the completion of any assignment, have students post their completed work or responses on large Post-it notes on the walls around the room. Have all students stand and conduct Gallery Walks around the room, examining the responses. Sticky notes can be provided for students to use to comment on the work of their peers.

WHO:	Elementary/Middle/High
WHEN:	During a lesson
CONTENT AREA(S):	Music

- Have students sit in chairs representing the lines (EGBDF) on the treble clef. Other students stand in spaces between the chairs and represent the spaces (FACE) on the treble clef. When a note is called out or played on an instrument, have students stand if seated or squat, and if standing, have them stand if their position on the scale corresponds to the note played. Once familiar with the treble clef notes, engage them in the same activity using the lines and spaces on the bass clef.

WHO:	Elementary/Middle/High
WHEN:	During the lesson
CONTENT AREA(S):	Mathematics

- Engage students in the *circumference conga* to teach students the concepts of *circumference, radius,* and *diameter.* Have all students in class form a circle. Stand in the middle of the circle. Have them do the conga by putting their hands on the shoulders of the person in front of them and moving to the salsa music. The circle represents the *circumference.* When you say, "Turn," have them reverse the circle. Then say, "Freeze," and the circle stops. Then, point to a student in the circle and appoint them as the *radius*. The radius then dances (or walks) over to you and then back to its original position (because the radius only extends to the center of the circle). The circle (circumference) then moves again. Say, "Freeze." Then, point to a different student in the circle who can be the *diameter.* The diameter dances (walks) over to you and then straight to the opposite side (because the diameter goes all the way through the circle). Repeat this dance for as long as you desire. Gloria Estefan's song "Conga" is the perfect music for this activity.

WHO: Elementary/Middle/High

WHEN: During a lesson

CONTENT AREA(S): Cross-curricular

- When teaching sequential order (such as events in history, action in a story, or steps in the scientific process), put the separate events or steps on pieces of paper, and then pass them out to students in class. Put on fast-paced music, such as the theme from *The Price Is Right*, and have students place themselves in sequential order before the music ends. Then, have the class decide if students have placed themselves correctly.

WHO: Middle/High

WHEN: During a lesson

CONTENT AREA(S): Mathematics

- Have students do the "Number Line Hustle." Draw a number line on the board. Explain the position of the positive and negative integers on the number line. Have students stand, and tell them they will do the "Number Line Hustle" by moving along the number line. Have each student stand in a place in the room where they have space to move to the left and the right. They should all be facing in the same direction, turning toward the board's number line. You may use any appropriate disco music, such as Van McCoy's "The Hustle." Put on the music, and then position yourself in front of the class. Lead the class in the movements necessary to solve the following problems:

(Problem I: +5 + –3 = ?) Have students move with you to the music five steps in a positive direction (+5). Then, have them move three steps in a negative direction (–3). Ask them what number they landed on. The class should say +2.

Ask the class what they would have to do to get back to zero. (They should say move two steps in a negative direction.) Have them move back to zero.

(Problem II: –6 + +10 = ?) Starting at zero, have students move six steps in a negative direction (–6). Then, have them move +10 steps in a positive direction. Ask the class, "What number are you on?" (+4)

Have the class sit down. Put the same problems you danced out on the board so students can see the connection between the concrete and the abstract. Then, provide five additional problems for students to work either individually or in pairs. Give students the option of going to the back of the classroom and dancing along the number line to solve the additional problems while the music continues to play softly in the background. I have actually taught students this lesson multiple times, and it works every time.

Action Plan for Incorporating MOVEMENT

WHAT ARE MY PLANS FOR INCORPORATING MORE *MOVEMENT* INTO MY LESSONS TO ACCELERATE LEARNING?

RECOMMENDATIONS	ALREADY DOING	PLANNING TO DO
Ask students to stand and move around the room, swatting and naming the words they recognize on the walls.		
Have students stand and associate a phoneme with its corresponding body part.		
Ask students to stand and clap or jump rope while skip counting.		
Have students make appointments with others to discuss content.		
Ask students to stand if they agree with the answer of a peer.		
Ask students to stand while discussing content.		
Engage students in a choral reading while standing.		
Involve students in a *Sit/Stand* to distinguish two attributes of a concept.		
Have students participate in a Gallery Walk to observe the work of their peers.		
Have students in music represent notes on the treble clef by moving.		
Engage students in the Circumference Conga.		
Have students place events in the proper sequential order using movement.		
Engage math students in the Number Line Hustle to add positive and negative integers.		
Goals and Notes:		

Strategy 10 • Movement

Source: istock.com/FangXiaNuo

Certain structures in the auditory cortex of the brain respond only to the tones of music (Sousa, 2022).

STRATEGY 11

Music, Rhythm, Rhyme, Rap

💡 WHAT: DEFINING THE STRATEGY

Imagine a world without music! I would not want to live in such a world! When one pursues research on the power of music for the brain, it appears to divide itself into three main ideas. First, the state of the brain can be changed with the type of music that is played. In other words, a person can be made happy, sad, angry, or agitated by the type of music to which they listen (Gregory & Chapman, 2013; Jensen, 2005). Television and movie producers realize this. Have you ever noticed that you are in tears simply by listening to the music played in a sad movie? On the other hand, songs like "Happy" by Pharrell Williams or the theme from the movie *Rocky* can be very motivational. In the movie *Jaws*, the music creates suspense whenever the shark appears. You do not even see the actual shark until the three main characters are in the ocean and the movie is half over. Teachers can use the right type of music to change students' brains. As a mood enhancer, music can calm or cheer stressed or grumpy students and motivate those who are reluctant (Allen & Scozzi, 2012). It can make the hyperactive student less hyper or the angry child less angry.

A second main idea regarding music is its relationship to a person's mathematical ability. Some research (Bergee & Weingarten, 2021; Sousa, 2022) also suggests that the same spatial part of the brain that is activated when one is playing a musical instrument or sight-reading music is also activated when one is solving higher-level math problems. In a study by Catterall et al. (1999), the mathematics scores of low socioeconomic students more than doubled for those who took music lessons compared to those who did not. My daughter, Jessica, who took more than 10 years of piano lessons, played in the band and sang in the chorus in high school and college, did very well on the SAT math section. A coincidence? I think not!

A third main idea has to do with the brain's ability to remember the lyrics of songs. Senior citizens, even those with dementia who may have difficulty remembering people's names and faces, can still remember the lyrics to songs they once knew. Students, who teachers tell me cannot retain their teaching content, walk down the hall singing the lyrics to every song they love. Having students put content to music increases the likelihood that they will remember that content long after the tests have ended.

WHY: THEORETICAL FRAMEWORK

It is well researched that playing a musical instrument and long-term musical training can build the brain since those actions improve executive function on important tasks such as processing and retaining information, controlling behavior, solving problems, and making decisions (Jensen, 2022).

While research on the *Mozart effect* is inconclusive, listening to appropriate background music can enable students to stay focused and enhance their recall, attention, concentration, and visual imagery (Sousa, 2022).

The subject areas of math and reading appear to both correlate with achievement in music (Bergee & Weingarten, 2021).

Learning to play a musical instrument can cause important and permanent changes in the structure of the brain since students must learn and coordinate new motor skills and distinguish tone patterns and groupings (Sousa, 2022).

Numerous studies are continuing to show that musical training improves verbal memory (Taylor & Dewhurst, 2017); working memory (Gagnon & Nicoladis, 2020); and visual, spatial, and executive memories (Anaya et al., 2017).

Some mathematical concepts that are basic to music include the following: patterns, counting, geometry, ratios, proportions, equivalent fractions, and sequences (Sousa, 2022).

The enhancement of Broca's area in the brain, which is recruited by musicians and also needed to develop sight-reading skills, may generally allow musicians to become better readers (Sousa, 2022).

The motor cortex, the cerebellum, the auditory cortex, and the corpus callosum appear to be larger in musicians than in nonmusicians (Angulo-Perkins et al., 2014; Schlaug, 2015).

There are certain structures in the auditory cortex of the brain that respond only to the tones of music (Sousa, 2022).

Music has the remarkable ability to energize, relax, set the daily mood, stimulate student brains, inspire, and make the learning fun (Jensen, 2009).

Since music can act as a volume barrier, playing it while students are collaborating can keep the noise level low (Allen & Currie, 2012).

Music activates neural networks in the brain, which stimulate both the intellect and the emotion (Sousa, 2011).

Music can be used as a signal, when students are moving, to match a theme, during small-group discussions, or after class (Allen & Scozzi, 2012).

Fast music with 100 to 140 beats per minute can be energizing for the brain, while calming music at 40 to 55 beats per minute can be relaxing (Jensen, 2005).

The rhythms, contrasts, and patterns of music help the brain encode new information, which is why students easily learn words to new songs (Jensen, 2005).

HOW: INSTRUCTIONAL ACTIVITIES

WHO:	Elementary/Middle/High
WHEN:	Before, during, or after a lesson
CONTENT AREA(S):	Cross-curricular

- A rule of thumb for using music in class is less than one-third of your class time. I never play music when I am doing direct instruction to my class. It can be very distracting to have music playing in the background when you want students to pay rapt attention to what you are saying. I might use music if students are writing creatively or solving math problems, but I would choose music without lyrics and keep the volume low. I even find on an airplane that I can still simultaneously read my book when music without lyrics is played before our departure. However, when music with lyrics is played, I struggle to focus and pay attention.

WHO:	Elementary/Middle/High
WHEN:	Before, during, or after a lesson
CONTENT AREA(S):	Cross-curricular

- To maximize instructional time and minimize transition time, play music. Music with approximate beats of 40 to 55 per minute line up with the heart and calm the brain. This music can include classical, jazz, New Age, Celtic, Native American, or nature sounds. Have this type of music playing as students enter your room to help ensure appropriate behavior for the beginning of class. Teach students that if you can hear their voices over the music, they are talking too loudly.

WHO:	Elementary/Middle/High
WHEN:	Before, during, or after a lesson
CONTENT AREA(S):	Cross-curricular

- Rather than calming music, high-energy music is often the day's order. Music with beats of 100 to 140 per minute energizes the brain and body and can bring excitement to your lesson. This type of music can include salsa, rhythm and blues, rock and roll, positive rap, and fast-paced country. High-energy music is often needed for the afternoon classes when students have eaten lunch and appear to display the mnemonic device *TEGO (The Eyes Glaze Over!)*. One art teacher used the high-energy song "Car Wash" to get students to clean up after they completed their projects. Each student's area had to be spotless by the

122 Engaging the Brain

time the song ended. By the way, do you know what you get if you play a country song backward? You get your house back, your wife back, your dog back, your alimony payments stop, and you get out of jail.

WHO: Elementary/Middle/High

WHEN: Before, during, or after a lesson

CONTENT AREA(S): Cross-curricular

- Below are just a few musical resources that can be used to teach content across the curriculum.
  - Dr. Jean (Feldman) (primary grades; www.drjean.org)
  - Jack Hartmann (primary grades; https://jackhartmann.com)
  - Hopscotch Songs (primary grades; https://www.youtube.com/c/hopscotchsongs.com)
  - *The Green Book of Songs by Subject* (5th ed.) by Jeff Green (all levels; www.greenbookofsongs.com)
  - Flocabulary (all levels; www.flocabulary.com)
  - Mr. Betts (social studies, all levels; www.mrbettsclass.com)
  - Warren Phillips (science, all levels; www.wphillips.com)
  - Mr. Parr (science, all levels; www.youtube.com/user/ParrMr/videos)

(Tate, 2022)

WHO: Elementary/Middle/High

WHEN: During a lesson

CONTENT AREA(S): Cross-curricular

- Find appropriate music to accompany your lesson, and incorporate it directly into your teaching. For example, Billy Preston's "Will It Go Round in Circles" is perfect for teaching circumference in math, and Billy Joel's "We Didn't Start the Fire" can accentuate your history lesson.

WHO: Elementary/Middle/High

WHEN: Before or after a lesson

CONTENT AREA(S): Cross-curricular

- If you do not want to go to the trouble of downloading your own music, consult the following websites for music appropriate to the classroom: www.di.fm, www.radiotunes.com, www.Live365.com, www.pandora.com, and www.lastfm.com.

WHO: Elementary/Middle/High

WHEN: Before a lesson

CONTENT AREA(S): Cross-curricular

- Music can change the state of students' brains. Consult books that contain the research and can assist you with your selection of music. Two such books are *Top Tunes for Teaching* by Jensen (2005) and *The Rock 'n' Roll Classroom: Using Music to Manage Mood, Energy, and Learning* by Allen and Wood (2013). The following sections list some of my favorite artists and selections that I use when teaching students and adults.

CALMING MUSIC FOR THE BRAIN

CLASSICAL MUSIC

- *The Most Relaxing Classical Album in the World*
- *The Most Relaxing Classical Album in the World—Ever!* (Disc 1)

NEW AGE MUSIC

- *The Most Relaxing New Age Music in the Universe*
- *Tribute to Enya*

PIANO MUSIC—EMILE PANDOLFI

- *An Affair to Remember*
- *By Request*
- *Days of Wine and Roses*
- *Secret Love*
- *Some Enchanted Evening*

JAZZ

- *At Last . . . The Duet's Album* (Kenny G.)
- *The Ultimate Kenny G.*
- *Best of Hiroshima*
- *The Best Smooth Jazz Ever!* (Disc I)
- *Boney James*
- *The Greatest Hits of All* (George Benson)
- *Stardust . . . The Great American Songbook: Vol. III* (Rod Stewart)

HIGH-ENERGY MUSIC FOR THE BRAIN

ARTISTS' GREATEST HITS

- *Doobies*
- *Earth, Wind and Fire: Greatest Hits*
- *Greatest Hits (Gloria Estefan)*
- *Hits (Phil Collins)*
- *Song Review: A Greatest Hits Collection (Stevie Wonder)*
- *Sounds of Summer (Beach Boys)*
- *Suddenly '70s (Greatest Hits of the 1970s)*
- *The Hits (Faith Hill)*
- *The Very Best of Kool & the Gang*
- *The Very Best of Chic*
- *The Very Best of the Bee Gees*
- *Greatest Hits Chapter One (Taylor Swift)*
- *Best of Taylor Swift (2nd Edition): Big-Note Piano*

ARTISTS' SINGLE HITS FOR MOTIVATING STUDENTS

- "Ain't No Stopping Us Now!" (McFadden and Whitehead)
- "Best Day of My Life" (American Authors)
- "Celebration" (Kool & The Gang)
- "Don't Worry, Be Happy!" (Bobby McFerrin)
- "Eye of the Tiger" (Survivor)
- "Firework" (Katy Perry)
- "Girl on Fire" (Alicia Keys)
- "Happy" (Pharrell Williams)
- "Rather Be" (Clean Bandit)
- "Roar" (Katy Perry)
- "Shining Star" (Earth, Wind and Fire)
- "Rolling in the Deep" (Adele)
- "Something to Talk About" (Bonnie Raitt)
- "We Are the Champions" (Queen)
- "We Will Rock You" (Queen)
- "Stronger (What Doesn't Kill You)" (Kelly Clarkson)

WHO:	Elementary/Middle/High
WHEN:	After a lesson
CONTENT AREA(S):	Cross-curricular

- To assist students in recalling information following a lesson, have them walk, march, or dance around the room to high-energy, fast-paced music. Periodically, stop the music and have students form groups of three or four with other students standing in close proximity. Have them recall a major concept covered in the lesson and discuss it with their respective groups. Then, start the music again and have them walk in a different direction so they do not stand next to the same students when they stop. Have them repeat the procedure with another group and another major concept.

WHO:	Elementary/Middle/High
WHEN:	Before or after a lesson
CONTENT AREA(S):	Cross-curricular

- Appoint a disc jockey in each class whose job is to play the music you request when you request it. One student can fulfill that role for one week, and at the end of the week, the responsibility shifts to another student who is interested in being employed. Make playlists on *Spotify* or *YouTube Music* for your disc jockey to make the job easier. Be judicious about the type of music you choose to play. Any songs with profanity or negative lyrics should never be used. Frequently, students will ask to use their earphones and listen to the music they select. They would not have my approval since they may be choosing songs that do not create the positive mindset I want to engender in their brains as they learn. However, if students wish to recommend songs to be added to the playlist and they meet your approval, by all means, add them to your lists!

WHO:	Elementary/Middle/High
WHEN:	Before a lesson
CONTENT AREA(S):	Cross-curricular

- Put your creative talents to work! Write an original song, rhyme, or rap to symbolize your understanding of a concept you have previously taught the class. Perform your creative effort for your students and teach it to them so they can use the powerful effects of music to remember your content. The books, *100 Brain-Friendly Lessons for Unforgettable Teaching and Learning (K-8) and (9-12)* are replete with the original songs of two of the most prolific teachers ever—Simone Philp Willingham, Language Arts and Warren Phillips, Science (Tate, 2020a, 2020b). Several samples of each of their creative efforts is included at the end of this chapter.

WHO:	Elementary/Middle/High
WHEN:	After a lesson
CONTENT AREA(S):	Cross-curricular

- Have students work in cooperative groups to write a cinquain that symbolizes their understanding of a concept previously taught or content read. The format of a cinquain is as follows: first line—one word, second line—two words, third line—three words, fourth line—four words, last line—one word.

EXAMPLE

Brain

Social organism

Thinking, linking, connecting

Necessary for life itself

Life

WHO:	Elementary/Middle/High
WHEN:	After a lesson
CONTENT AREA(S):	Cross-curricular

- Following instruction in a major concept, have students write an original song, rhyme, or rap to symbolize their understanding of the concept previously taught. Students can be assigned this task for homework if class time does not permit. Then, on the following day, all students in a social studies class, for example, can attend the talent show, where volunteers pretend to be on *American History Idol* rather than *American Idol* and get up and perform their original effort for the class. What a fun way to review content! By the way, when students are taking content and putting it into a different form, such as a song, rhyme, or rap, they are using one of the highest-level thinking skills available to them—synthesis.

Action Plan for Incorporating MUSIC, RHYTHM, RHYME, and RAP

WHAT ARE MY PLANS FOR INCORPORATING MORE *MUSIC, RHYTHM, RHYME,* AND *RAP* INTO MY LESSONS TO ACCELERATE LEARNING?

RECOMMENDATIONS	ALREADY DOING	PLANNING TO DO
Use music less than one-third of your class time and not during direct instruction.		
Play music of 40–55 beats per minute to calm students' brains.		
Play high-energy music of 100–140 beats per minute to motivate students' brains.		
Consult the list of musical resources to assist students in remembering content.		
Incorporate appropriate music into your lessons.		
Consult the recommended websites for appropriate music.		
Consult the references and lists of my favorite artists and musical selections.		
Engage students' brains by having them walk around the room to fast-paced music and review content.		
Appoint a class disc jockey to assist you with playing your music.		
Write an original song, rhyme, or rap to incorporate into your lesson.		
Have students work together to write a cinquain related to content previously taught.		
Have students write an original song, rhyme, or rap to review content previously taught.		
Goals and Notes:		

128 • Engaging the Brain

INFERENCE SONG

By Simone Willingham

To the tune of *Are You Sleeping*

Read the question

Read the passage

To see what it's about!

What can it be about?

Find the facts and opinions

They help you answer the questions

Think about the clues

Bring in your own knowledge

What does your evidence say

What does your knowledge suggest

Think about it slow

What do I really know?

Then draw an inference right away

With process of elimination

What can you conclude?

What can you infer?

STATES OF MATTER

By Warren G. Phillips

© 2018

Sung to *Battle Hymn of the Republic*

Available on iTunes

The states of matter come from atoms' energy they store *(Students vibrate fists in fixed positions)*
And it's constantly exerted as they vibrate back and forth
As the energy accumulates, the atoms vibrate more
Phase changes can occur!

Solid, Liquid, Gas, and Plasma *(Students vibrate fists in fixed positions, then revolve them, then outstretch them, then open fingers)*
Solid, Liquid, Gas, and Plasma
Solid, Liquid, Gas, and Plasma
And now Bose-Einstein! *(Students clap their hands)*

Solids have less energy with atoms locked in place *(Students vibrate fists in fixed positions)*
Liquid atoms move around and take up different shapes *(Students revolve fists)*
Gaseous atoms move apart and fill up any space *(Students outstretch fists)*
And Plasma photons glow! *(Students open fists to show fingers)*

Solid, Liquid, Gas, and Plasma *(Students vibrate fists in fixed positions, then revolve them, then outstretch them, then open fingers)*
Solid, Liquid, Gas, and Plasma
Solid, Liquid, Gas, and Plasma
And now Bose-Einstein! *(Students clap their hands)*

Now Einstein hypothesized another state exists *(Students clap their hands)*
And more recently a scientist has found what he had missed
A state at real cold temperatures that aren't in our midst
Bose found it could subsist!

Solid, Liquid, Gas, and Plasma *(Students vibrate fists in fixed positions, then revolve them, then outstretch them, then open fingers)*
Solid, Liquid, Gas, and Plasma
Solid, Liquid, Gas, and Plasma
And now Bose-Einstein! *(Students clap their hands)*
And now Bose-Einstein!
And now Bose-Einstein!

DNA

Written by Warren G. Phillips

© 2018

Sung to *Ta-Ra-Ra Boom-De-Ay*

Available on iTunes

I made some DNA!
I just learned how today!
You take some adenine
And add some cytosine.

Thymine and guanine, too
Are added to the brew,
Then they're connected to
Long sugar molecules.

And I can hardly wait
For it to replicate:
First it's unraveling
And then assem-bl-ing.

I'll take my DNA
And find a mate today
I'll make genetically
A brand new family tree!

My baby's DNA
It will display some day,
A handsome phenotype
And perfect genotype.

My children's DNA
It will create some day
Grandchildren that will be
Looking a lot like me!

Source: istock.com/Halfpoint

"The more complex the problem, the more complex the brain activity becomes" (Fogarty, 2009, p. 167).

STRATEGY 12

Project-based and Problem-based Learning

💡 WHAT: DEFINING THE STRATEGY

When I teach math, if the objective involves problem solving, I never use the problems in the book as my initial examples. Most do not have any real meaning for students. Generic problems can be used for practice later, but students need to know how this skill appears in the real world. If they cannot see the correlation between what you teach in class and their lives, they will often ask you *Why do we have to learn this?* Therefore, I try to figure out where this concept shows up in the students' world, and I even integrate the names of some of the students into the problem.

Here's a specific problem-based example: When students are trying to figure out the number of ways that various events can occur, they can use the fundamental counting principle in geometry. In teaching this principle, tell them they can multiply event *a* by event *b*. If there are multiple events *for a* and *b*, then those must be taken into consideration. For example, give students the following real-life problem:

For lunch, you can choose an entrée, a drink, and a side dish. No problem! However, there are three entrees (chicken, pizza, hamburger), four drinks (milk, juice, tea, water), and three side dishes (beans, salad, fruit). Question: How many different choices might students have? The answer would be (3 × 4 × 3), equalling 36 choices.

Once students have understood the concept, have them tackle the following more complicated real-life problem:

In a state, a license plate consists of three digits followed by three letters. The letters I and O are not used; every digit or letter can be used multiple times. How many different license plates are possible? See if you can figure this problem out without looking at the answer revealed at the end of this chapter* (Tate, 2020b).

When real-life problems are used as examples and students are engaged in true-to-life projects, content becomes more meaningful and easier to understand. That is what project-based and problem-based learning do very well for the brain!

WHY: THEORETICAL FRAMEWORK

Problem-based learning works much more successfully when students possess the content or surface knowledge to make the necessary connections (Hattie, 2023).

When students are given tasks to determine what they do not know to gain their attention, they are more likely to be receptive to problem-solving activities (Hattie, 2023).

Project-based learning is a crucial teaching strategy for increasing student engagement and includes student inquiry and student choice within the decision-making process (Bender, 2017).

Research shows that it is critical to define a problem by restating it in as many different ways as possible prior to solving it (Jensen, 2022).

When teachers are creating opportunities for students to observe, make inferences, and share their discoveries with peers, they are building the problem-solving skills advocated by the national standards for social studies (Melber & Hunter, 2010).

Problems stimulate brain activity as it seeks patterns, makes sense, finds connections, and functions effectively while bringing harmony to the dissonance it senses in the problem (Fogarty, 2009).

"The more complex the problem, the more complex the brain activity becomes" (Fogarty, 2009, p. 167).

Problem solving to the brain is what aerobic exercise is to the body since solving challenging, complex problems creates a flourish of neural activity. Synapses form, blood flow increases, and neurotransmitters are activated (Jensen, 2008).

Teaching problem-solving strategies using the interest of students of all abilities and grade levels keeps them involved and capitalizes on their natural inclination to solve meaningful problems in the context of real life (Algozzine et al., 2009).

When engaged in project-based learning, students are working at abstract and complex levels while still addressing their individual skill levels and rates of learning (Gregory & Chapman, 2013).

Project-based learning is a 21st century approach that differentiates instruction while simultaneously encouraging high levels of student engagement (Bender, 2012).

One of the highest correlations in a meta-analysis regarding the quality of teaching and student learning comes when teachers challenge students by encouraging them to think through and solve problems, either as a group or individually (Hattie, 2009).

Rigorous and creative problem solving has a strong effect size of 0.93 (Ma, 2009).

HOW: INSTRUCTIONAL ACTIVITIES

WHO: Elementary/Middle/High

WHEN: During a lesson

CONTENT AREA(S): Mathematics

- Have students work in groups and follow these steps when solving math problems:
  - Read the problem.
  - Comprehend the problem.
  - Analyze the problem.
  - Plan an approach that can be used to solve the problem.
  - Explore the approach to ascertain whether it will work.
  - Use the plan to solve the problem.
  - Verify the solution.
  - Listen to and observe other students while solving the problem (Posamentier & Jaye, 2006).

These steps could be put in a graphic organizer and placed as an anchor chart on the wall for students to follow when solving math problems.

WHO: Elementary/Middle/High

WHEN: Before a lesson

CONTENT AREA(S): Mathematics

- Have students create their own math problems for other students to solve. When students enter the room, one student's problem is on the board as a *sponge activity*. The problem could provide a review of a problem-solving strategy already taught and could supply some needed practice. Students could earn extra points by solving one another's problems correctly, either individually or with a partner.

WHO: Elementary/Middle/High

WHEN: During a lesson

CONTENT AREA(S): Cross-curricular

- Identify multiple objectives from a number of content areas. Create a real-life project for students that will address all of the chosen objectives. For example, a project in which students write and produce a news program could address multiple objectives in a real-world, memorable context. Objectives for this project could include the following: researching major current or historical events to determine the stories to be included in the broadcast, writing news copy that is grammatically correct with a main idea sentence in each paragraph, or broadcasting the news using appropriate public speaking skills.

WHO: Elementary

WHEN: During a lesson

CONTENT AREA(S): Mathematics

- Have students construct a class cookbook to apply their understanding of multiplying fractions. Have students find recipes for their favorite foods with fractions of servings: 2½ cups of flour, 2¼ cups of sugar, and ¾ teaspoon of vanilla. Students then rewrite the recipe, cutting it in half and doubling and tripling it. Students can choose one version of the recipe to make as a project for homework.

WHO: Elementary/Middle/High

WHEN: After a lesson

CONTENT AREA(S): Science

- To help them recall the parts of an animal cell, have students complete a project for a homework assignment. Have them make a pizza that displays their knowledge of the parts of the cell. Students will decide what toppings will be used to replicate parts of the cell, such as pepperoni for the nucleus or the cytoplasm. On a designated day, have students bring their pizzas to school and evaluate one another's pizzas based on a rubric students helped to develop. Following the evaluation, be sure the class eats their pizzas and enjoys a "Cellebration!"

WHO: Elementary/Middle/High

WHEN: Before or during a lesson

CONTENT AREA(S): Cross-curricular

- Have students use advanced searches to gather information from a variety of print and digital sources that could aid them in solving a problem or completing an assigned project. Students could evaluate the usefulness of each source in light of the problem or project and the audience. Have students integrate the information, without plagiarism, into the text so that they are not overly dependent on any one source (Tate, 2014a).

WHO: Elementary/Middle/High

WHEN: During a lesson

CONTENT AREA(S): Mathematics

- When introducing a new concept in math class, create real-world problems incorporating the students' names. As you solve the problem, talk aloud so students can follow the thought processes involved. For example, when teaching the concept of elapsed time, have a student in class, let's say her name is Denise, share her typical daily schedule, such as what time she gets up, gets to school, arrives home, eats dinner, goes to bed, and so forth. Write the schedule on the board. Then, have students figure out how much time elapses from when Denise does one thing to when she does something else. Using the context of a student's real-world experiences makes the content more relevant and meaningful. After showing three or more examples where you model the thought processes, have students work individually, in pairs, or in small groups to solve additional problems.

WHO: Elementary/Middle/High

WHEN: During a lesson

CONTENT AREA(S): Science

- Have students create a timeline that shows a geologic history of life. One meter on the timeline could equal one million years. This scale will show the vast amount of time with no life on earth and the relative success of sustained life for the dinosaurs. Younger students could draw rather than write out timeline events (Tate & Phillips, 2011, p. 102).

WHO: Middle/High

WHEN: During a lesson

CONTENT AREA(S): Cross-curricular

- Engage students in interdisciplinary cooperative learning projects such as the following. The class forms into student teams of four to six. Each team selects one football, basketball, or baseball team to follow for 10 to 20 games of the regular season. Each team will choose the most valuable player of the team for the 10- to 20-week period, but they must be ready to justify the choice using vital statistics as evidence. The team will plan and deliver a broadcast, including a PowerPoint presentation, during which they will report analysis and interpretation of the stats. They will also submit journals in which they have tracked the team's statistics.

WHO: Middle/High

WHEN: During or after a lesson

CONTENT AREA(S): Mathematics

- To assist students with the real-life skill of building a budget, have them work in cooperative groups. Give each group an allotted yearly income of, for example, $40,000. Have students plan a budget that allows for living expenditures such as housing, utilities, food, car payments, gas for car, car and health insurance, and so forth. Have students research the average cost of each expenditure and build a realistic annual budget. This project goes a long way toward helping students realistically understand just how much money it actually takes to live.

WHO: Elementary/Middle/High

WHEN: During a lesson

CONTENT AREA(S): Cross-curricular

- Have students conduct short research projects to answer a question. Have them draw research from multiple sources and generate additional related questions that call for them to explore additional print and digital sources for information.

WHO: Elementary/Middle/High

WHEN: During or after a lesson

CONTENT AREA(S): Social Studies

- Have students create a newspaper that displays their understanding of a particular period of history. My daughter, Jessica, will never forget her authentic *Civil War Newspaper,* which had to contain a slogan, a front-page news story, an ad, a crime story, and so on. Jessica's slogan was *If you don't get the news from us, you don't get it!* Her front-page story was the assassination of Abraham Lincoln, her ad sold horseshoes, and her crime story was the fact that John Wilkes Booth had been accused of Lincoln's murder. Jessica's teacher laminated her newspaper, and she kept it. She still remembers this project even though it was over 30 years ago.

WHO: Elementary/Middle/High

WHEN: During a lesson

CONTENT AREA(S): Cross-curricular

- Place students in cooperative groups of four to six. Give each group a real-world problem to solve. Problems could include such topics as the following:
  - How would you increase parental participation in this school?
  - How would you decrease the unemployment rate in the country?
  - How can we increase the number of students taking advanced placement classes in this school?

Have students collect and analyze data and work together to derive the best solution to the problem. Have each group write a paper outlining the problem and possible solution(s) and make an oral presentation to the class.

WHO: Elementary/Middle/High

WHEN: During a lesson

CONTENT AREA(S): Cross-curricular

- When solving problems during class discussions, allow students to take turns sharing their ideas. Have them use sample sentence starters such as the following:
    - I realized that . . .
    - I agree with your thinking and would like to add . . .
    - I don't understand what you meant when you said . . .
    - I solved the problem this way . . .

WHO: Elementary/Middle/High

WHEN: During the lesson

CONTENT AREA(S): Cross-curricular

- During a science or technical experiment, have students formulate a hypothesis. Have them collect data and use corroborating sources to verify the data. Have students then analyze the data to determine if they support or disprove the hypothesis. Have them draw conclusions and, if possible, use other sources of information to support those conclusions (Tate, 2014a).

*The answer to the license plate problem at the beginning of this chapter is 13,824,000.

Action Plan for Incorporating PROJECT-BASED and PROBLEM-BASED LEARNING

WHAT ARE MY PLANS FOR INCORPORATING MORE *PROJECT-BASED* AND *PROBLEM-BASED LEARNING* INTO MY LESSONS TO ACCELERATE LEARNING?

RECOMMENDATIONS	ALREADY DOING	PLANNING TO DO
Have math students follow appropriate steps when solving problems.		
Have math students create their own problems for peers to solve.		
Create a real-life project that will address cross-curricular objectives.		
Have students construct a class cookbook to apply their knowledge of fractions.		
Have science students make a pizza displaying the parts of a cell.		
Have students gather information from print and digital sources.		
Create real-life math problems involving students.		
Have science students create a timeline showing a geological period of history.		
Engage students in an interdisciplinary cooperative learning project.		
Assist students with building a real-life budget.		
Have students conduct short research projects.		
Have social studies students create a newspaper regarding a period of history.		
Have students work in cooperative groups to solve a real-world problem.		
Teach students to use sample sentence starters for sharing their ideas.		
Have students formulate and test a hypothesis.		
Goals and Notes:		

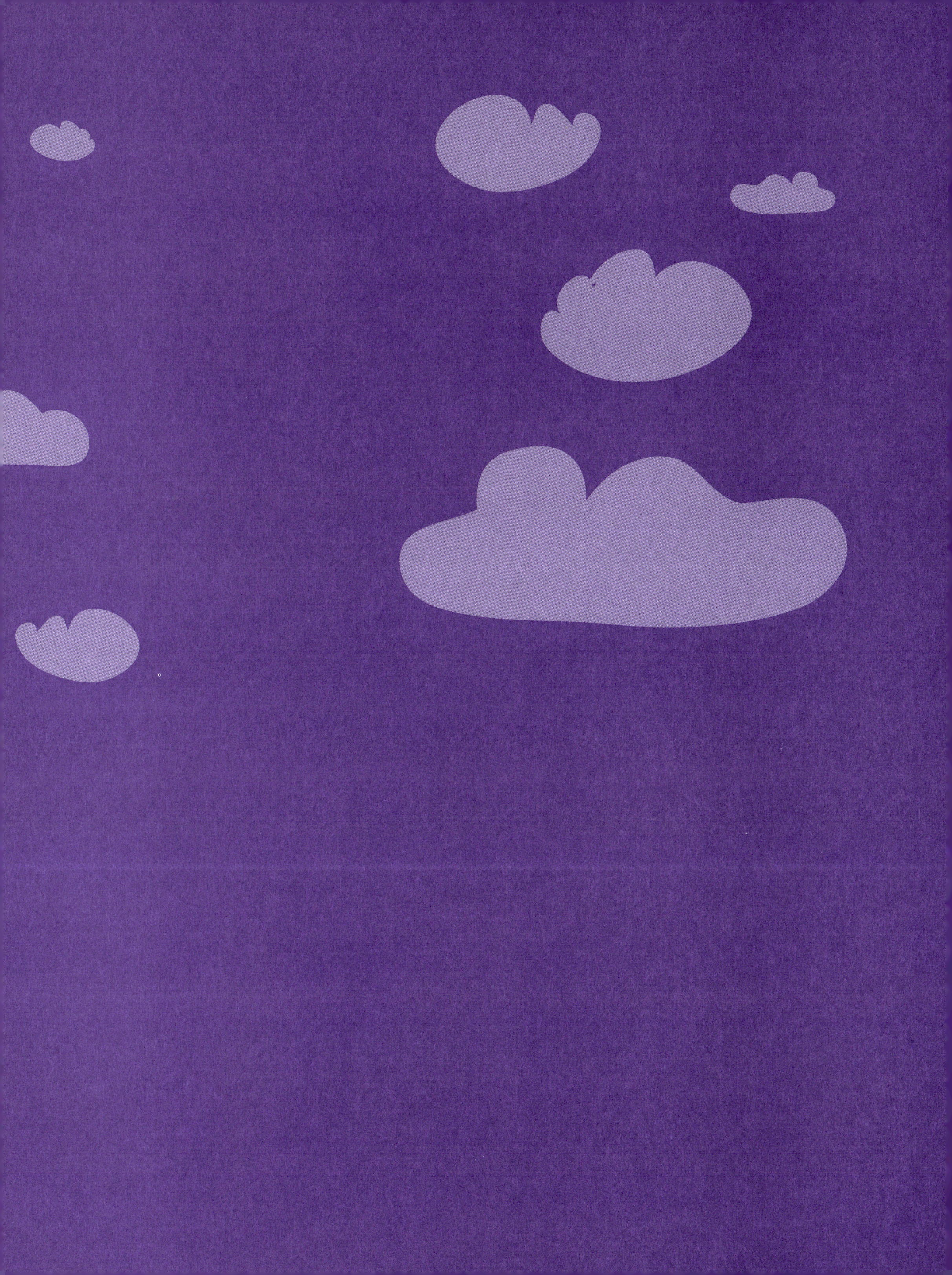

Source: istock.com/vitchanan

Peer tutoring is one of the most effective teaching strategies for raising academic achievement (Hattie, 2023).

STRATEGY 13

Reciprocal Teaching and Cooperative Learning

WHAT: DEFINING THE STRATEGY

When I was taught to teach almost 50 years ago, if two students were talking together about content, they were accused of cheating. Yet, I think that college students instinctively knew that they stood a better chance of remembering what they talked about. That is why they would form discussion groups outside of class. Students should not have to talk outside of class. They should be conversing about the content in class.

Reciprocal teaching and cooperative learning are two of the best ways to have conversations about content. In the original definition of reciprocal teaching (Palincsar & Brown, 1984), the process is as follows: students make predictions about a part of a text to be read. Once the text is read, the group's discussion leader has the group discuss questions raised. A group member then summarizes the content read thus far, and others clarify difficult concepts and make predictions about the following portion of the text. Then, the process continues. However, my definition is much simpler. Stopping during class time and having students reteach what they are learning to a student sitting nearby is time well spent! After all, we learn at least 70% of what we say as we talk about content (Ekwall & Shanker, 1988).

Very little is done in the world of work by oneself. Most jobs are done while working with a team or, at the very least, a partner. What better way to help students develop those interpersonal skills they will need in the workplace than by having them complete some tasks in class cooperatively? According to Rios (2020), the top attributes in job advertisements today include the ability of the employee to communicate orally and in writing, problem solve, and collaborate. According to Willis (2021), collaboration experiences have never been more valuable than they are now since students have had less interpersonal contact and collaboration during remote learning. Remember this motto: *Some of us are better than others of us, but none of us is better than all of us* (Johnson et al., 1994).

WHY: THEORETICAL FRAMEWORK

Collaborative learning benefits achievement since students can experience new ideas that may conflict with their own conceptions and can even generate new approaches for problem solving that students were not aware of prior to working together (Hattie, 2023).

Students with learning difficulties are very successful when working in teams since they are practicing their interpersonal skills, finding meaning, and rehearsing new learnings while actively engaged (Sousa, 2016).

Students can foster the growth mindset in one another if a teacher encourages them to collaborate, thereby noticing, explaining, encouraging, and serving as a resource for growing together (Jensen, 2022).

Reciprocal teaching is an effective method for dealing with English language learners who may have limited English proficiency when solving math problems (Sousa, 2022).

As students develop collaborative skills, they learn that their contribution is necessary for the success of the group as they learn to work with one another, share responsibility, and compromise, when necessary, to achieve a common outcome (Sousa, 2022).

Peer tutoring appears to result in a fairly dramatic increase in student engagement and is one of the most effective teaching strategies for raising academic achievement (Bender, 2017; Hattie, 2023).

In peer-to-peer tutoring, the student doing the teaching is gaining because to teach something is to remember it, and the learner is gaining because of the individual instruction that is tailored to them personally (Gregory & Chapman, 2013).

While competition is learned naturally, cooperation has to be taught (Allen & Currie, 2012).

Cooperative learning is one major strategy for creating a culturally responsive classroom for students of poverty and color (Tileston, 2011).

Diversity (mixing boys and girls and high and low achievers) within a cooperative group results in a better exchange of ideas (Feinstein, 2004).

Inhibiting students from talking decreases the likelihood that any new material will be processed and embedded into long-term memory (Hattie, 2009).

Cooperative group activities improve the learning for diverse students because they teach crucial social skills and reinforce concepts by allowing group members to discuss a variety of ideas (Algozzine et al., 2009).

Because humans are social beings, working collaboratively elicits thinking that is superior to individual effort (Costa, 2008).

Individual students' abilities can be nurtured when those students, with or without learning disabilities, belong to a community of learners who engage in peer tutoring and working collaboratively to make sense of mathematics (Posamentier & Jaye, 2006).

Without the metacognitive process of group debriefing following a cooperative activity, there is only minimal improvement in the group's ability to use a specific collaborative or social skill (Gregory & Parry, 2006).

HOW: INSTRUCTIONAL ACTIVITIES

WHO: Elementary/Middle/High

WHEN: Before, during, or after a lesson

CONTENT AREA(S): Cross-curricular

- When students are working with peers in small groups or talking to a partner, it is often difficult to get their attention. Create a signal, and use it whenever students need to pay attention to you. The signal can be a chime, raised hand, rain stick, chant, bell, clap, or anything soothing that would not be abrasive to your students' brains. Change the signal periodically since students' brains appreciate novelty.

WHO: Elementary/Middle/High

WHEN: During a lesson

CONTENT AREA(S): Cross-curricular

- There is a technique I use called *My Turn, Your Turn*. Since the brain can only pay conscious attention to one thing at a time, tell students that when you are addressing the class, this is the teacher's turn to talk. This time would be called *My Turn*. When the time comes for students to talk to a partner or a cooperative group, this time would be considered *Your Turn*.

WHO: Elementary/Middle/High

WHEN: Before a lesson

CONTENT AREA(S): Cross-curricular

- I am often asked how teachers keep students on task when they are allowed to talk to a partner or in a cooperative group. The tactic *of My Stuff, Your Stuff* has worked for me. Tell students that when they are given an assignment, that is considered the teacher's stuff. Students should attend to the teacher's stuff first and be prepared in case they are called upon. Then, if time permits, partners or groups can talk about anything they choose. This conversation would be considered *Your Stuff*. When students know they may have the opportunity to talk about their wishes, they are more likely to concentrate on what the teacher wants first. According to Allen (2008), it is natural for student conversations to get off the topic. Adults in my workshops do so as well! He suggests letting them finish their personal discussion and then having them bring the conversation back around to the topic at hand.

WHO:	Elementary/Middle/High
WHEN:	During a lesson
CONTENT AREA(S):	Cross-curricular

- Have each student select a close partner (CP), a peer who sits so close in class that they can talk with this person whenever necessary and not have to get out of their seat. Stop periodically during a lesson and have students discuss a concept, brainstorm an idea, or review content prior to a test. Close partners can also re-explain a concept that might not be clear or easily understood by their partner. According to Gregory and Parry (2006), children learn best when they have the opportunity to discuss ideas with their peers in a nose-to-nose and toes-to-toes interaction.

WHO:	Elementary/Middle/High
WHEN:	During a lesson
CONTENT AREA(S):	Cross-curricular

- Consult Strategy 10 (Movement) for a way to integrate reciprocal teaching with movement by having students make clock, seasonal, timeline, or quadrant appointments to discuss pertinent content.

WHO:	Elementary/Middle/High
WHEN:	During a lesson
CONTENT AREA(S):	Cross-curricular

- Have students work together in cooperative groups, or *families*, of four to six. They may be seated in groups already or taught to pick up their desks and arrange them into groups for a cooperative learning activity and to put them back once the activity is over. It is recommended that the groups be of mixed ability levels or capitalize on students' various multiple intelligences or talents.

WHO:	Elementary/Middle/High
WHEN:	During a lesson
CONTENT AREA(S):	Cross-curricular

- Give each cooperative group of students the same task. Have them discuss the thought processes involved in completing the task and reach a consensus as to the correct answer. Once the answer is agreed upon, have each person in the group sign the paper that the answer is written on, verifying that they agree with the answer and, if called on randomly, could explain how the solution was derived to the entire class. This individual accountability helps to ensure that one person does not do all the work while other students watch and applaud their efforts.

WHO: Elementary/Middle/High

WHEN: During a lesson

CONTENT AREA(S): Cross-curricular

- When students have difficulty working together as a cooperative group, you may want to teach some social skills necessary for effective functioning. For example, construct a T-chart similar to the one shown in Figure 13.1 where each social skill is considered from two perspectives: (1) what it looks like and (2) what it sounds like. Social skills could include paying undivided attention, encouraging one another, or critiquing ideas and not peers.

Observe each group and make a tally mark on a sheet every time the social skill is practiced by any student in the group. Provide feedback to the class during a debriefing following the cooperative activity. You may also assign a student in each group to fulfill the function of a *process observer* who collects the data for the group. The process observer cannot talk and only observes the group. Therefore, it may be beneficial to make your more talkative student in each group the process observer (Tate, 2014a).

FIGURE 13.1 • T-Chart

Paying Attention

Looks Like	Sounds Like
Eye contact	One person speaking at a time
Leaning forward	Asking appropriate questions
One person speaking	Paraphrasing what is being said
Not distracted	Summarizing what is being said

WHO:	Elementary/Middle/High
WHEN:	During a lesson
CONTENT AREA(S):	Cross-curricular

- Another way to help ensure individual accountability is to assign group roles for students to fulfill during the cooperative learning activity. Some of the following roles can be given:
  - **Facilitator**—Ensures that the group stays on task and completes the given activity
  - **Scribe**—Writes down anything the group has to submit in writing
  - **Time Keeper**—Tells the group when half the time is over and when there is one minute remaining
  - **Reporter**—Gives an oral presentation to the class regarding the results of the group's work
  - **Materials Manager**—Collects any materials or other resources that the group needs to complete the task
  - **Process Observer**—Provides feedback to the group on how well they practiced their social skills during the cooperative learning activity

WHO:	Elementary/Middle/High
WHEN:	During a lesson
CONTENT AREA(S):	Cross-curricular

- One way to have students navigate through narrative or expository text is to have them engage in *partner reading*. Students could take turns participating in the 3-Ps by reading a *page or paragraph* or *passing* their turn until the selection is complete. They could take turns quizzing their partners regarding what was just read.

WHO:	Elementary/Middle/High
WHEN:	During a lesson
CONTENT AREA(S):	Cross-curricular

- When students need to memorize facts in any content area, have them pair with a *drill partner*. Students work together to drill one another on the content (such as multiplication facts or content-area vocabulary definitions) for several minutes each day until both partners know and can recite the facts from memory. Give bonus points on the subsequent test if both partners score above a certain percentage or improve their score over a previous test.

WHO:	Elementary/Middle/High
WHEN:	During a lesson
CONTENT AREA(S):	Cross-curricular

- Have students use the *think, pair, share* technique. Students first individually *think* about how to respond to a question or solve a problem; then, they *pair* with another student and *share* their thought processes and/or answers to the problem. Both students reach a consensus as to the correct solution or answer. If their original answers differ, the discussion involved in convincing their partner that they are correct is invaluable to learning.

WHO:	Elementary/Middle/High
WHEN:	During a lesson
CONTENT AREA(S):	Cross-curricular

- Place students in cooperative groups. Have them participate in an activity called *Jigsaw*. Jigsaw's name is derived from the fact that each student has only one piece of the puzzle, and it will take all students to make a whole. Each student in the cooperative group is accountable for teaching one section of a chapter. The procedure is as follows:
  - Give students time to prepare their part in class or for homework individually.
  - Have them confer with a student in another group, who has the same part they do, to get and give ideas before teaching their original group.
  - Give each student a required number of minutes to teach their part to their original cooperative group. Individuals in each group start and stop teaching at the same time. If they finish before time is called, the student can quiz group members for understanding.
  - Conduct a whole-class review that outlines the pertinent points that should have been made during each student's instruction. In this way, the entire class gets to hear the content at least twice, once from a group member and once from the teacher.

WHO:	Elementary/Middle/High
WHEN:	During a lesson
CONTENT AREA(S):	Cross-curricular

- While checking homework, in-class assignments, or brainstorming ideas, have students take their paper in hand and walk around the room to fast-paced music. Every time you stop the music, have each student pair with another student standing close by, give one answer to their partner, and *get* one answer from their partner. Repeat the procedure for a specified period of time or until the song has ended.

Action Plan for Incorporating RECIPROCAL TEACHING and COOPERATIVE LEARNING

WHAT ARE MY PLANS FOR INCORPORATING MORE *RECIPROCAL TEACHING* AND *COOPERATIVE LEARNING* IN MY LESSONS TO ACCELERATE LEARNING?

RECOMMENDATIONS	ALREADY DOING	PLANNING TO DO
Create a signal for getting students' attention when needed.		
Use the technique of *My Turn, Your Turn* to let students know when to talk and when to listen.		
Use the technique of *My Stuff, Your Stuff* to enable students to be ready if called upon.		
Have students select a *close partner*, a peer who sits so close that they will be easy to talk with.		
Consult Strategy 10: Movement for ways to integrate reciprocal teaching with activity.		
Have students work together in *families* of four to six when needed.		
Make students accountable for responding if called upon.		
Teach students the social skills necessary for effective functioning.		
Assign group roles for students to fill during cooperative learning.		
Engage students in *partner reading* and implement the *3Ps*.		
When needed, have students pair with a drill partner.		
Have students use the *think, pair, share* technique.		
Implement *Jigsaw* to have students teach content to one another.		
Have students move around the room giving answers and getting them from one another.		
Goals and Notes:		

Engaging the Brain

Source: istock.com/FatCamera

Roleplay uses the body in a physical way to understand and recall a difficult concept (Sousa, 2022).

STRATEGY 14

Roleplays, Drama, Pantomimes, and Charades

💡 WHAT: DEFINING THE STRATEGY

I go into classrooms when requested and teach model lessons to the students. Teachers observe the lesson while I use brain-compatible strategies to provide instruction on a concept the teacher is teaching. I used roleplay to engage English II students in a lesson regarding the genre of drama as it relates to Scene 3 of Sophocles's *Antigone*. Each student was asked to select a partner and, as a review, take turns retelling the major events in Scenes 1 and 2 of the play. I then conducted a whole-class discussion of the salient events and informed students that by the time the lesson was completed, they would be able to make inferences regarding the structure and elements of *Antigone* and cite evidence to support their understanding. The best part of the lesson, however, occurred when I asked four different duos of students to volunteer to assume the roles of Creon and Haemon, stand, and come to the front of the room to read those parts. I told them that they would need to read with fluency and expression since the class did not need to be bored immediately after lunch. One duo attempted to outdo the previous one in their abilities to read dramatically as if they were the actual characters. The remainder of the class became the Choragos, a chorus of the elders of Thebes, who stood and read in a choral response each time the chorus spoke.

Having students take turns standing and acting out the steps in a math word problem, a scene from history, or the definition of a vocabulary word helps to ensure that the content is remembered long after the subsequent tests are over. This strategy takes advantage of one of the brain's strongest memory systems, procedural or muscle memory, and results in much fun in the classroom!

WHY: THEORETICAL FRAMEWORK

When students put the skills into practice that they have learned in theory through roleplay, a deeper cognitive link to the material is created, making the material easier to learn (Elmore, 2024).

Drama, or music-based teaching, can result in improvements in nondrama content such as reading and math as well as drama-specific content (Hattie, 2023).

The strategy of roleplay uses the body in a physical way to understand and recall a difficult concept (Sousa, 2022).

Researchers have found roleplay useful in getting students to grasp practical cognitive skills (Elmore, 2024).

Roleplaying games assist students in taking on different personas and helping them understand those personas as part of a larger system of thought, thereby considering alternate points of view (Nguyen, 2021).

Roleplay can develop speaking skills as well as conflict resolution skills, and increase reading comprehension and the ability to communicate. It also appeals to varying learning styles and injects creativity and fun into learning (Williams, 2019).

The effects of numerous studies conducted in Turkey found a 0.99 effect size of creative drama-based learning on the math success of elementary students and an effect size of 0.87 across various subjects (Hattie, 2023).

When students are engaged in drama, specific areas of the cerebrum focus on acquiring spoken language while calling on the emotional control center of the brain known as the limbic system (Sousa & Pilecki, 2013).

Test scores for classes where students were involved in mini-dramas or vignettes were significantly higher than scores in three additional classes taught next door with traditional methods (Allen, 2008).

Roleplays use visual, spatial, linguistic, and bodily modalities and, therefore, not only access students' emotions but also enable students to comprehend at much deeper levels than a lecture would (Gregory & Parry, 2006).

Roleplay is a form of rehearsal that enables students to demonstrate skills and process their knowledge in an emotional context (Gregory & Chapman, 2013).

In simulation or roleplay contexts, learning is more enjoyable and meaningful, choice and creativity come into play, and pressure from negative evaluation is minimized (Jensen, 2008).

Roleplays are most effective when illustrating key events, demonstrating critical roles of historical figures, and showing the process of concepts that come in sequential order (Udvari-Solner & Kluth, 2008).

HOW: INSTRUCTIONAL ACTIVITIES

WHO: Elementary/Middle/High

WHEN: During a lesson

CONTENT AREA(S): Cross-curricular

- Follow the steps below when engaging students in a simulation or roleplay:
  - Define what a roleplay or simulation is, and present the topic that is to be role-played.
  - Give students the roleplay's procedures, rules, roles, scoring, and goals.
  - Monitor, facilitate, and provide feedback as students work through the roleplay.
  - Debrief the activity, and have students discuss applying what they learned during the roleplay (Gregory & Herndon, 2010).

WHO: Elementary/Middle/High

WHEN: During a lesson

CONTENT AREA(S): Cross-curricular

- As a motivating review activity, have students play Charades. Have them take turns coming to the front of the room and acting out the definition of a content-area vocabulary word given to them. The student cannot speak but must use roleplay to get classmates to shout out the word. The first student to guess the word is the winner.

WHO: Elementary/Middle/High

WHEN: During a lesson

CONTENT AREA(S): Science

- Warren Phillips, an exemplary former science teacher, has students participate in the following roleplay to learn about states of matter. Have students use two shaking fists to represent two atoms in a solid. The fists maintain their position just as atoms retain their definite shape. Have them revolve their fists to indicate two atoms in a liquid, taking the shape of whatever container it is in. Having students wiggling outstretched fists represents a gas filling its container. Opening fingers represent the heat and light given off by plasma. Clapping hands represent the collapsed atoms of Bose-Einstein. Students can sing Warren's song "States of Matter" while demonstrating the actions. The lyrics to this song can be found in Strategy 11: Music, Rhythm, Rhyme, and Rap.

WHO:	Elementary/Middle/High
WHEN:	During a lesson
CONTENT AREA(S):	Cross-curricular

- Have students *body spell* the letters of their content-area vocabulary words. First, provide them a visual or have them visualize the word. Then, have them move their bodies according to the placement of the letters in the word. For example, suppose the word we need to spell is *play*. The lowercase *p* in *play* falls below the line, so to body spell it, the student should bend toward the floor from the waist with the arms extended as if to touch the toes. The *l* in *play* extends above the line, so to body spell it, students should put both arms up and reach for the sky. The *a* in *play* falls on the line, so the student should put both arms out to the side. Finally, the y in *play* falls below the line (just like the *p*), so the arms are once again positioned to touch the toes. The student then puts it all together and spells the entire word, *play*. They say each letter of the word as they body spell it. Once students learn the technique, they can spell any word. Have them spell content-area vocabulary such as *Mississippi* or *photosynthesis*. As students become more confident with their body spelling, they enjoy spelling words faster and faster, and because the words are being placed in procedural memory, their spelling during writing improves.

WHO:	Elementary/Middle/High
WHEN:	During a lesson
CONTENT AREA(S):	Cross-curricular

- Have students take turns role-playing as if they are newscasters reporting current events. They could broadcast an editorial representing their point of view on an issue or historical event. They could also interview a peer regarding a controversial cross-curricular concept.

WHO:	Elementary/Middle/High
WHEN:	During a lesson
CONTENT AREA(S):	Mathematics/Social Studies

- Have students develop and participate in a simulated economic system for the classroom where they are asked to design their own classroom currency and create a system for using the currency to buy and sell goods and services for the classroom (Tate, 2012).

WHO:	Elementary/Middle/High
WHEN:	During a lesson
CONTENT AREA(S):	Mathematics

- To more clearly understand the steps in a multistep word problem, have students take turns getting up and acting out each step of the word problem. This roleplay will work with a large number of math problems and can go a long way in helping students who need a visual depiction of the problem.

WHO:	Elementary/Middle/High
WHEN:	During a lesson
CONTENT AREA(S):	Social Studies

- Following a lesson on a significant historical event, such as the signing of the Declaration of Independence or the Gettysburg Address, have students create and present a dramatic presentation of the event, incorporating major characters and details in sequential order.

WHO:	Elementary
WHEN:	During a lesson
CONTENT AREA(S):	Science

- Have students show their understanding of a biological process, such as digestion, or a process of nature, such as the rotation and revolution of the planets, by acting it out. For example, divide students into groups of nine. One student in each group pretends to be the sun and stands in the middle of a circle. The other eight form a circle and revolve around the sun from closest to the sun to farthest from it while simultaneously rotating on their axis. Give students signs to hold up for the planets they represent so that other students can visualize them.

WHO:	Elementary/Middle/High
WHEN:	During a lesson
CONTENT AREA(S):	Language Arts

- Have students participate in *Reader's Theater* by dramatizing a story previously read. Assign parts to class members, and have them act out their respective parts. This roleplay goes a long way toward improving comprehension of narrative text. I had a group of eighth graders do a roleplay of one scene from *The Outsiders*. They did an excellent job and made the text so much more memorable!

WHO: Elementary/Middle/High

WHEN: During a lesson

CONTENT AREA(S): Mathematics

- Teach geometric terms, ensuring that students understand their meanings—terms such as *line, line segment, ray, right angle, obtuse angle,* and *acute angle*. Show students an action for each definition. Then, have students stand beside their desks and role-play the definitions you just demonstrated. For example, to demonstrate the term *line*, have students point both arms out to their sides and point their fingers to indicate that a line has no endpoints. To demonstrate *line segment*, have them point their arms straight out but ball their fingers into fists to show that a line segment has two endpoints. Have them demonstrate a *ray* by pointing the arms out and making the left fingers into a fist while pointing the right fingers out straight because the ray only has one endpoint. Students can role-play angles by extending both arms to simulate right, obtuse, and acute angles. Involve students in a game by having them use their arms to make the terms as you randomly say them. This game is a lot of fun while putting the terms into procedural or muscle memory.

WHO: Middle/High

WHEN: During a lesson

CONTENT AREA(S): English/Social Studies

- Following a discussion of the judicial system, have students establish a peer court where they try a character in a novel or a historical figure for a predetermined offense. Roles of the judge, bailiff, jury, witnesses, prosecuting attorney, and defense attorney are assigned and carried out by members of the class.

WHO: Elementary/Middle/High

WHEN: During a lesson

CONTENT AREA(S): Cross-curricular

- Have students take turns role-playing that they are you, the teacher. Have them volunteer to come to the front of the room and pretend, as the teacher, to reteach the lesson previously taught. Give each student a maximum of two minutes. This activity will give you an idea of which concepts have been understood by your students and which may need reteaching. Remember that you learn what you teach and that most brains need to hear something a minimum of three times before the information actually sticks. As a side benefit, you will see your teaching through your students' eyes. At the end of one lesson I taught, I had a fourth grader come to the front of the room and reteach what I had taught about solving multistep math word problems. I went and sat in the student's desk. When it was time for me to get up, I couldn't! I was literally stuck in the fourth-grade desk. We had a good laugh about that one!

Action Plan for Incorporating ROLEPLAYS, DRAMA, PANTOMIMES, and CHARADES

WHAT ARE MY PLANS FOR INCORPORATING MORE *ROLEPLAY, DRAMA, PANTOMIMES,* AND *CHARADES* INTO MY LESSONS TO ACCELERATE LEARNING?

RECOMMENDATIONS	ALREADY DOING	PLANNING TO DO
Follow the steps for involving students in the strategy of roleplay.		
Play Charades by having students act out the meaning of content-area vocabulary words.		
Teach science students to role-play to understand the states of matter.		
Use body spelling to improve the spelling abilities of students.		
Have students pretend to be newscasters reporting current or historical events.		
Have students develop and implement a simulated economic system.		
Have math students act out each step of a multistep word problem.		
Have social studies students dramatize a historical event.		
Ask science students to act out a biological process or a process of nature.		
Have students participate in a *Reader's Theater* by dramatizing a story read.		
Show math students how to role-play geometric terms.		
Have students form a peer court and assume the accompanying roles.		
Ask students to take turns becoming the teacher and reteaching a concept previously taught.		
Goals and Notes:		

Strategy 14 • Roleplays, Drama, Pantomimes, and Charades

Source: istock.com/monkeybusinessimages

Telling good stories is like weightlifting for the brain, since stories force listeners to make connections between their world, feelings, and ideas (Stibich, 2014).

STRATEGY 15

Storytelling

WHAT: DEFINING THE STRATEGY

People are always bragging about their ability to multitask. Many see nothing wrong with talking or texting on their cell phones while driving. Brain research tells us that the concept of multitasking is a misnomer. When I teach the workshop that accompanies this book, I tell the following true story to illustrate that the brain can only pay conscious attention to one thing at a time:

> My daughter, Jennifer, was going to the store to get food for dinner when the woman in front of her ran through the stoplight and into three teenagers who were innocently standing on the sidewalk. Jen stopped her car to see if she could render aid to the three young people who had been hit and was even holding the hand of one of the boys when he passed away. She later discovered that this woman was arguing with her husband while driving and was oblivious to anything happening around her. She ended up killing all three of the teenage boys since all of them eventually died.

This story helps ensure that workshop participants begin to change their conception of multitasking since the story is long remembered. Stories have a beginning, a middle, and an end. The content is connected, and the ability to remember it is strengthened when there is also an emotional connection. Storytelling, one of the oldest forms of instruction, was the only way for people to pass information from one generation to the next. Tell stories as you teach content. When they remember your story, they recall the content you are teaching.

WHY: THEORETICAL FRAMEWORK

When a teacher values students' lives, cultures, and stories, students will feel it and be amenable to making changes in their lives (Jensen, 2022).

Human brains seek the meaning and coherence of convenient stories called packages of thoughts. (Hagoort, 2020).

Storytelling addresses the needs of all three types of learners. Visual learners love the mental pictures; auditory learners, the words and voice of the storyteller; and kinesthetic learners, the feelings and emotional connections (Boris, 2017).

When one is listening to a narrative, not only are the language neural circuits activated but so are the brain networks involved in movement and emotions arising from sounds (Renken, 2020).

Psychologist Peg Neuhauser found that the learning which comes from a story well-told is remembered longer and more accurately than learning which comes from figures and facts (Boris, 2017).

When students are immersed in storytelling, the larger portions of their brains, that is, creativity, imagination, problem solving, and remembering, are stimulated simultaneously (Early Impact Learning, n.d.)

According to cognitive psychologist Jerome Bruner, facts are 20 times more likely to be recalled if those facts are part of a story (Boris, 2017).

According to Hasson, a professor of neuroscience at Princeton, during storytelling, regions of the brain that do complex information processing appear to be engaged (Renken, 2020).

People love good stories, whether real or make-believe, because stories usually resemble the reality with which we are familiar but find difficult to define (Scott & Marzano, 2014).

Telling good stories is like weightlifting for the brain, since stories force listeners to make connections between their world, feelings, and ideas (Stibich, 2014).

Storytelling is an effective way to enhance a student's emotional connection to the content and conceptual understanding and helps students' *digital brains* become more attentive (Sprenger, 2010).

Students often remember stories better when they create original ones (Allen, 2008).

HOW: INSTRUCTIONAL ACTIVITIES

WHO: Elementary/Middle/High

WHEN: Before or during a lesson

CONTENT AREA(S): Cross-curricular

- Have a story stool or bench in your classroom, and sit on it whenever you tell students stories related to a concept being taught. No notes are taken during storytelling so that students can give their undivided attention to you in this nonthreatening environment. Remember, never tell a story unless its purpose is to teach or reinforce a curricular concept to be remembered.

WHO: Elementary

WHEN: Before a lesson

CONTENT AREA(S): Social Studies

- Tell your students the following story to teach the continents. It will take you less than one minute.

  There once was a man named **North**. His last name was **America**.

  He fell in love with a beautiful woman named **South**. They got

  married and she took his name so she became South **America**.

  They honeymooned in **Europe**. This couple was blessed to have

  four daughters whose names all began with the letter A. Their

  names were **Africa, Antarctica, Asia,** and **Australia**.

  The End

By the time you have told this story aloud at least three times and students have gotten up and retold the story to several partners in the room, students remember the continents. Why? Because the continents are not learned in isolation. They are learned within the context of a story.

WHO: Elementary/Middle/High

WHEN: During a lesson

CONTENT AREA(S): Cross-curricular

Strategy 15 • Storytelling

- The brain needs a purpose. Whenever giving students either narrative or informational text to read silently or orally, always give them the purpose for reading. For example, say to students, *We are reading the next two pages to find out why . . .*

WHO: Elementary/Middle/High

WHEN: During a lesson

CONTENT AREA(S): Cross-curricular

- Create factual or fictional stories that can illustrate a cross-curricular concept you are teaching. Integrate the stories into your lesson delivery, and watch students more easily retain the concept. If your story is humorous or emotional, the recall value is enhanced. For example, use the following cross-curricular stories to teach students to remember the 13 original colonies in social studies (written by Gloria Caracas, El Oro Way Elementary School) and the concept of natural selection in science (written by Warren Phillips, Plymouth Middle School).

- There once was a cow named <u>Georgette</u> **(Georgia)**. She was a <u>Jersey</u> **(New Jersey)** cow and gave lots of milk. She was strange because she liked to wear yellow <u>underwear</u> **(Delaware)**. One day, she went up the <u>Empire State Building</u> **(New York)**. Up there she sang two Christmas <u>carols</u> **(North Carolina, South Carolina)**. Then she came down and walked down the <u>road</u> **(Rhode Island)**. She was carrying a <u>massive</u> **(Massachusetts)** <u>Virginia</u> **(Virginia)** <u>ham</u> **(New Hampshire)**. She bent down to pick up a <u>pencil</u> **(Pennsylvania)** and proceeded to do a <u>connect-a-dot</u> **(Connecticut)** of <u>Marilyn</u> **(Maryland)** Monroe (Tate, 2012, pp. 121–122).

- The light-colored form of the moth was the predominant form in England prior to the beginning of the Industrial Revolution. Then, darker-colored forms of the moth became much more prevalent. In areas where pollution had darkened the landscape, the darker moths were better camouflaged and less likely to be eaten by birds. Later, after the use of coal declined under less-polluted conditions, the light-colored moths prevailed again. Go figure! (Tate & Phillips, 2011, p. 125).

WHO: Elementary/Middle

WHEN: During a lesson

CONTENT AREA(S): Cross-curricular

- Have students create stories, fictional or factual, that can be used to remember a concept that has been taught. Stories are particularly helpful when recalling a multistep process or events that happen in sequential order. Have students retell their stories several times to their classmates. Have them recall their original stories each time they attempt to remember the key concept on which the story is based.

WHO: Elementary/Middle/High

WHEN: During a lesson

CONTENT AREA(S): Mathematics

- Read aloud to the class any of the appropriate books in the bibliography, *Have You Read Any Math Lately?* found on page 147 of *Mathematics Worksheets Don't Grow Dendrites: 20 Numeracy Strategies That Engage the Brain* (Tate, 2009). These include Neuschwander's series of books about *Sir Cumference* and Scieszka's book, *Math Curse*. The first time you read the books aloud, do so for the enjoyment of the literature. Then revisit the book at another time, and select a math skill or strategy from the story. The context of the story will help students remember the skill being taught.

WHO: Elementary/Middle/High

WHEN: During a lesson

CONTENT AREA(S): Language Arts

- Select literary works that contain numerous examples of language arts skills and strategies from the curriculum to be taught. Although a few titles are listed below as examples, any story or poem that contains examples of the skill can be used. Consult pages 98–103 of my book, *100 Brain-Friendly Lessons for Unforgettable Teaching and Learning (K-8)*, compiled by Simone Willingham, for an extensive list of literary texts that teach story elements and skills. Read the story or poem aloud to the class initially for enjoyment. Reread parts of the story on a subsequent day, pointing out examples of the skill or strategy to be taught. Have students look for examples in this or other literary works.

TITLE	AUTHOR	CONCEPTS
The Important Book	Margaret Wise Brown	Main idea and details
The Day Jimmy's Boa Ate the Wash	Trinka Hayes Noble	Cause and effect
Thomas' Snowsuit	Robert Munsch	Sequence of events
The Pain and the Great One	Judy Blume	Point of view
Encounter	Jane Yolen	Point of view
My Brother's Flying Machine	Jane Yolen	Point of view
The King Who Rained	Fred Gwynne	Figurative language
Amelia Bedelia series	Judy Blume	Figurative language
The Parts of Speech series	Brian Cleary	Parts of speech
The Parts of Speech series	Ruth Heller	Parts of speech
The Doorbell Rang	Pat Hutchins	Concept of division
Counting on Frank	Rod Clement	Real-world math
Math Curse	John Scieszka	Real-world math
Science Alphabet Books series	Jerry Pallotta	Science concepts

WHO:	Elementary/Middle/High
WHEN:	During a lesson
CONTENT AREA(S):	Cross-curricular

- Following a read-aloud or the silent reading of a story or content-area unit of study, have students retell the story to a partner with story events in the correct sequential order.

WHO:	Elementary/Middle/High
WHEN:	During a lesson
CONTENT AREA(S):	Cross-curricular

- Have students work individually or in cooperative groups to use the *narrative chaining* method by creating an original story linking unrelated terms, concepts, or words in a list.

WHO:	Middle/High
WHEN:	During a lesson
CONTENT AREA(S):	Mathematics

- Tell students "The Story of the Algebraic Equation" to help them understand one step in solving equations. This story also incorporates the strategies of movement, roleplay, and metaphor. Seven students hold cards representing the numbers and signs in the algebraic equation $3y + 10 = 2y + 18$. $3y$ and $2y$ should be female students. *Ten* and *18* should be male students. The cards for 10 and $2y$ should have -10 and $-2y$ written on the backs, respectively. Students role-play the story as it is read.

"THE STORY OF THE ALGEBRAIC EQUATION"

$$3y + 10 = 2y + 18$$

Once upon a time, two families lived on either side of a busy street called Equal Street. Each family had two children (one teenage daughter and one younger son). One day the teenage daughters, $3y$ and $2y$, made a date to go to the mall. However, there was a problem. Each daughter had been asked to babysit a younger brother. $3y$ had to babysit 10 and $2y$ had to babysit 18.

The girls desperately wanted to get together to go to the mall. Therefore, daughter $3y$ suggested that she send her younger brother 10 to cross Equal Street so he could play with her friend's brother, 18. Now, there was one peculiar thing about this particular town. Whenever anyone crossed Equal Street, they had to turn around and cross it backward. So, younger brother

10 turned backward and crossed the street. The two boys were very happy because now they could play together.

There was only one problem. To be all alone with no one to bother them, the boys had to get rid of big sister 2y. That was all right with big sister 2y because she wanted to go to the mall with her friend 3y anyway. So she said goodbye to her brother and crossed Equal Street, backward of course, and she and her friend 3y could be all alone to proceed to the mall. The girls had a wonderful time, and so did the boys.

When the girls returned from the mall, they were in a world of trouble because their parents had told them repeatedly never to leave their younger brothers unattended. But you know as well as I do that for generations, older sisters have left younger brothers unattended. That's just the way the story goes!

Action Plan for Incorporating STORYTELLING

WHAT ARE MY PLANS FOR INCORPORATING MORE *STORYTELLING* INTO MY LESSONS TO ACCELERATE LEARNING?

RECOMMENDATIONS	ALREADY DOING	PLANNING TO DO
Put a story stool or bench in your classroom.		
Tell the story of the continents to enable students to remember them.		
Give students a purpose for reading narrative or expository texts.		
Create original stories to illustrate a cross-curricular concept.		
Have students create their own fictional or factual stories.		
Read aloud books from the bibliography, *Have You Read Any Math Lately?*		
Select literary works with numerous examples of language arts skills and strategies to be taught.		
Following a read-aloud or silent reading of a story, have students retell the story to a partner.		
Have students use the *narrative chaining* method to create an original story.		
Tell students *The Story of the Algebraic Equation* to enable them to begin solving equations.		
Goals and Notes:		

168 • Engaging the Brain

Source: istock.com/monkeybusinessimages

When digital literacy is infused within each content area, relevant subject matter is taught with 21st century technology (Summey, 2013).

STRATEGY 16

Technology

💡 WHAT: DEFINING THE STRATEGY

What would we have done without this strategy over the last few years? Thanks to an unprecedented pandemic, content that was once taught only face-to-face was relegated to virtual delivery via technology. Teachers like me were forced to master online previously unfamiliar platforms like Zoom or GoToMeeting. However, the large majority of students we teach are classified as *digital natives*. Most have never known life without this strategy—cell phones, iPads, email, streaming television channels, TikTok, Snapchat, Instagram, and social media sites abound. I have even watched my grandchildren, as early as two, instinctively know what to do with their iPads without guidance or instruction.

Eighty-nine percent of 18- to 24-year-old Americans are online. While experts suggest that between 30 minutes and two hours per day should be the maximum amount of time spent on social media (Hui, 2024), average Americans are spending seven hours and four minutes daily looking at a screen. According to the Pew Research Center (2023), the share of teenagers who say they are online constantly has doubled since 2014–2015.

I, on the other hand, am a "digital immigrant" (Prensky, 2009), and though I was late to learn to Google, my children now call me the Google *queen*. I search Google for everything—the weather in a city to which I will be going, the score of a sporting event, or a topic I must teach when planning a model lesson.

Technological advances have revolutionized all aspects of our lives, including how educators teach and students learn. Technological literacy is crucial and one of the five competencies that high school students should be proficient with to succeed in the work world (Secretary's Commission on Achieving Necessary Skills [SCANS], 1991). This strategy will deal with the amazing and engaging impact that can be made on a lesson when technology is integrated.

However, the longer I am around today's students, the more convinced I am that the strategy of technology should be considered only one of 20 and needs to be balanced with the other 19. A combination of strategies helps foster the interpersonal skills essential for meaningful personal and professional relationships in the real world. The overdependence on technology can also lead many brains to crave the uniqueness and overstimulation engendered. Research from studies in China found that addiction to the Internet can actually lower the density of gray matter in the adolescent brain (Park et al., 2011; Zhou et al., 2011). Balance, then, appears to be the key.

WHY: THEORETICAL FRAMEWORK

Computers are used effectively in the classroom when (a) there are a variety of teaching strategies; (b) teachers and students are pretrained in the use of computers for the purpose of teaching and learning; (c) many learning opportunities exist; (d) the student is in control of their own learning; and (e) student feedback is optimized (Hattie, 2023).

Technology is rewiring the brains of teenagers since they are spending more time with media than interacting with their parents, teachers or even sleeping (Sousa, 2022).

Teachers must adjust their teaching to the rapidly changing environment in which today's student brains are existing (Sousa, 2022).

Effective technology integration should answer three questions: (1) Will the technology encourage communication between students? (2) Will the technology give students the possibilities for choice in completing the assignment? and (3) Is the technology providing useful data that can help inform holistic assessments of students' learning (Kavanagh & Bernhard, 2023)?

The pros of having technology in the classroom include (1) providing a variety of useful resources; (2) making day-to-day tasks more efficient; (3) preparing students for success in college and the world of work; (4) having immediate access to up-to-date information; (5) giving students more control over their learning; and (6) making learning more engaging and motivating (Brown, 2019).

The cons to avoid of having technology in the classroom include (1) increasing the already excessive amount of screen time; (2) keeping students on task with the large number of online distractions; (3) having students cheat by plagiarizing other people's work; (4) minimizing the time for face-to-face interaction; and (5) lacking access to the technology (Brown, 2019).

Thanks to the brain's neuroplasticity, children have responded to technology by changing the brain's organization and function to allow for the large amount of information in today's environment (Sousa, 2016).

Infusing digital literacy within each content area not only teaches relevant subject matter with 21st century technology but also addresses vital literacy skills (Summey, 2013).

Students become excited and challenged to find answers to problems and create unique ways of presenting information when they are allowed to use their gadgets at appropriate times (Gregory & Chapman, 2013).

Technology is not an end unto itself but should be used to enrich, enhance, and present content in a more efficient manner (Sousa, 2011).

Students of all ability levels can use technology to process, demonstrate, retain, and share information and communication (Karten, 2009, p. 196).

> Assistive technology can support the participation of students with disabilities in whole-class and small-group discussions (Udvari-Solner & Kluth, 2008).
>
> When the inquiry-based learning model is paired with dynamic geometric software programs, math students are able to discover relationships, make hypotheses, and defend assumptions (Posamentier & Jaye, 2006).

HOW: INSTRUCTIONAL ACTIVITIES

WHO: Elementary/Middle/High
WHEN: During a lesson
CONTENT AREA(S): Cross-curricular

- The *SAMR* model is a good guide to refer to when planning the most effective use of technology. SAMR is a mnemonic device for *Substitution, Augmentation, Modification,* and *Redefinition* and represents a hierarchy of the different levels of technology integration from simplest to most complex. The Table 16.1 shows how technology can enhance and even transform classroom activities.

TABLE 16.1 • The SAMR Model

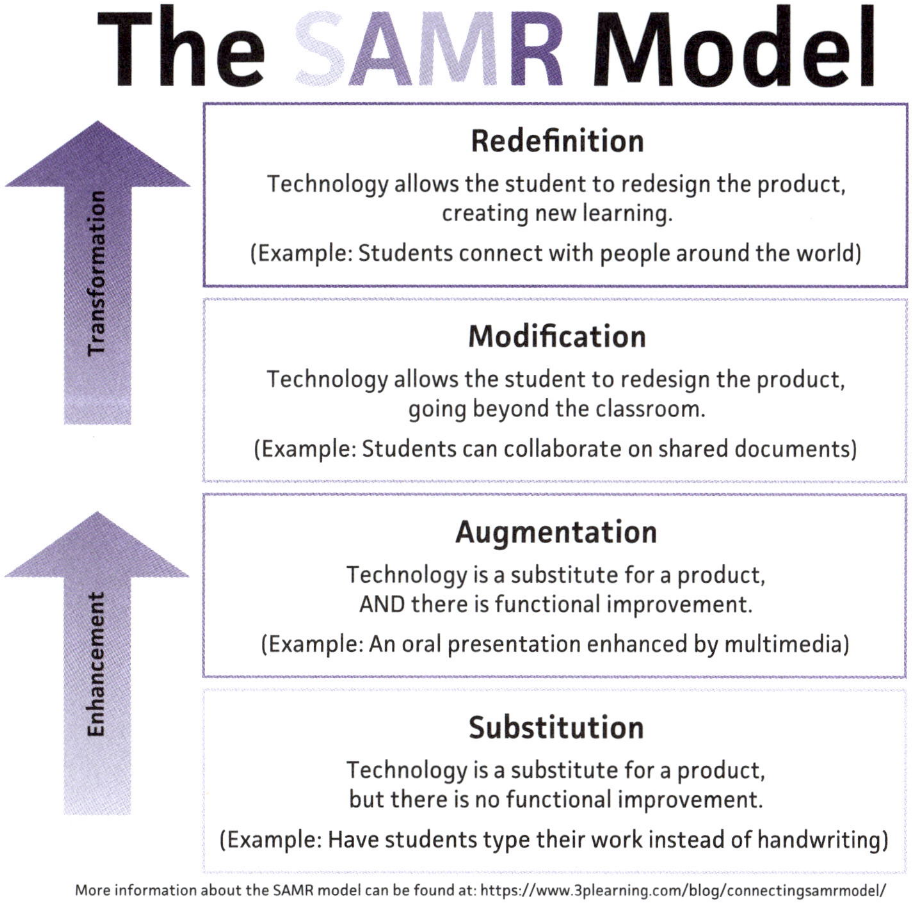

The SAMR Model

Transformation

Redefinition
Technology allows the student to redesign the product, creating new learning.
(Example: Students connect with people around the world)

Modification
Technology allows the student to redesign the product, going beyond the classroom.
(Example: Students can collaborate on shared documents)

Enhancement

Augmentation
Technology is a substitute for a product, AND there is functional improvement.
(Example: An oral presentation enhanced by multimedia)

Substitution
Technology is a substitute for a product, but there is no functional improvement.
(Example: Have students type their work instead of handwriting)

More information about the SAMR model can be found at: https://www.3plearning.com/blog/connectingsamrmodel/

Source: Created by Warren Phillips. Used with permission.

WHO:	Elementary/Middle/High
WHEN:	During a lesson
CONTENT AREA(S):	Cross-curricular

- Use the following types of technology to address the major memory pathways of students:
  - **Semantic**—mind maps, blogging, texting, searching online
  - **Episodic**—story searches, use of a computer lab setting
  - **Procedural**—step-by-step software programs, PowerPoint presentations, programs with drag-and-drop features, organizational classroom routines
  - **Automatic**—memory games, computerized flashcards, and using software to create poems
  - **Emotional**—blogging, texting, group computer time (Sprenger, 2010)

WHO:	Elementary/Middle/High
WHEN:	During a lesson
CONTENT AREA(S):	Cross-curricular

- Personal technology devices such as smartphones, smartwatches, or tablets can be a distraction in class, or they can be incorporated into the instruction. Plan opportunities for students to use their personal gadgets to accomplish a curricular objective. Place QR codes around the classroom. When scanned, students are directed to websites with more information to read or a task to complete for an assignment. The Goosechase app can be used to create scavenger hunt challenges for students to complete. When these devices are not in use, ask for them to be stored away safely so that students' conscious attention is not divided.

WHO:	Elementary/Middle/High
WHEN:	During a lesson
CONTENT AREA(S):	Cross-curricular

- An interactive whiteboard (you may know them as SMART or Promethean) is a powerful tool for the classroom. It serves as the gateway to learning for students who rely on the visual display. They allow for writing, brainstorming, editing, and encouraging student interaction, all of which can be captured and saved for later. And, of course, they can be used as a display for slides or videos you'd like to present.

WHO: Elementary/Middle/High

WHEN: During or after a lesson

CONTENT AREA(S): Cross-curricular

- Use one of many technology tools to help keep students organized with tasks and homework from different classes. A digital calendar, Google Keep Notes, or Padlet all provide the means for tasks to be entered by date, class, color, and subject and to be visually appealing.

WHO: Elementary/Middle/High

WHEN: During or after a lesson

CONTENT AREA(S): Cross-curricular

- A collaborative spreadsheet is a great way to gather examples from students during a lesson. At the beginning of the lesson, provide a shared spreadsheet with the first column prefilled with all student names. As the lesson proceeds, you may ask students to give an example of something and put their response in a different column. The responses will provide students with a variety of examples to consider, and the teacher can use the spreadsheet both as an indication of participation and a formative assessment.

WHO: Elementary/Middle/High

WHEN: During or after a lesson

CONTENT AREA(S): Cross-curricular

- Wakelet is a free, versatile platform students and educators use to curate and organize digital content. Students can use Wakelet to compile research materials, organize class notes, and create visually appealing presentations by incorporating links, images, videos, and text. For educators, Wakelet serves as a collaborative tool for lesson planning, enabling you to gather and share resources with students.

WHO: Elementary/Middle/High

WHEN: During or after a lesson

CONTENT AREA(S): Cross-curricular

- Part 1-Graphics: Have students use the process of digital storytelling by integrating technology. Have them create images or build infographics that represent the main idea and details of informational text or the elements of a narrative story. These tools are easy to learn and free for users: Canva and Genially.
- Part 2-Video: Give students the opportunity to take photographs or have them use the images created in Part 1 for this task. Students will

import these images into a digital storytelling tool such as iMovie, Movie Maker, or Screencastify. Add narration. Use this activity to motivate struggling writers or English language learner students (McLaughlin & Overturf, 2013).

WHO: Elementary/Middle/High

WHEN: During or after a lesson

CONTENT AREA(S): Cross-curricular

- Use technology for interactive formative assessments with students. Many tools are available for you to create activities for instruction and formative assessment. Some tools even gamify learning! These tools all have free versions available: Blooket, Flippity, Gimkit, Kahoot, Quia, Quizlet, and Quizziz.

WHO: Elementary/Middle/High

WHEN: During or after a lesson

CONTENT AREA(S): Cross-curricular

- Why present static slides to your students when you could present dynamic, interactive slides? Using tools such as Nearpod or Peardeck will pull your students into the lesson with activities that serve as attention-getters and formative assessments for content knowledge. Slides created in various programs can be imported and modified using tools like Nearpod and Peardeck to add interactive components, such as polls, free response questions, quizzes, collaborative boards, and more. The paid versions allow for self-paced student access to lessons.

WHO: Elementary/Middle/High

WHEN: During or after a lesson

CONTENT AREA(S): Cross-curricular

- Have students access websites, such as Newsela, which allow them to explore news stories at a variety of reading levels and take differentiated quizzes on the stories. Fisher (2013) refers to this instructional strategy as *digital differentiation*. The website Wordle enables teachers to create tag clouds of different news stories. This allows students to compare and contrast the treatment of the same news stories by different news agencies. A service called Newspapermap compares news stories from the United States with those from around the world (Fisher, 2013).

WHO: Elementary/Middle/High

WHEN: During or after a lesson

CONTENT AREA(S): Cross-curricular

- Even notetaking can be digitized. Have individual students use writing apps or software on their computers to save digital versions of their notes, which can be modified and shared by way of email. Apps and tools such as Google Docs, Draftin, and TodaysMeet allow students to contribute notes, media, and hyperlinks to other students in real-time (Fisher, 2013).

WHO: Elementary/Middle/High

WHEN: During a lesson

CONTENT AREA(S): Cross-curricular

- Have students design a Facebook page for a fictional or historical character. The Facebook page should include personal biographical information, a listing of family members, personal likes and dislikes, social affiliations, and a timeline of important life events. Students can then decide which other people living at that time would have been Facebook friends with the original character (Tate, 2014a).

WHO: Middle/High

WHEN: After a lesson

CONTENT AREA(S): Cross-curricular

- Have students create an original song, rhyme, or rap to demonstrate their understanding of course content, as suggested in Strategy 11 (Music, Rhythm, Rhyme, and Rap). Select the best creative efforts, and have those students follow the necessary directions to post their songs, rhymes, or raps on YouTube for others to enjoy.

Action Plan for Incorporating TECHNOLOGY

WHAT ARE MY PLANS FOR INCORPORATING MORE *TECHNOLOGY* INTO MY LESSONS TO ACCELERATE LEARNING?

RECOMMENDATIONS	ALREADY DOING	PLANNING TO DO
Consult the *SAMR* model when planning the most effective way to integrate technology into your lessons.		
Use appropriate technology to address students' memory pathways.		
Incorporate students' personal technology into instruction.		
Use interactive whiteboards as visual displays.		
Help keep students organized with technology tools.		
Use a collaborative spreadsheet to gather student examples in a lesson.		
Have students use Wakelet to organize digital content.		
Have students integrate technology into the process of digital storytelling.		
Use technology for interactive formative assessments with students.		
Use technology to present dynamic, interactive slides.		
Have students access websites to explore news stories.		
Help students make notetaking digitized.		
Have students design a Facebook page for a fictional or historical character.		
Have students post original songs, rhymes, or raps on YouTube		
Goals and Notes:		

Source: istock.com/Jacob Wackerhausen

When one visualizes the things they want, neural pathways are created in the brain as if the person had actually done those things (Better Help Editorial Team, 2023).

STRATEGY 17

Visualization and Guided Imagery

WHAT: DEFINING THE STRATEGY

I was watching the 2024 National Championship Game between my Alma Mater, the University of Michigan, and Washington. In an interview following the Michigan win, the quarterback, J. J. McCarthy, related all the times he had visualized himself winning this championship. I immediately thought about this all-important strategy. It is used in at least two places in the real world—sports and medicine. Coaches have always advised players to picture themselves scoring the touchdown or hitting the home run before the game even begins. This practice increases the likelihood that the same action will happen in the game, which it did for J. J. According to Caine et al. (2005), like great athletes (e.g., skiers and golfers) and actors, students can also visualize a performance before it happens.

The second place that the strategy of visualization appears is in medicine. Doctors often advise their cancer patients who are taking chemotherapy to visualize the chemotherapy medicine knocking out the cancer cells in the body. This strategy seems to increase the effectiveness of the medicine.

Visualization refers to the mind's ability to form mental images and involves imagining experiences, objects, or solutions in detail (Warren, 2023). It can work for your students and you. Visualize when you were young and you went outside and played. Remember that you saw yourself as someone else and your friend as another person. The tree in your yard was not a tree but your house. In other words, you imagined. One reason that some of today's students have difficulty comprehending what they read is that in this world of vivid visuals found on computer screens and in video games, students have had little opportunity to use their imaginations. And yet, if there are no pictures in a novel, good readers have to visualize the action in the story. Otherwise, there is little or no comprehension. This strategy provides opportunities for students to use their imaginations to facilitate understanding across the curriculum.

Visualize every one of your students experiencing success this year. This is the first step toward ensuring that it happens!

WHY: THEORETICAL FRAMEWORK

Visualization, a powerful technique for making learning more meaningful, involves creating mental images of the processes, scenarios, or outcomes desired to be achieved (Linkedin, 2023).

When one visualizes the things they want, neural pathways are created in the brain as if the person had actually done those things (Better Help Editorial Team, 2023).

Visualization assists in holding information in working and long-term memory, and improves students' comprehension, attention, and motivation (Warren, 2023).

Visualization creates associations between new knowledge and the knowledge that already exists since it engages your emotional, sensory, and cognitive facilities (Linkedin, 2023).

The classroom teaching strategy of visualization is one of many factors that can separate struggling teachers from those who are successful (Jensen, 2022).

Visualizing movement changes how the networks of the brain are organized, creating additional connections between various regions (Lohr, 2015).

There is evidence that visualization during prelearning and postlearning can reduce the loss of the significant number of neurons that adolescent brains produce and lose within weeks (Curlik & Shors, 2013).

Learning new skills and associations through visualization or your trained imagination can increase the survival of new cells (Dalla et al., 2007).

Since visualized note taking combines on paper verbal information in sequence with symbols and visual patterns, it is a strategy that associates language with visual imagery (Sousa, 2011).

When important events in history are too abstract to remember, visual imagery facilitates the retention of those events (Melber & Hunter, 2010).

"If a picture is worth a thousand words, perhaps drawing and visualization can help science students enhance their learning potential" (National Science Teachers Association [NSTA], 2006, p. 20).

Visualization enhances learning and retention of information because, during mental imagery, the same sections of the brain's visual cortex are activated as when the eyes are actually processing input from the real world (Sousa, 2006).

The image is the greatest instrument of instruction. If the majority of classroom time was spent ensuring that students are forming proper images, the instructor's work would be indefinitely facilitated (Dewey, 1938).

HOW: INSTRUCTIONAL ACTIVITIES

WHO: Elementary/Middle/High

WHEN: Before a lesson

CONTENT AREA(S): Cross-curricular

- Students in every classroom should visualize themselves as successful! That visualization helps build confidence, and since success builds success, teachers need to do everything within their power to help students experience those initial positive experiences. It even worked for me. I visualized all of my eight books in the *Worksheets Don't Grow Dendrites* series as bestsellers. Seven of eight books are bestsellers! One teacher told me that at the beginning of every school year, she has students write the word *can't* on a piece of paper and then ball it up and throw it into the trash. Then she teaches them this motto: *Success comes in cans, not in can'ts!* After all, *If you believe you can or you believe you can't, you're right!*

WHO: Elementary/Middle/High

WHEN: During a lesson

CONTENT AREA(S): Mathematics

- To provide practice in visualizing, as you read a word problem aloud, have students imagine each step of the problem. Have them see in their mind what is happening and then determine what operations are needed to solve the problem. Stop periodically, and have students draw what they are visualizing. Visualization is one of the strategies students in Singapore are encouraged to use when solving problems. Their test scores in mathematics speak for themselves!

WHO: Elementary/Middle/High

WHEN: During a lesson

CONTENT AREA(S): Cross-curricular

- Read aloud to students at all grade levels for purposes of information, enjoyment, or to teach a skill or strategy. As you read, have students visualize what is happening. As you read, they should imagine what they see, hear, feel, touch, and taste. Stop periodically, and have students describe the scenes in their minds to one another and then compare them to the original text.

WHO:	Elementary/Middle/High
WHEN:	During a lesson
CONTENT AREA(S):	Cross-curricular

- As students read a novel or content-area passage independently, teach them how to visualize the scenes or events using each of their senses. Have them answer the following question: *What do you see, hear, feel, touch, and taste as you visualize the passage you read?*

WHO:	Elementary/Middle/High
WHEN:	During a lesson
CONTENT AREA(S):	Cross-curricular

- Have students work individually or in groups to create visual images that link a word to its definition or, as in social studies, a state to its capital. The more absurd the visual image, the easier it is for the brain to remember the connection. For example, to remember that the capital of Minnesota is St. Paul, have students visualize a saint sipping on a little bitty soda (Tate, 2012).

WHO:	Elementary/Middle/High
WHEN:	During a lesson
CONTENT AREA(S):	Mathematics

- Have students visualize what a given shape would look like rotated 180 degrees, flipped vertically, or turned 90 degrees. Have them describe or draw the resulting figure.

WHO:	Elementary/Middle/High
WHEN:	During a lesson
CONTENT AREA(S):	Cross-curricular

- When students must recall concepts, events, or objects in sequential order in any content area, have them visualize the items in the sequence connected together in novel ways. Have them imagine the items upside down, backward, tossed about, crashing into one another, dancing together, or positioned uniquely. Since these items are visualized in novel ways, the brain can remember them better. Brains pay attention to novelty (Tate, 2012)!

WHO:	Elementary/Middle/High
WHEN:	During a lesson
CONTENT AREA(S):	Science

- As you use guided imagery to orally describe a bodily function, have students visualize themselves involved in the process, such as a red blood cell coursing through the body or a piece of food involved in the process of digestion. As a red blood cell, have them imagine the salty taste, warm temperature, or wetness they would experience.

WHO:	Elementary/Middle/High
WHEN:	During a lesson
CONTENT AREA(S):	Physical education

- To improve the quality of their physical performance, have students visualize themselves as being successful, such as getting the base hit, making the basket, completing the pass, or jumping the farthest. These positive images help increase brain confidence and improve physical prowess. When the confidence level in sports changes from one team to another, that is known as a momentum shift and often results in a positive change in the game's score for the team that is now the most confident.

WHO:	Elementary/Middle/High
WHEN:	During a lesson
CONTENT AREA(S):	Social Studies

- Have students mentally transport themselves into a specific period of history being studied, such as the Civil War or the French Revolution, and visualize themselves in that period. Have them ask and answer the following questions: What do you see? How are you dressed? What's going on around you? These images will help to make history more relevant and memorable.

WHO:	Elementary/Middle/High
WHEN:	During a lesson
CONTENT AREA(S):	Cross-curricular

- Show students a content-area visual such as a math formula, vocabulary word, or science process, such as the process of a flower from pollination to seed production. After a while, remove the visual, ask them to visualize the concept, and write or draw it from memory. Repeat the process several times since the brain needs that repetition.

WHO: Elementary/Middle/High

WHEN: During a lesson

CONTENT AREA(S): Cross-curricular

- To alleviate anxiety prior to any test, have students take deep breaths and visualize themselves successfully completing each item on the test. This activity, in addition to well-taught lessons incorporating brain-compatible strategies, gives students the confidence they need to do well!

Action Plan for Incorporating VISUALIZATION and GUIDED IMAGERY

WHAT ARE MY PLANS FOR INCORPORATING MORE *VISUALIZATION* AND *GUIDED IMAGERY* INTO MY LESSONS TO ACCELERATE LEARNING?

RECOMMENDATIONS	ALREADY DOING	PLANNING TO DO
Have students visualize themselves having a successful school year.		
When reading a math word problem aloud, have students imagine each step.		
As you read aloud, have students visualize the action in the story.		
As students read silently, have them visualize the scenes or events.		
Have students create visual images linking words to their definitions.		
Ask students to visualize a given shape rotated or flipped.		
To remember sequential order, ask students to visualize items connected together in novel ways.		
Have science students use guided imagery to describe a scientific process.		
Have physical education students visualize themselves succeeding.		
Ask social studies students to transport themselves to a specific period of history.		
Have students visualize a content area visual after viewing it.		
Prior to testing, have students visualize themselves experiencing success.		
Goals and Notes:		

Source: istock.com/Anna Usova

The human eye can register 36,000 visual messages per hour, even if the visual message lasts for only 13 milliseconds (Jandhyala, 2017).

STRATEGY 18

Visuals

WHAT: DEFINING THE STRATEGY

Have you flown in an airplane recently? If so, you will remember that it is not sufficient for the flight attendants to simply *tell* you what to do with your seat belt and the other myriad instructions they must give. They have to *show* you. They either get out in the aisle and demonstrate while holding the apparatus or show you what to do via a video. Why? Even airline personnel know that merely telling human beings what they need to know is probably the least effective form of getting the information across to them. Brains need a visual to accompany the information. I fly so frequently that I have memorized the dialogue of what to do and can physically show you where the exits are. If you ever attend one of my workshops, I will gladly demonstrate this crucial information to you (smile). Southwest Airlines has even added the strategy of *humor* to the flight instructions to increase passengers' attention and retention.

The Chinese knew the power of visuals thousands of years ago when they created the following proverb:

Tell me, I forget.

Show me, I remember.

Involve me, I understand!

At least 50% of students in any classroom will be predominately visual learners (Willis, 2006). Look at all the information that today's students are taking in visually. They text on their cell phones, play video games, watch television, and spend hours on social media. These activities strengthen the visual modality for many of your students. There is even physical evidence to support that the visual cortex in students' brains today is physically thicker than in my brain when I was their age. That is why the strategy of visuals is essential.

WHY: THEORETICAL FRAMEWORK

When teaching new concepts, visual models should accompany discussion, increasing the likelihood that students will be able to accurately recall the information later (Sousa, 2022).

Visual supports in the classroom are particularly effective for students with Autism spectrum disorder, have dyslexia, are hard of hearing or deaf, or are simply visual learners (Turner, 2022).

Small meaningful segments of a video presentation should be shown, then the video stopped, followed by discussion (Sousa, 2022).

According to the Visual Teaching Alliance, 90% of information transmitted to the brain is visual, which is processed 60,000 times faster than text (Jandhyala, 2017).

Visuals are essential in the classroom since they lend support to classroom instruction, encourage students to associate one piece of information with another, function to aid memory, and quickly soak up pieces of content (Bowman, 2018).

The human eye can register 36,000 visual messages per hour, even if the visual message lasts for only 13 milliseconds (Jandhyala, 2017).

Pictures, graphs, diagrams, and other types of visual organizers are very effective learning and retention devices for today's students since they are continuously inundated with visual stimuli from their digital devices (Sousa, 2016).

Using visual representations (i.e., models, diagrams, photographs) enables scientists to present phenomena that can be complex and not able to be observed in any other ways (Evagorou et al., 2015).

The part of the brain that processes words is very small compared to the part that processes visual images, making the brain an image, not a word, processor (Kouyoumdjian, 2012).

After about two weeks, the effects of direct instruction diminish on the brains of students, but the effects of visuals and those images taken in peripherally continue to increase during the same period of time (Jensen, 2007).

Even though rote learning plays some part, students in Singapore comprehend abstract concepts by using visual tools (Prystay, 2004).

Because the eyes can take in 30 million bits of information per second, teachers should provide images and moving pictures when instructing students (Jensen, 2007).

Visual aids provide students with a point of focus and improve learning as students encounter the following stages of acquiring new concepts: acquisition, proficiency, maintenance, and generalization (Algozzine et al., 2009).

Visuals, such as concept maps, flow charts, cartoons, sketches, and drawings, can often help to communicate a teacher's message in a more powerful way than words because visuals can be taken in quickly and remembered by the brain (Allen, 2008).

HOW: INSTRUCTIONAL ACTIVITIES

WHO: Elementary/Middle/High

WHEN: During a lesson

CONTENT AREA(S): Cross-curricular

- Gain and keep students' visual attention by changing your location in the room. Begin your lesson in the front of the class and then shift to other areas. This tactic will not only keep students interested but also put you in close proximity to all students and communicate to them that you care about their well-being and are interested in what they are doing. *Remember to teach on your feet, not in a seat!*

WHO: Elementary/Middle/High

WHEN: Before, during, or after a lesson

CONTENT AREA(S): Cross-curricular

- An anchor chart represents an artifact representing what students have learned. Like an anchor, it holds students' and teachers' ideas, thoughts, and processes in place. Display anchor charts around the room to remind students of prior learning and to build upon the charts in subsequent lessons.

WHO: Elementary/Middle/High

WHEN: Before a lesson

CONTENT AREA(S): Cross-curricular

- Before reading content-area texts, have students survey the chapter or unit of study and peruse any visuals such as maps, charts, graphs, pictures, chapter titles, subtitles, or bold headings. Have them make predictions as to what the chapter or unit will include. This survey technique, called SQ3R (Survey, Question, Read, Recite, Review), should facilitate comprehension.

WHO: Elementary/Middle/High

WHEN: Before a lesson

CONTENT AREA(S): Cross-curricular

- Place visuals on the classroom bulletin boards and walls that introduce or reinforce concepts being taught. For example, display a visual of the *periodic table* on the wall in a science class or the eight parts of speech in a language arts class. Even if those visuals are removed during testing, students can still visualize them.

    WHO: Elementary/Middle/High

    WHEN: During a lesson

    CONTENT AREA(S): Cross-curricular

- PowerPoint can be a great visual tool when lecturing, but it is overused. I have watched students disengage when too many slides are shown. Remember the following 10–20–30 rule of good PowerPoint: (1) no more than 10 slides, (2) no more than 20 minutes, and (3) each line on the slide should be at least 30 font. Remember to intersperse activity within your lecture. Have a miniature copy of your slides for your students, if necessary, since they will not be listening to you if they simultaneously have to do too much writing.

    WHO: Elementary/Middle/High

    WHEN: During a lesson

    CONTENT AREA(S): Cross-curricular

- Facilitate lecture or discussion with visuals by writing keywords and phrases or drawing pictures on a dry-erase or SMART board. Positioning information vertically indicates a step, time, or hierarchical sequence. Writing information horizontally implies a relationship that is parallel (Sousa, 2022). For example, write the word "noun" and the words "person," "place," "thing," and "idea" as you explain their definitions, or draw and label a picture of the heart as you describe its function. The use of color leaves its imprint on the brain. Write with a blue marker, which works well for most students' brains. Emphasize keywords or phrases in red.

    WHO: Elementary/Middle/High

    WHEN: During a lesson

    CONTENT AREA(S): Cross-curricular

- As you deliver a lecturette or minilecture, provide students with a visual by filling in a semantic map or creating an appropriate graphic organizer emphasizing the lecturette's main ideas and key points. Place the map or organizer on the board. Have students draw the visual along with you. Lecturettes typically last less than seven minutes. (See Strategy 5, Graphic Organizers, Semantic Maps, and Word Webs, for specific examples.)

WHO: Elementary/Middle/High

WHEN: During a lesson

CONTENT AREA(S): Cross-curricular

- Find and show students a visual or a real-life artifact to clarify a concept being taught. For example, bring in a live chrysanthemum as you teach the vocabulary word for this flower, show a picture of the Great Wall of China as you teach about its history, or bring in a pizza to teach the concept of fractional pieces.

WHO: Elementary/Middle/High

WHEN: During a lesson

CONTENT AREA(S): Mathematics

- When introducing a new math concept, work a minimum of three problems on the SMART or dry-erase board so that all students can see the steps involved. Most brains need at least three examples before they begin to understand the procedure. As you work on each problem, talk aloud so students can hear you modeling the thought processes and become more metacognitive.

Adaptation: Have students come to the dry-erase or SMART board and work on math problems that can serve as visuals for the remainder of the class. Have them explain the steps in solving the problem so that students have an auditory link to the visual problem.

WHO: Elementary/Middle/High

WHEN: After a lesson

CONTENT AREA(S): Cross-curricular

- Create a *word wall* by categorizing basic sight words or content-area vocabulary words and placing them on the wall under the appropriate alphabet letter or by the parts of speech they represent as they are taught.

WHO: Elementary/Middle/High

WHEN: During a lesson

CONTENT AREA(S): Social Studies

- During the course of the school year, add specific historical events to a timeline placed around the wall as they are taught so that students can visually see the relationships between sequential events in history.

Action Plan for Incorporating VISUALS

WHAT ARE MY PLANS FOR INCORPORATING MORE *VISUALS* INTO MY LESSONS TO ACCELERATE LEARNING?

RECOMMENDATIONS	ALREADY DOING	PLANNING TO DO
Change your physical location in the classroom to maintain students' attention.		
Create and display anchor charts around the room to remind students of previous learning.		
Have students survey a chapter before reading it.		
Provide visuals on bulletin boards and walls that introduce or reinforce concepts.		
Utilize the 10-20-30 rule of effective PowerPoint.		
Facilitate lecture or discussion by writing keywords or phrases or drawing pictures that serve as visuals.		
Have students draw a graphic organizer along with you to accompany your lecturette.		
Locate and show a visual or real-life artifact to clarify a concept being taught.		
Work or have math students work on at least three problems on the SMART board as examples.		
Create a word wall of sight or content-area words for display.		
In social studies, construct and add to a timeline of historical events placed on the wall.		
Goals and Notes:		

Source: istock.com/VichienPetchmai

Well-designed Career Technology Education programs enable students to get college or career-ready by interconnecting the skills needed for both (Rix, 2022).

STRATEGY 19

Work Study and Apprenticeships

WHAT: DEFINING THE STRATEGY

I have rarely been as impressed as when I had the privilege of conducting the workshop accompanying this book to the phenomenal educators at the Hollenstein Career and Technology Center in Eagle Mountain-Saginaw ISD, Fort Worth, Texas. I walked into a beautiful edifice with an open area that looked like an amphitheater, perfect for plays or other presentations. My workshop commenced, and the morning flew by as we talked to one another and moved around the room to learn about the 20 engaging strategies. When the participants went to lunch, I was taken on a field trip, a guided tour of the facility. The building houses approximately 1,200 high school students who spend part of their day in their local schools, where they can take their content classes and participate in extracurricular activities, and a second part at the technology center. You see, by the time these students finish the Hollenstein Career and Technology Center, they will not only have a high school diploma but certification and training in many areas, including architectural design, business marketing and finance, health science, hospitality and tourism, pharmacy technician, law and public service and culinary arts, to name only a few. These students can walk directly into the world of work as EMTs, dental hygienists, welders, phlebotomists, cosmetologists, graphic artists, and many other professionals.

Think back to when you finished high school. No doubt you can recall the names of many students in your senior class who did not have the grades or the SAT scores to place in the top 25th or even the 50th percentile of graduating seniors. However, fast-forward to your 10-year class reunion. How many of these so-called nonachievers became highly successful in the actual world of work? Could it be that much of the knowledge and skill one acquires in school may have little relationship to the essential knowledge and skill required for success in real life? Could it be that on-the-job training may be infinitely more valuable for some occupations than memorizing and regurgitating isolated facts, which seem to earn the As in school? Students who may not succeed academically or have discipline problems at their neighborhood schools appear to succeed at Hollenstein and will graduate with a marketable skill that enables them to become employed immediately.

Work study, apprenticeships, practicums, and internships may be instructional strategies that afford students the best of both worlds: exposure in school to a wide variety of experiences that help students determine possible career choices and actual on-the-job work experiences that prepare students for success in the real world.

WHY: THEORETICAL FRAMEWORK

An apprenticeship is a pathway for a high school graduate to a specific long-term career that does not require a four-year degree and includes such occupations as skilled trades, information technology, healthcare, hospitality, and business and management (Indeed Editorial Team, 2022).

With an expansion of courses from culinary arts to landscaping, Career Technology Education (CTE) is a vibrant national approach to increasing high school graduation rates and preparing students for jobs that pay well (Rix, 2022).

Nearly six in ten (or 56%) of parents opt for apprenticeships when asked to choose between a full-tuition college scholarship and a three-year apprenticeship that leads to a lucrative job (Manno, 2023).

Well-designed Career Technology Education programs enable students to get ready for college or for a career by interconnecting the skills needed for both (Rix, 2022).

More than two-thirds (or 65%) of Gen Z high schoolers related that post-high school learning should be on the job through apprenticeships or internships (Manno, 2023).

To prepare students for their life after they have completed high school is the actual purpose of schooling (Sousa & Pilecki, 2013).

When students encounter experiential learning, their brains are led to higher levels of recall and retention (Sousa & Tomlinson, 2011).

One of the problems with high schools is their propensity to cover a great deal of content without providing students the opportunity to use that content in the context of authentic situations (Wiggins & McTighe, 2008).

When the learning is applicable to students' lives, students not only become more engaged, but they also feel more responsible for finishing assignments and they understand the relationship between their success in school and success in the real world (Algozzine et al., 2009).

> Educated adults often have difficulty finding a job or meeting job expectations because large gaps can exist between the performance needed to be successful in a business setting and those required for school success (Sternberg & Grigorenko, 2000).
>
> When students learn under the supervision of an expert in the field, they build technical skills and share tasks that relate those technical skills to their knowledge and interpretation (Wonacott, 1993).
>
> Learning should be organized around cognitive-apprenticeship principles that stress subject-specific content and the skills required to function within the content (Berryman & Bailey, 1992).

HOW: INSTRUCTIONAL ACTIVITIES

WHO: Middle/High

WHEN: Before a lesson

CONTENT AREA(S): Cross-curricular

- There are a number of different instruments that can assess a student's interest in and aptitude for a variety of professions. If the school does not already administer one to students, find one and allow students to take it so that they can begin to think about which professions they may like to pursue. I knew that I wanted to be a teacher at six years of age. I would line my dolls up in my bedroom and teach them for hours. Funny, I didn't have a single behavior problem!

WHO: Elementary/Middle/High

WHEN: Before or after a lesson

CONTENT AREA(S): Cross-curricular

- Familiarize students with the U.S. Department of Labor Secretary's Commission on Achieving Necessary Skills (SCANS, 1991), which delineates the five competencies and three foundational skills essential for high school graduates to possess if they were expected to be successful in the world of work in the year 2000. Even though this report was first issued over 30 years ago, in 1991, my daughter Jessica was asked to demonstrate six of them when she applied for and received a promotion to head chef of the banquet staff at the Ritz Carlton Hotel in Atlanta. The competencies and skills are as follows:
  - **Five Competencies:** Allocation of Resources, Interpersonal Skills, Information, Systems Thinking, and Technology
  - **Three Foundational Skills:** Basic Skills, Thinking Skills, and Personal Qualities

Jessica now works in Human Resources. She and my daughter Jennifer, an elementary principal, relate that they continue to look for these same competencies and foundational skills in the people they hire.

WHO: Elementary/Middle/High

WHEN: During a lesson

CONTENT AREA(S): Cross-curricular

- Initiate a career day in the school. Invite parents, scientists, historians, writers, mathematicians, dignitaries, local celebrities, radio station hosts, and other persons of interest to talk about their vocations and avocations. Have students research the careers in advance to be more knowledgeable and brainstorm pertinent questions to be asked during the visits. This career day can be done schoolwide or in an individual classroom.

WHO: Elementary/Middle/High

WHEN: After a lesson

CONTENT AREA(S): Cross-curricular

- As students complete various curricular objectives, invite professionals who use the given skills or knowledge in their daily jobs to speak to the class. For example, as math students complete a chapter on types of angles, have architects demonstrate to the class how angles play a part in building bridges or houses. After these presentations, students are less likely to ask, *Why do we have to learn this?* When Jessica was a chef at the Ritz Carlton, she came to her sister Jennifer's second-grade class and talked about the importance of math in following recipes. They even made chocolate-covered pretzels during the presentation.

WHO: Elementary/Middle/High

WHEN: After a lesson

CONTENT AREA(S): Cross-curricular

- Have students research professions of interest and create reports or projects to share their knowledge with the class. In this way, students glean information regarding an occupation of interest. They can create a timeline of what specific schooling, job training, or apprenticeships would be required to fulfill that position. Students need to realize that, without adequate training and preparation, they will not awaken one day and occupy the position of computer tech, teacher, doctor, lawyer, writer, or anything else.

WHO: High

WHEN: After a lesson

CONTENT AREA(S): Cross-curricular

- Partner with local businesses that can make it possible for students to engage in internships, apprenticeships, or work-study projects during the school year or the summer months to experience firsthand the knowledge and skills essential for the workplace. Allow them to spend time with professionals who use course content or skills in their daily occupations.

WHO: Elementary/Middle/High

WHEN: During a lesson

CONTENT AREA(S): Cross-curricular

- Engage students in a service-learning project where they are providing a service for their school or community while mastering curricular objectives. For example, math students could organize a fundraiser for a nonprofit organization, and all students could tutor or mentor younger students or participate in a community clean-up project. Service learning is one of the best vehicles for combining character, interdisciplinary instruction, and real-world skills and strategies.

WHO: Middle/High

WHEN: Before, during, or after a lesson

CONTENT AREA(S): Mathematics

- Have students adopt a local business and track its success or lack thereof over a specified time. Have students interview employees of the business in an effort to ascertain information about what product or service the business provides, what demands exist for the product, how the business supplies the product, and the current state of the business. Have students write about these experiences and, based on research, make recommendations as to how the business could make changes to increase its revenue (Tate, 2014a).

WHO: Elementary/Middle/High

WHEN: During a lesson

CONTENT AREA(S): Cross-curricular

- Take your students on a field trip to a job site related to your teaching content. For example, Warren Phillips, an exemplary science teacher and coauthor of the *Science Worksheets Don't Grow Dendrites* book, always took his middle school students to the Massachusetts Institute of Technology (MIT) annually, where they could visit various science laboratories and talk to scientists about their work. Following the trip, several of his students each year would decide that they wanted to be scientists or conduct laboratory work (Tate & Phillips, 2011).

WHO: Middle/High

WHEN: Before or after a lesson

CONTENT AREA(S): Mathematics

- Under the direction of a teacher, have students plan and operate a school bank where fellow students can deposit money. Use this real-life experience to enable students to master math concepts such as bank deposits and withdrawals, loans with interest rates, percentages, and so forth. Have students take turns serving as apprentices in the banking business.

WHO: High

WHEN: During a lesson

CONTENT AREA(S): Cross-curricular

- Research school-to-work programs as a part of the School-to-Work Opportunities Act of 1994. This learning experience at an employer's worksite includes all of the following elements:
  - a planned program of job training and work experience commensurate with a student's abilities;
  - a sequence of activities that increase in complexity and promote mastery of basic skills;
  - a learning experience that exposes the student to all aspects of an industry, promotes the development of transferable skills; and
  - a learning experience that provides for real or simulated tasks or assignments that cause students to develop higher-order thinking and problem-solving skills.

Action Plan for Incorporating WORK STUDY and APPRENTICESHIPS

WHAT ARE MY PLANS FOR INCORPORATING MORE *WORK STUDY* AND *APPRENTICESHIPS* INTO MY LESSONS TO ACCELERATE LEARNING?

RECOMMENDATIONS	ALREADY DOING	PLANNING TO DO
Administer an inventory to ascertain students' interests and aptitude for certain professions.		
Familiarize students with the competencies and skills on the SCANS report.		
Initiate a career day.		
Invite professionals to come and relate course content to their professions.		
Have students research a profession of interest, and share the findings with classmates.		
Partner with local businesses that can engage students in internships or work-study projects.		
Engage students in a service learning project.		
Have students adopt a local business and track its success.		
Take students on field trips to talk with various professionals while on the job.		
Have students plan and operate a school bank.		
Research School-to-Work programs.		
Goals and Notes:		

Source: istock.com/mussi87

Recent research is finding that students recall, understand, and apply more of what they write in longhand on paper than what they type digitally (Sousa, 2022).

STRATEGY 20

Writing and Journals

WHAT: DEFINING THE STRATEGY

With all the emphasis on technology, perhaps this chapter should be deleted, or the title, at the very least, changed to "Typing and Journals." Not so fast! Teachers ask this question of me a great deal, *What is more memorable to the brain—typing on a computer or writing in long hand?* Guess which one! If you said *writing*, you would be correct. Research (Mueller & Oppenheimer, 2014; Sousa, 2022) appears to indicate that the things that we write down tend to stick to the brain better than the things we type on a computer. Allow me to share a true story. When I worked for the DeKalb School System, my administrative assistant, Carol, had typed a memo regarding the time that a meeting I scheduled for reading specialists would be starting. When I could not remember the time I set, I asked Carol. *What time is the reading specialist meeting scheduled to begin?* Carol said something to me that made no sense at the time, but now it does. She responded, *I don't remember the time. I don't read your memos. I just type them.* How many students today are going through the motions of typing notes and important content without giving any conscious thought to what they are doing?

A word of caution about writing: Many middle and high school teachers have students taking copious notes while they are lecturing. What's wrong with this picture? Since the brain can only pay conscious attention to one thing at a time, students are either attempting to write the notes and missing part of the lecture or attempting to listen to the lecture and miss many of the notes. Don't expect them to do both simultaneously! According to Jensen and Nickelsen (2008), having students write notes or copy them from the board while the teacher continues talking can be a distraction. That would make multitasking a misnomer since if we are doing several things simultaneously, only one of those things is conscious. Everything else is done unconsciously!

WHY: THEORETICAL FRAMEWORK

The results of studies with large effect sizes show that it is powerful to teach students the strategies and processes involved in writing, have students working together in an organized fashion, and set specific and clear goals regarding the purpose of the writing (Hattie, 2023).

Journal writing, whether on paper or a digital device, is a very useful technique for the closure of a lesson or the transfer of information in the brain (Sousa, 2022).

There is a great deal of support for the substantial benefits of teaching reading through writing, teaching writing through reading, and teaching writing about other curricular areas, that is, mathematics, social studies, and science (Graham, 2020).

Recent research is finding that students recall, understand, and apply more of what they write in longhand on paper than what they type digitally (Sousa, 2022).

More thought processing and summarizing of content is required when one is writing versus the mechanical process of typing (Mueller & Oppenheimer, 2014).

Despite the push from technology to abandon cursive writing, the research supports cursive writing as an important device for improving motor skills, attention, reading, and academic achievement (Sousa, 2016).

Three separate studies indicated that high school students and college freshmen who took handwritten notes were better able to remember, integrate, and apply new learning when compared to those who used a laptop to take notes (Mueller & Oppenheimer, 2014).

Students stand a better chance of recognizing letters and characters, a skill necessary for reading, if they write the letters while they are being learned rather than typing them on the computer (Longcamp et al., 2008).

When the kinesthetic activity of writing is used to communicate math concepts, more neurons are engaged and students are made to organize their thoughts (Sousa, 2007).

In a large study by Graham and Perin (2007), if students are struggling writers, it is recommended that teachers provide direct instruction in strategies for planning, revising, and editing.

Students understand that notes are a work in progress and a valuable tool for memory when they have an opportunity to revise and review those notes (Dean et al., 2012).

When students were given written model solutions (examples that had been worked out) to refer to when solving math practice problems, they made fewer errors than a comparable group who solved a greater number of practice problems without the written model solutions (Posamentier & Jaye, 2006).

> "Write to argue and persuade readers and write to convey information" are tied as the two most important types of writing required of incoming college students (ACT Inc., 2009).
>
> Rubrics created and scored by students enable them to focus their writing and think more critically about it (Algozzine et al., 2009).
>
> Writing enables the brain to reverse the reading process. Rather than responding initially to external visual stimuli, during the writing process the brain starts with internal thoughts, chooses appropriate vocabulary to express those thoughts, and then produces the symbols for the words in writing (Wolfe & Nevills, 2004).

HOW: INSTRUCTIONAL ACTIVITIES

WHO: Elementary/Middle

WHEN: During a lesson

CONTENT AREA(S): Cross-curricular

- Engage students in a prewriting activity called *four square writing* (see Figure 20.1) according to the following guidelines:
  - Take a piece of 8- by 11-inch white paper and fold it both vertically and horizontally so that when you open it, the paper forms four squares.
  - Draw a rectangle in the middle of the paper and label it with a small *Box 1*. Box 1 would contain a topic sentence for a paragraph to be written.
  - Label the top left square as *Box 2*, the top right square as *Box 3*, the bottom left square as *Box 4*, and the bottom right square as *Box 5*.
  - Boxes 2–4 would each contain one detail or reason in support of the topic sentence in Box 1. Additional sentences could be written in Boxes 2–4 in support of the details already recorded in each box.
  - Box 5 would contain either a conclusion, summary, or feeling statement in support of the topic sentence.
  - From this prewriting activity, students can then form paragraphs. Students in kindergarten who are not yet writing can draw pictures in each box or dictate their sentences to the teacher who can then record them (Tate, 2014a, pp. 154–155).

FIGURE 20.1 • Four Square Writing

Four Square Writing

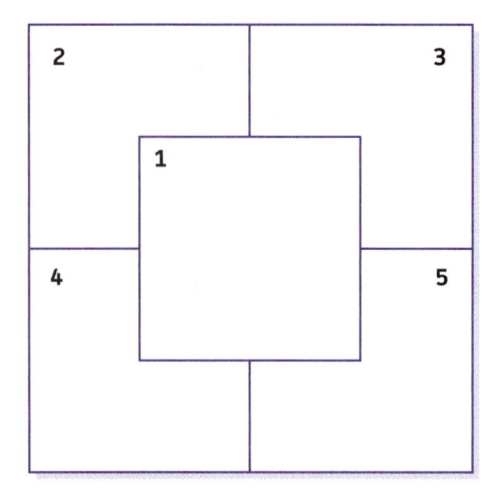

```
┌──────────────┬──────────────┐
│ 2            │ 3            │
│     ┌────────┼────────┐     │
│     │   1    │        │     │
│     │        │        │     │
├─────┤        │        ├─────┤
│ 4   │        │        │  5  │
│     └────────┼────────┘     │
│              │              │
└──────────────┴──────────────┘
```

WHO:	Elementary/Middle/High
WHEN:	During a lesson
CONTENT AREA(S):	Cross-curricular

- As you present a lecturette (a minilecture of five to seven minutes), have students write key concepts and phrases that will help them remember your content. Be sure to give them time to write so that their brains will not have to engage in two behaviors simultaneously—listening to your continued talk and trying to remember what to write. Provide time later for students to review and revise the notes.

WHO:	Elementary/Middle/High
WHEN:	During a lesson
CONTENT AREA(S):	Cross-curricular

- Give students many opportunities to write for a variety of real-world, cross-curricular purposes. Reasons for writing should proceed naturally during instruction and include the following: to persuade, to inform, to express, and to entertain (PIE). For example, have students write an essay about one event that changed the course of their lives. Watch the emotional reaction that this activity can engender! Then, use their essays to teach them about the writing process in language arts.

WHO: Elementary/Middle/High

WHEN: During a lesson

CONTENT AREA(S): Cross-curricular

- Give students a variety of media that provide them with opportunities to express their ideas in writing. These could include, but not be limited to, posters, brochures, scripts for plays, book jackets, commercials, and graphic organizers. Consult Strategy 5 (Graphic Organizers, Semantic Maps, and Word Webs) for examples of various mind maps.

WHO: Elementary/Middle/High

WHEN: During a lesson

CONTENT AREA(S): Language Arts

- Expand students' reading and writing vocabularies by identifying "tired words" that are overused in students' writing, such as said, like, good, and pretty. Have students brainstorm a list of synonyms that give them alternative vocabulary words to make their writing more interesting and appealing. For example, for the word "said," the brainstormed list could include "replied," "exclaimed," "declared," "responded," and "stated." Compile a class list of alternative words, and post it on the wall for students to use during future writing assignments. If students cannot think of alternative words, appoint a resident thesaurian, a student who possesses the thesaurus and can provide more rigorous vocabulary words. Forbid students from using the tired words, and have them incorporate the new words appropriately into their writing.

WHO: Middle/High

WHEN: During a lesson

CONTENT AREA(S): Mathematics

- Have students keep math journals in which they could write the steps when solving computational or word problems. Not only will the written steps assist the student in remembering the sequence of the solution, but it will also provide insight to the teacher into the thinking of the student during problem solving.

WHO: Elementary/Middle/High

WHEN: During a lesson

CONTENT AREA(S): Cross-curricular

- Incorporate *Quick Writes* throughout a lesson. Stop periodically during the lesson, and have students write a concept just taught. Writing, even for a minute, will help to reinforce the content. For example, stop your lesson and have students do the following: *Write the steps in the scientific process. Write the three causes of the Civil War.* Quick Writes can be used as daily exit slips. Immediately prior to the end of class, have students do a *Quick Write* regarding something you want them to remember from the day's content. The exit slip is given to you as they leave the classroom. Assess the exit slips to ascertain the amount of content retained.

WHO: Elementary/Middle/High

WHEN: During a lesson

CONTENT AREA(S): Cross-curricular

- Have students carry a piece of writing through the following five stages of the writing process for publication in a class book.
    - **Prewriting**—Have students brainstorm a list of ideas regarding an original composition or related to an assigned topic.
    - **Writing**—Have students write a rough draft of the composition according to teacher guidelines.
    - **Editing**—Have students assess one another's writing according to a rubric developed by the class.
    - **Revising**—Have students revise their composition in light of peer feedback from the rubric.
    - **Final Draft**—Have students produce a written or typed final draft that is ready for publication in the class book.

WHO: Elementary/Middle/High

WHEN: During a lesson

CONTENT AREA(S): Cross-curricular

- In an effort to improve the students' quality of cross-curricular writing, have them brainstorm an *alphabet book* that would include vocabulary chunked according to the letters of the alphabet yet pertinent to a unit of study. For example, during a unit of geometry, a *geometry alphabet book* could look like the following: *acute, base, circumference, diameter, equilateral, figure,* and so forth. Post these words as a visual or have students include them in their notebooks for ready reference.

WHO: Elementary/Middle/High

WHEN: After a lesson

CONTENT AREA(S): Cross-curricular

- Following a unit of study in any content area, have students record their thoughts regarding the unit in their personal journals. The following open-ended question starters may serve to spark the thinking of students:
  - State at least three major concepts you learned in this unit.
  - What was your favorite activity in which the class participated?
  - What was your least favorite activity in which the class participated?
  - How can you apply what you have learned to your personal life or to a future career choice?
  - If this unit were taught again, what things would you change?

WHO: Elementary/Middle/High

WHEN: Before or after a lesson

CONTENT AREA(S): Cross-curricular

- Provide time daily for students to write in a personal journal regarding topics of choice, including descriptions of incidents that have happened at home, personal reflections on class assignments, or feeling or emotions expressed. Journals are not graded, and students can indicate whether they want their entries read by the teacher by leaving the page unfolded if it is to be read or folding the page lengthwise if it is not to be read.

Action Plan for Incorporating WRITING and JOURNALS

WHAT ARE MY PLANS FOR INCORPORATING MORE *WRITING* AND *JOURNALS* INTO MY LESSONS TO ACCELERATE LEARNING?

RECOMMENDATIONS	ALREADY DOING	PLANNING TO DO
Engage students in four-square writing.		
Have students write key concepts and phrases as you lecture.		
Give students opportunities to write for a variety of real-world cross-curricular purposes.		
Give students a variety of media that provide them with opportunities to express their ideas in writing.		
Expand students' reading and writing vocabularies by identifying "tired (overused) words."		
Have students keep math journals for writing the steps when solving computational or word problems.		
Incorporate *Quick Writes* throughout a lesson.		
Have students carry a piece of writing through the five stages of the writing process.		
To increase vocabulary, have students brainstorm an alphabet book.		
Have students record their thoughts regarding a unit previously taught in their personal journals.		
Provide opportunities for students to write in their personal journals.		
Goals and Notes:		

Resource A: Brain-Compatible Lesson Plans

In this fourth edition of the original bestseller, a brain-compatible lesson plan continues to serve as a resource since teachers have found it very helpful as they work to include the 20 instructional strategies into their lesson design. In fact, an adaptation of this plan is currently being used nationwide as school systems revise curriculum and ensure that teachers are planning lessons that not only accelerate student achievement and help students meet content standards but also go a long way toward enabling students to retain content long after the examinations are over. It answers the following question: *How can I incorporate the 20 brain-compatible strategies into my daily lesson plans so that students will understand and remember the content?* The sample lesson plan is displayed at the end of Resource A.

It does not matter whether you use this particular lesson plan template as you put your lessons together. In fact, a lengthy written response to each question would be very time-consuming. You may even have your own unique lesson plan design, and it is not necessary to change from the form that you are currently using. What does matter is whether you can honestly ask and answer the five questions on the plan that are delineated in the paragraphs that follow.

SECTION 1: LESSON OBJECTIVE: WHAT DO YOU WANT YOUR STUDENTS TO KNOW AND BE ABLE TO DO?

The first question of Section 1 has changed since the original lesson plan was developed. As a teacher of the *7 Habits of Highly Effective People* (Covey, 2020), it makes sense that all lessons should *Begin With the End in Mind* (Habit 2). Obviously, when teachers are planning lessons, the first question they should ask themselves should be, *What do I want students to know and/or be able to do by the time the lesson is completed?*

As I travel the United States, many teachers tell me that they know that they should incorporate the brain-compatible strategies during instruction, but they simply do not have the time. Teachers express their frustration at being asked to teach more and more content every year in the same amount of time with nothing being eliminated.

For example, an American History teacher told me that his curriculum expects him to cover the Vietnam War in one day. How in the world can you teach such an important war in one class period? I empathized with his plight, but I wanted to tell him what a famous educator, Madeline Hunter, said years ago. She related that if all teachers are doing is covering content, then they should get a shovel and cover it with dirt since it is dead to memory as far as the brain is concerned. The question should be, *What do you want your students to know regarding the Vietnam War?* That becomes what you teach.

During my international travels and teaching in other countries, many of whom outscore us on tests of achievement, *less appears to be more*. Their textbooks are about one-third the size of ours, and content is chunked together into relevant concepts to be taught. Why can't we in the United States look at our content that way?

I also pray that the days are gone when teachers are solely dependent on their textbooks. They have students open the textbook to page one at the beginning of the school year and conclude instruction with the last page of the book prior to summer vacation. The days should be over when teaching content consists solely of round-robin oral reading the chapter as the class follows along in their textbooks and then having the class answer the questions at the end of the chapter. Content may be covered but retention is compromised. In order to answer the question regarding the Vietnam War, the textbook may not even be necessary!

A better way of teaching calls for a paradigm shift on the part of many professionals who look at their subject matter as content to be covered or isolated skills to be mastered. Instead, the question should be, *What should my students be responsible for knowing or doing by the end of the lesson?*

In the second scenario in this book, students are being asked to analyze the meaning, importance, and relevance of the Bill of Rights.

SECTION 2: ASSESSMENT: HOW WILL YOU KNOW STUDENTS HAVE MASTERED ESSENTIAL LEARNING?

When planning a lesson, if you wait until the completion of the plan to decide how you will assess your students, you have actually waited too long. I can still visualize myself as a student in school. I remember being stressed on test days because assessment sometimes meant trying to guess what my teachers were going to put on their tests. If I guessed correctly, I would manage to make an A. However, if I guessed incorrectly, even if I studied feverishly, my grade was not so good. The current research tells us to tell students what you expect. Your expectations should not be kept a secret.

Tell students what they should know and be able to do at the culmination of a lesson or unit of study. In this way, your assessment may be a challenge to the brains of students but never a high stressor or threat. Consider this analogy: How can a pilot file a flight plan without knowing the destination? Tell students their destination, and they will stand a better chance of arriving there.

In the sample lesson, the assessment is both traditional and authentic. Students' graphic organizers at each station will be assessed as will their drawings or skits to determine if they truly understand the relevance of the Bill of Rights.

SECTION 3: WAYS TO GAIN/MAINTAIN ATTENTION: HOW WILL YOU GAIN AND MAINTAIN STUDENTS' ATTENTION?

(Consider need, novelty, meaning, or emotion.)

There are so much stimuli in the environment that brains are very particular regarding what they choose to pay attention to. When you are teaching, you are vying for that attention. But your lesson may be competing with a text message from their smartphone, a conversation with a peer, a noise in the hall, a colorful leaf on a tree outside the window, or reflections of an argument the student had with his girlfriend before he came to class. Students can even be quietly staring you in the face and not paying a bit of attention to what you are teaching.

There is also a structure in the brain called the hippocampus that pretty much determines whether a lesson will be remembered. If the hippocampi of your students determine that your lesson is not worth remembering, then when your students fall asleep at night, the delete button of the brain is pushed and your lesson ends up in the trash. Let me tell you one way you can tell that your lesson was deleted. Your students return the next day and, when you review, it is like they were not present when the information was taught. Either the lesson never entered the brain or it was deleted while students slept! By the way, when students do not get enough quality sleep since that is the time that their brains are less active, those brains do not have time to process what they learned during the day.

Good news! There are four major ways to gain and maintain your students' attention. Do you have to grab students' attention using all four ways in every lesson you teach? Absolutely not! Do you have to grab students' attention using at least one way? Absolutely so! The ways are *need, novelty, meaning,* or *emotion*.

NEED

The first way to grab the attention of your students is through need. When students do not see the need for learning what you are teaching, they just may not pay attention. If students see the purpose in what you are teaching, they will see the need to learn it.

Here is a true story. People today may not see the purpose in memorizing important phone numbers. If you are old enough, you may remember January 15, 2009, when U.S. Airways flight 1549 made an emergency landing on the Hudson River after birds blew an engine. There was a passenger on that plane whose phone was underwater when the plane landed. She could have easily asked another passenger to borrow their cell phone to call her daughter and tell her she was safe and not to worry. She did not know her daughter's number. It was on her phone, and her phone was inoperable. Even in this age of technology, there are some things that we need to keep hidden in our brains for immediate retrieval. Important phone numbers are one of those things.

When students see the purpose of your lesson, they will see the need to learn the content. Simply telling them they will need the information for a subsequent test may not be enough motivation for many students. Some couldn't care less!

In the second scenario in our Introduction, the teacher impresses upon students the need to know which of their rights and the rights of their teachers are protected in the constitution.

NOVELTY

Sometimes need is simply not sufficient for engaging students in the lesson. You may know that your students need the information, but your students don't share your sense of urgency. The good news is that you have three more ways to gain their attention. A second way is by teaching your content in a novel or interesting way. The brain tends to pay attention to things in the environment that are new or different. As I stated earlier, I pay no attention to the initial flight instructions when I am on an airplane. I know I should, but I have heard it so many times that I could actually recite it myself. In my workshops, I actually show people where the exits are, like they do in the visual. There are a few exceptions. Some Southwest Airlines flight attendants give the flight instructions using the strategy of music or humor. On one flight, they were singing the flight instructions to the tune of the theme of the television show, *The Beverly Hillbillies*. Whatever I am doing at the time when this happens, I stop and pay attention. Why? Because the instructions are presented in a new and different way. On another flight, one teacher who flew Southwest told me they had a very hard landing on the tarmac. The flight attendant came on the intercom and apologized for the rough landing. She stated, *It was not the pilot's fault. It was not the weather's fault. It was the asphalt.* This flight attendant made the flight memorable with the strategy of humor.

While you certainly want consistency in your class rituals and procedures, you will want to vary your lesson delivery. When you change your location in the room, your voice inflection, or the strategies you use to deliver your lesson, you are being novel and stand a better chance of gaining and maintaining your students' attention. Providing them with the same sets of worksheets or a similar lecture just won't hold the attention of most students.

The 20 strategies provide you with many ways to be novel. Think of all the novel stories you and your students can tell, the variety of songs you can play, the projects in which you can engage your students, and all the different movements you can use to put information into procedural memory. Although there are only 20 strategies, the use of those strategies for novel lessons is endless!

The lesson in our scenario incorporates the brain-compatible strategies of discussion, movement, graphic organizers, writing, drawing and artwork, and roleplay. Incorporating a variety of strategies helps to make the lesson novel.

MEANING

Because the brain's purpose is survival in the real world, when you are connecting your content to real life, you are making it meaningful. When you are not, students will raise their hands and ask this question: *Why do we have to learn this?* As I teach, I take every opportunity to use real-life examples to illustrate my points. When I tell students the true story about the fact that my father had the trait of sickle-cell anemia and how that trait has been passed on to my sister and her daughter, that story goes a long way toward giving my science lesson on dominant and recessive genes more meaning. When teachers have students write about one decision that they made that changed the course of their lives, the writing lesson becomes unforgettable! Even mathematics isn't a scary and abstract mystery when everyday life applications are used to teach it (Posamentier & Jaye, 2006).

By beginning the lesson with a discussion of student and teacher rights, the Bill of Rights becomes more meaningful.

EMOTION

Of all the ways to gain and maintain students' attention, emotion may be the most powerful! Emotion places experiences in reflexive memory, one of the strongest memory systems in the brain and helps to ensure retention. In fact, you will not soon forget anything that happened to you in your personal life or the world at large that was emotional. I bet you can even remember where you were when it happened. For example, if you were old enough, where were you on January 28, 1986, when you were informed that the *Challenger* had exploded? We lost seven astronauts that day, including a teacher by the name of Christa McAuliffe.

You do not, however, want to use a negative definition of emotion when talking about teaching and learning. If you were ever in the classroom of a teacher you did not like, you will never forget being in that teacher's room. Those memories stay with you. However, chances are you will not remember the content that the teacher taught. While you were sitting there, your brain was in survival mode, and when the brain is under threat only information crucial to survival is recalled.

Teachers who are emotional about their content are passionate and enthusiastic! No doubt, you remember a math teacher who influenced you to love math or a science teacher, like Warren Phillips, whose hands-on lessons were unforgettable! How can we expect students to become excited about our content if we are not excited about our content? This emotion enables students to place the content into reflexive memory and still recall it long after tests are completed.

As students created their original drawings and designed and presented their skits regarding the Bill of Rights, positive emotions emerged. Students laughed and cheered one another's creative efforts!

Need, novelty, meaning, or *emotion* are four ways to gain the brain's attention. You do not need to have all four working for you in one lesson. Even one, used appropriately, will work as you compete with the multitude of stimuli surrounding your students during your lesson presentation.

SECTION 4: CONTENT CHUNKS: HOW WILL YOU DIVIDE AND TEACH THE CONTENT TO ENGAGE STUDENTS' BRAINS?

Many years ago, Madeline Hunter asked another question: *How do you eat an elephant?* The answer, of course, was *one bite at a time.* The adult brain can only hold approximately seven bits of information (plus or minus two) simultaneously, which is why so much in the real world comes in a series of seven. There are seven days in a week, numbers in a phone number minus the area code, colors in the rainbow, notes on the scale, wonders of the ancient world, continents, *Habits of Highly Effective People,* and dwarfs, to name a few. The way to get the brain to remember more than seven isolated bits would be to connect or chunk those bits together. This is why the Social Security number, which is more than seven digits, is in chunks. It is nine digits and, therefore, needs to be connected together into three chunks. A telephone number with an area code is 10 digits. However, it is also divided into three chunks to make it easier for you to remember. Even your lengthy credit card numbers are chunked. You see, the brain remembers a chunk as if it were one piece of information, rather than separate numbers.

Your job is to determine how many chunks or lesson segments are needed for you to get across the objective to your students. The chunking for a class of gifted students may be different from a group of special education students. Just determine how much your students' brains can hold at one time.

I have added another question to Madeline Hunter's original question: *How do you digest an elephant?* The answer, of course, is that you have to *chew it up.* Activity enables the brain to *chew up* information. Chew is a metaphor for the fact that the activity embedded in each chunk enables the brain to process or *digest* what it is learning. A classroom where there is little opportunity for students to process what they are learning is a classroom where students are not performing at optimal levels or may not be comprehending or retaining much at all.

In the sample lesson as the objective is addressed, only one chunk is necessary. However, a variety of activities are incorporated which may span more than one class period.

SECTION 5: BRAIN-COMPATIBLE STRATEGIES: WHICH WILL YOU USE TO DELIVER CONTENT?

By the time a teacher completes a lesson plan, the activities included in the lesson should reflect the 20 brain-compatible strategies outlined in this book. In fact, at the bottom of the sample lesson plan template, all 20 strategies are listed so that teachers have a ready reference for their use.

In every lesson I teach, regardless of which grade level or content area, I attempt to incorporate at least four of the strategies, one from each of the four modalities—visual, auditory, kinesthetic, and tactile—knowing that I probably have all four modalities represented in that class. (Refer to Table 0.1 in the Introduction for a correlation of the strategies to the learning modalities.) In this way, regardless of student preferences, there is an activity in the lesson for every student, and instruction can be differentiated based on students' learning needs. It also appears that if the same information is taught using multiple strategies, the student has several places in the brain from which to choose when it is time to recall that information.

In our sample lesson, strategies that were used to teach the objective included the following: (1) whole group and small group discussion, drawing and artwork, graphic organizers, humor, movement, roleplay, and writing.

Following the blank lesson plan template, you will find four cross-curricular sample lessons designed by content specialists. These and 196 additional lessons appear in my books, *100 Brain-Friendly Lessons for Unforgettable Teaching and Learning (K-8)* and *(9-12)*. If you come to the end of a planned lesson and cannot check off any of the instructional strategies contained in the lesson plan, it is not a brain-compatible lesson and will probably not accelerate learning or be remembered by your students! No one is asking you to teach **harder**. Teaching is difficult business! I have first-hand knowledge since my daughter Jennifer, son-in-law Lex, sister Ann, and niece Erica all have education careers. I am suggesting that you teach **smarter**! In summary, teaching smarter means

- identifying what you want students to know and be able to do and telling them what that is at the beginning of the lesson;
- determining how you will know when students have mastered that essential learning;
- deciding how you will gain and maintain students' attention throughout the lesson;
- figuring out how many different lesson segments (chunks) are necessary to teach the objective; and
- integrating the appropriate instructional strategies into each chunk.

BRAIN-COMPATIBLE LESSON PLAN

Lesson Objective(s): *What do you want students to know and be able to do?*

Assessment (Traditional/Authentic): *How will you know students have mastered essential learning?*

Ways to Gain/Maintain Attention (Primacy): *How will you gain and maintain students' attention? Consider need, novelty, meaning, or emotion.*

Content Chunks: *How will you divide and teach the content to engage students' brains?*

LESSON SEGMENT 1:
- **Activities:**

LESSON SEGMENT 2:
- **Activities:**

LESSON SEGMENT 3:
- **Activities:**

Brain-Compatible Strategies: *Which will you use to deliver content?*

_____	Brainstorming/Discussion	_____	Music/Rhythm/Rhyme/Rap Project/Problem-Based Learning
_____	Drawing/Artwork	_____	Reciprocal Teaching/Cooperative Learning
_____	Field Trips	_____	Roleplays/Drama/Pantomimes/Charades
_____	Games	_____	Storytelling
_____	Graphic Organizers/Semantic Maps/Word Webs	_____	Technology
_____	Humor	_____	Visualization/Guided Imagery
_____	Manipulatives/Experiments/Labs/Models	_____	Visuals
_____	Metaphors/Analogies/Similes	_____	Work Study/Apprenticeships
_____	Mnemonic Devices	_____	Writing/Journals
_____	Movement		

Source: Reprinted from Tate, 2020

MATHEMATICS GRADES K–2 LESSON 4

CLASSIFYING SHAPES

Lesson Objective(s): *What do you want students to know and be able to do? Classify shapes based on attributes.*

Assessment (Traditional/Authentic): *How will you know students have mastered essential learning?*

Students will complete the graphic organizer *Straight Sides Shapes*.

Ways to Gain/Maintain Attention (Primacy): *How will you gain and maintain students' attention? Consider need, novelty, meaning, or emotion.*

Have students watch http://www.youtu.be/UDQDyx59QY4

Content Chunks: *How will you divide and teach the content to engage students' brains?*

LESSON SEGMENT 1: CLASSIFY SHAPES BY ATTRIBUTES

- **Activity 1: Straw Shapes**

Have students explore with straw pieces. Straw pieces consist of 4 straws—(2) full-length straws, (3) ½ length straws, and (2) ¼ length straws.

While exploration is happening and shapes are being made, avoid using shape names but focus on the number of straight sides and the number of corners. Shapes that are closed do not have openings. There is an inside and an outside. Both ends of every straw touch another straw. Have students continue to make closed shapes with their partners or groups.

- **Activity 2: Creating Shapes With Straws**

Have students make shapes with three straight sides and three corners. A ruler, pencil, and paper are needed.

Create a shape with straws and have students make the exact one. To record the shape, draw a dot at each corner. Demonstrate. Now move the straws away and connect the dots with a straight line using a ruler. Make another one. Encourage students to walk to see other students' work while music is playing softly. When the music stops, it is time to return to their seat. Repeat the activity with four straight sides and four corners.

- **Activity 3: Straight Sides Shapes**

Have students complete the graphic organizer *Straight Sides Shapes* in the plan.

Brain-Compatible Strategies: *Which will you use to deliver content?*

__X__	Brainstorming/Discussion	__X__	Music/Rhythm/Rhyme/Rap
__X__	Drawing/Artwork	_____	Project/Problem-Based Learning
_____	Field Trips	__X__	Reciprocal Teaching/Cooperative Learning
_____	Games	_____	Roleplays/Drama/Pantomimes/Charades
__X__	Graphic Organizers/Semantic Maps/Word Webs	_____	Storytelling
_____	Humor	__X__	Technology
__X__	Manipulatives/Experiments/Labs/Models	_____	Visualization/Guided Imagery
_____	Metaphors/Analogies/Similes	__X__	Visuals
_____	Mnemonic Devices	_____	Work Study/Apprenticeships
__X__	Movement	_____	Writing/Journals

Source: Reprinted from Tate, 2020

LANGUAGE ARTS GRADES 3–5 LESSON 6

CHARACTER TRAITS

Lesson Objective(s): *What do you want students to know and be able to do?*

Provide an in-depth description of a character while drawing on specific details in a text.

Assessment (Traditional/Authentic): *How will you know students have mastered essential learning?*

Students will create a character trait suitcase based on the events from a literary text.

Ways to Gain/Maintain Attention (Primacy): *How will you gain and maintain students' attention? Consider need, novelty, meaning, or emotion.*

Create a life-size silhouette of a body that represents the class. Using colored pencils, have students take turns writing a character trait word inside the body that best describes them. Instruct students to write their name next to their word. Define the word "character" and discuss what supporting evidence should look like.

Content Chunks: *How will you divide and teach the content to engage students' brains?*

LESSON SEGMENT 1: RECOGNIZE TRAITS OF A CHARACTER IN LITERATURE

- **Activity 1: Character Traits in Literature**

Read the story *Alexander and the Terrible, Horrible, No Good, Very Bad Day* to the class. The first time, have the students listen for enjoyment. The second time, read the first seven pages and ask students to listen for the character trait words to describe Alexander. On chart paper, write the character trait word on the left side. Then, ask students to think of two examples or evidence for each trait from the text. Write the examples on the right. The students should distinguish at least two traits from the text.

- **Activity 2: Character Portrait**

Distribute copies of the story *Alexander and the Terrible, Horrible, No Good, Very Bad Day* to pairs of students to create a *Character Portrait*. In the middle of the construction paper, draw a figure to represent Alexander. Label three parts of the portrait with an additional character trait word that describes him. Under each word, write two examples or evidence to support each trait.

- **Activity 3: Gallery Walk**

Once pairs have completed the character sketch, display their masterpieces on the walls around the room. Play upbeat music. Each time you play the music, have pairs rotate to each picture to see what their classmates created. Discuss differences in traits and the types of evidence used from the text.

- **Activity 4: Character Traits in Literary Texts**

Assign pairs of students a text that emphasizes a character and several traits. You may select a text from the *Literary Texts That Teach Story Elements* list. Students will take turns reading. Next, have students use the graphic organizer to distinguish at least four character traits from the story along with supporting evidence from the text.

- **Activity 5: Character Suitcase**

Use the graphic organizer to create a *Character Suitcase*. Distribute file folders, brown construction paper, and colored pencils to pairs of students. Have each pair draw a picture of a book character on the outside of the file folder. Using the colored pencils, have them write four words around the character. Inside, have them write each character trait word on the left side and the supporting evidence on the right. Finally, have students use the brown construction paper to create a handle to complete their suitcases.

As an extension, based on the character's personality, students can draw and cut out at least two items that the character would possibly take with them on a vacation. Place the items in their suitcase. Set time aside for students to share their suitcases and why they selected the items placed in the suitcases.

Brain-Compatible Strategies: *Which will you use to deliver content?*

X	Brainstorming/Discussion	X	Music/Rhythm/Rhyme/Rap
X	Drawing/Artwork	___	Project/Problem-Based Learning
___	Field Trips	X	Reciprocal Teaching/Cooperative Learning
___	Games	___	Roleplays/Drama/Pantomimes/Charades
X	Graphic Organizers/Semantic Maps/Word Webs	X	Storytelling
___	Humor	___	Technology
X	Manipulatives/Experiment/Labs/Models	___	Visualization/Guided Imagery
___	Metaphors/Analogies/Similes	X	Visuals
X	Mnemonic Devices	___	Work Study/Apprenticeships
___	Movement	X	Writing/Journals

Source: Reprinted from Tate, 2020

SOCIAL STUDIES GRADES 6–8 LESSON 1

MILITARY LEADERS

Lesson Objective(s): *What do you want students to know and be able to do?*

Describe the roles of Abraham Lincoln, Robert E. Lee, Ulysses S. Grant, Jefferson Davis, and Thomas "Stonewall" Jackson in the Civil War.

Assessment (Traditional/Authentic): *How will you know students have mastered essential learning?*

Students will select two of the historical figures and complete a compare and contrast graphic organizer. (See template, following this lesson.)

Ways to Gain/Maintain Attention (Primacy): *How will you gain and maintain students' attention? Consider need, novelty, meaning, or emotion.*

Display a picture of several military leaders, and ask students what these men have in common. Numerous images and photographs of Abraham Lincoln, Robert E. Lee, Ulysses S. Grant, Jefferson Davis, and Thomas "Stonewall" Jackson can be found online at the Library of Congress: https://www.loc.gov

Content Chunks: *How will you divide and teach the content to engage students' brains?*

LESSON SEGMENT 1: UNDERSTAND BIOGRAPHICAL INFORMATION

- **Activity 1: Strips of Information**

Retype a selection from a biography about the historical figure and cut it into strips. (Hint: Type *he* instead of the historical figure's name.) Distribute one strip to each student. Have students circulate and read their strips to each other. Then have students predict what they will learn about the historical figure based on the sentence strips.

- **Activity 2: Character Maps**

Have students create character maps regarding historical figures. (See template, following this lesson.) Possible information to include in the maps would be actions, feelings, appearance, words, symbols, and significance.

- **Activity 3: Grading Your Figure**

Have students evaluate the historical figure's significance by assigning them a letter grade. Tell students to include a teacher comment, in writing, to justify the grade they assign.

Brain-Compatible Strategies: *Which will you use to deliver content?*

__X__	Brainstorming/Discussion	_____	Music/Rhythm/Rhyme/Rap
_____	Drawing/Artwork	_____	Project/Problem-Based Learning
_____	Field Trips	__X__	Reciprocal Teaching/Cooperative Learning
_____	Games	_____	Roleplays/Drama/Pantomimes/Charades
__X__	Graphic Organizers/Semantic Maps/Word Webs	__X__	Storytelling
_____	Humor	_____	Technology
__X__	Manipulatives/Experiments/Labs/Models	__X__	Visualization/Guided Imagery
_____	Metaphors/Analogies/Similes	_____	Visuals
_____	Mnemonic Devices	__X__	Work Study/Apprenticeships
__X__	Movement	_____	Writing/Journals

Source: Reprinted from Tate, 2020

EARTH SCIENCE GRADES 9–12 LESSON 2

EARTH CLIMATE

Lesson Objective(s): *What do you want students to know and be able to do?*

Use a model to describe how variations in the flow of energy into and out of Earth's systems result in changes in climate.

Assessment (Traditional/Authentic): *How will you know students have mastered essential learning?*

Students will complete a simulation of the greenhouse effect. Students will complete a student assessment sheet during the simulation. Students will imitate the movements of the Earth. Students will be able to explain days, seasons, and precession.

Ways to Gain/Maintain Attention (Primacy): *How will you gain and maintain students' attention? Consider need, novelty, meaning, or emotion.*

Students will find the meaning of the importance of cycles in determining the earth's weather. The novelty of role-playing Earth's motions will help retain these concepts.

Content Chunks: *How will you divide and teach the content to engage students' brains?*

LESSON SEGMENT 1: DESCRIBE HOW CHANGES IN CLIMATE OCCUR

- **Activity 1: *Discussion of Earth's Systems***

Discuss cyclical natural changes in the Earth's systems over time (i.e., orbit around the sun, tilt of Earth's axis, Earth's wobble [precession] and large events [volcanic eruptions, comets, etc.]). Tell students that weather and climate are shaped by complex interactions involving sunlight, the ocean, the atmosphere, clouds, ice, land, and life-forms.

- **Activity 2: *Earth as an Apple* Metaphor**

Consider the earth as an apple:

Tilt the apple $23\frac{1}{2}$ degrees. Now have each student stand and tilt themselves $23\frac{1}{2}$ degrees.

Demonstrate a day (one rotation). Have each student stand and complete a rotation.

Demonstrate a year (one revolution). Have one student role-play the sun and a partner revolves himself around the sun. Wobble to show precession.

Slice the apple into quarters—$\frac{3}{4}$ represents the Earth's waters.

Identify the five oceans, Atlantic, Pacific, Arctic, Indian, and Southern, while eating three pieces.

Have students recite and repeat each of the world's oceans.

The remaining quarter $\left(\frac{1}{4}\right)$ is all of the continents. Identify the continents with a story: **North America** married **South America**—they went to **Europe** and got married. They had four kids—all beginning with the letter A—**Asia, Africa, Antarctica,** and **Australia**. Have students quiz each other on the names of the continents.

Now cut the quarter into $\frac{1}{2}$. One of these two pieces of land is inhospitable. What is $\frac{1}{2}$ of $\frac{1}{4}$? $\left(\frac{1}{8}\right)$ Throw the inhospitable piece away or eat it.

Cut the remaining $\frac{1}{8}$ into two pieces. What is $\frac{1}{2}$ of $\frac{1}{8}$? $\left(\frac{1}{16}\right)$ One of these pieces is livable but not good soil (too rocky, too wet/swampy, etc.) Throw it away or eat it.

Cut the remaining $\frac{1}{16}$ into $\frac{1}{2}$. What is $\frac{1}{2}$ of $\frac{1}{16}$? $\left(\frac{1}{32}\right)$ One of these pieces is not useful for food (parking lots, roads, parks, remote areas). Throw it away or eat it.

The remaining piece is $\frac{1}{32}$ of the Earth. Carefully peel off the underlying layer so that only the skin is remaining. We cannot live on the inside layer—throw it away or eat it.

The thin, flimsy piece left is the good fertile soil that is less than 5 feet thick. It supports all of the life on Earth—about 7 billion people. It is also the most polluted piece!

Wiggle the piece to show how fragile it is! Tell students that we must protect this piece and not pollute it!

- **Activity 3: *"Solution to Pollution" Song***

Sing the "Solution to Pollution" song, identify vocabulary, and discuss. A YouTube video is available at https://youtube/oaVY3Od9J-w.

- **Activity 4: *Greenhouse Effect* Metaphor**

Visit the website https://www.explorelearning.com* and select the lab (Gizmo) called Greenhouse Effect. Students should complete the "Student Exploration Sheet" and assessment questions. Within this simulated region of land, daytime's rising temperature and the falling temperature at night can be measured, along with heat flow in and out of the system.

- **Activity 5: *Sea Ice Video***

Show the video of sea ice area from 1979 to 2017 at https://youtube/Vj1G9gqhkYA.

*Explore Learning is a free trial website. https://www.explorelearning.com

Brain-Compatible Strategies: *Which will you use to deliver content?*

__X__	Brainstorming/Discussion	__X__	Music/Rhythm/Rhyme/Rap
_____	Drawing/Artwork	__X__	Project/Problem-Based Learning
_____	Field Trips	_____	Reciprocal Teaching/Cooperative Learning
_____	Games	__X__	Roleplays/Drama/Pantomimes/Charades
_____	Graphic Organizers/Semantic Maps/Word Webs	__X__	Storytelling
_____	Humor	__X__	Technology
__X__	Manipulatives/Experiments/Labs/Models	_____	Visualization/Guided Imagery
__X__	Metaphors/Analogies/Similes	__X__	Visuals
_____	Mnemonic Devices	_____	Work Study/Apprenticeships
__X__	Movement	__X__	Writing/Journals

Source: Reprinted from Tate, 2020

Resource B: Graphic Organizers

KWL Chart

Name: _____

Date: _____

Topic: _____

KNOW	WONDER	LEARNED
Before reading, write what you think you already know about this topic.	Before or during your research, write down questions you might have about this topic.	After finishing your reading, write what you learned about this topic.

Source: Reprinted from Tate (2020b)

Vocabulary Word Web

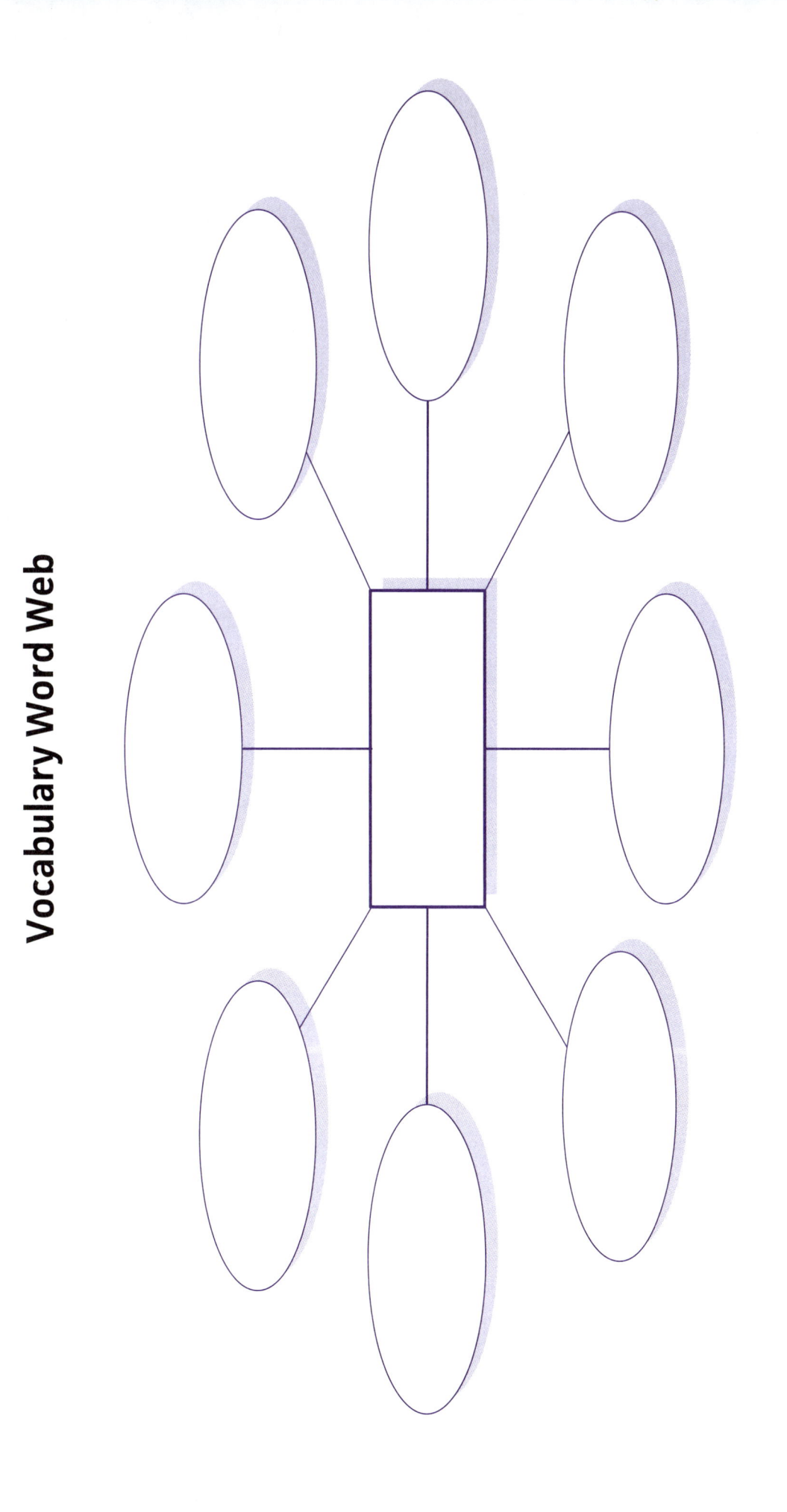

Frayer Model

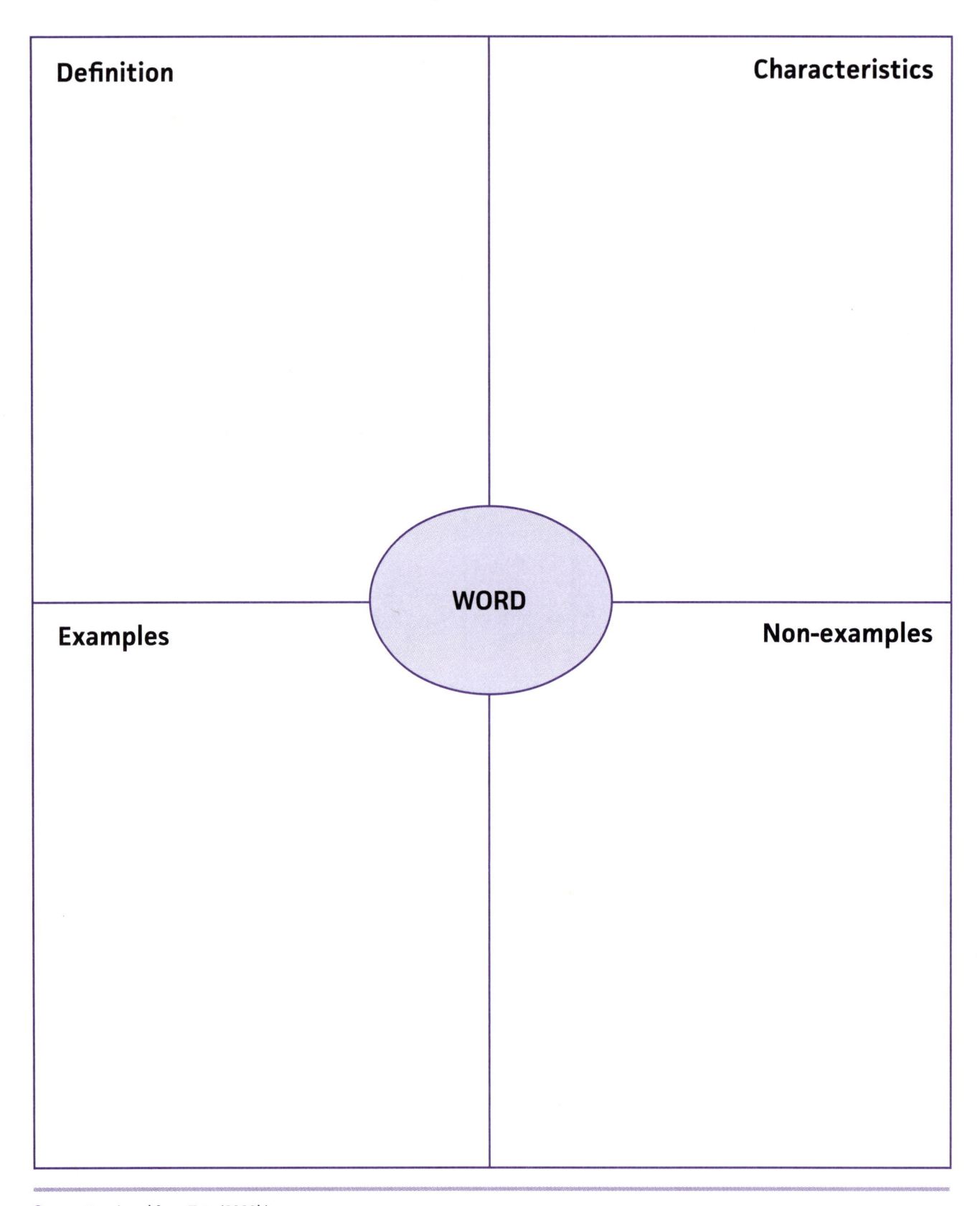

Definition	Characteristics

WORD

Examples	Non-examples

Source: Reprinted from Tate (2020b)

Story Map

Title _____

Setting

Characters _____ _____

_____ _____

_____ _____

Problem:

Event 1 _____

Event 2 _____

Event 3 _____

Event 4 _____

Solution

Resource B • Graphic Organizers

Main Idea Organizer

Main Idea

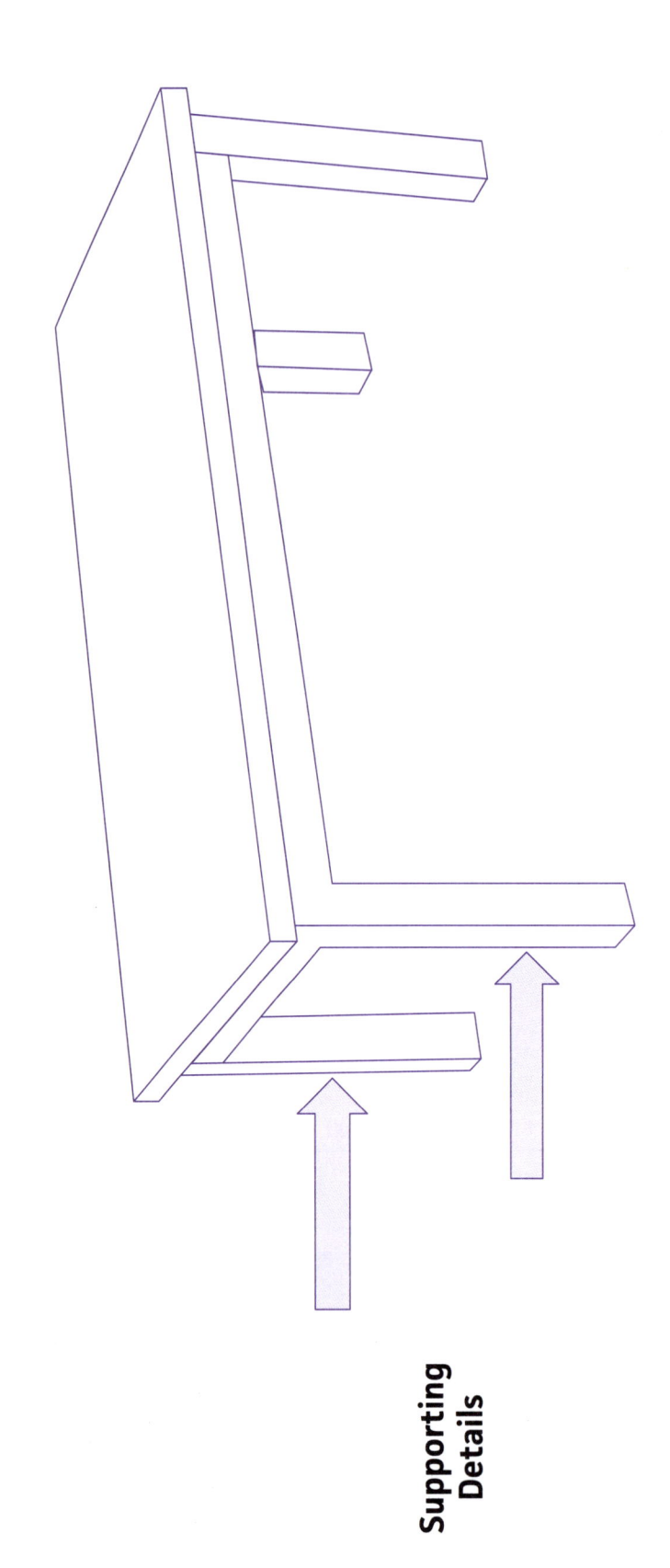

Supporting Details

Character Traits

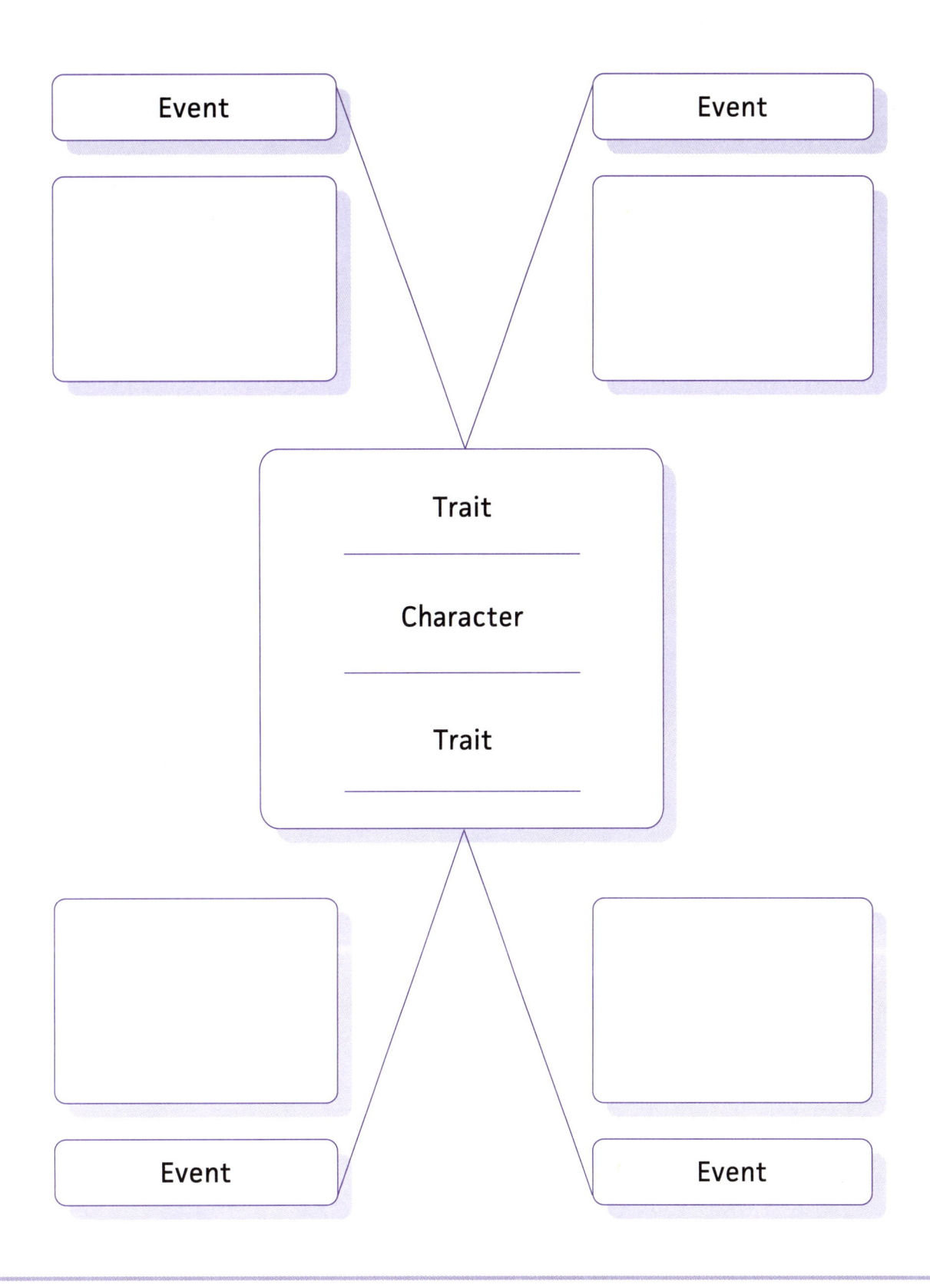

Event	Event

Trait
_____

Character
_____

Trait
_____

Event	Event

Source: Reprinted from Tate (2020a)

5 Ws and 1 H

Topic:

	Data
What	
Who	
When	
Where	
Why	
How	

Biography Research

Person's Name:

Picture:

Early Life:

Family Life:

Major Accomplishments:

3 Interesting Facts:

Source: Reprinted from Tate (2019)

Cause/Effect Organizer

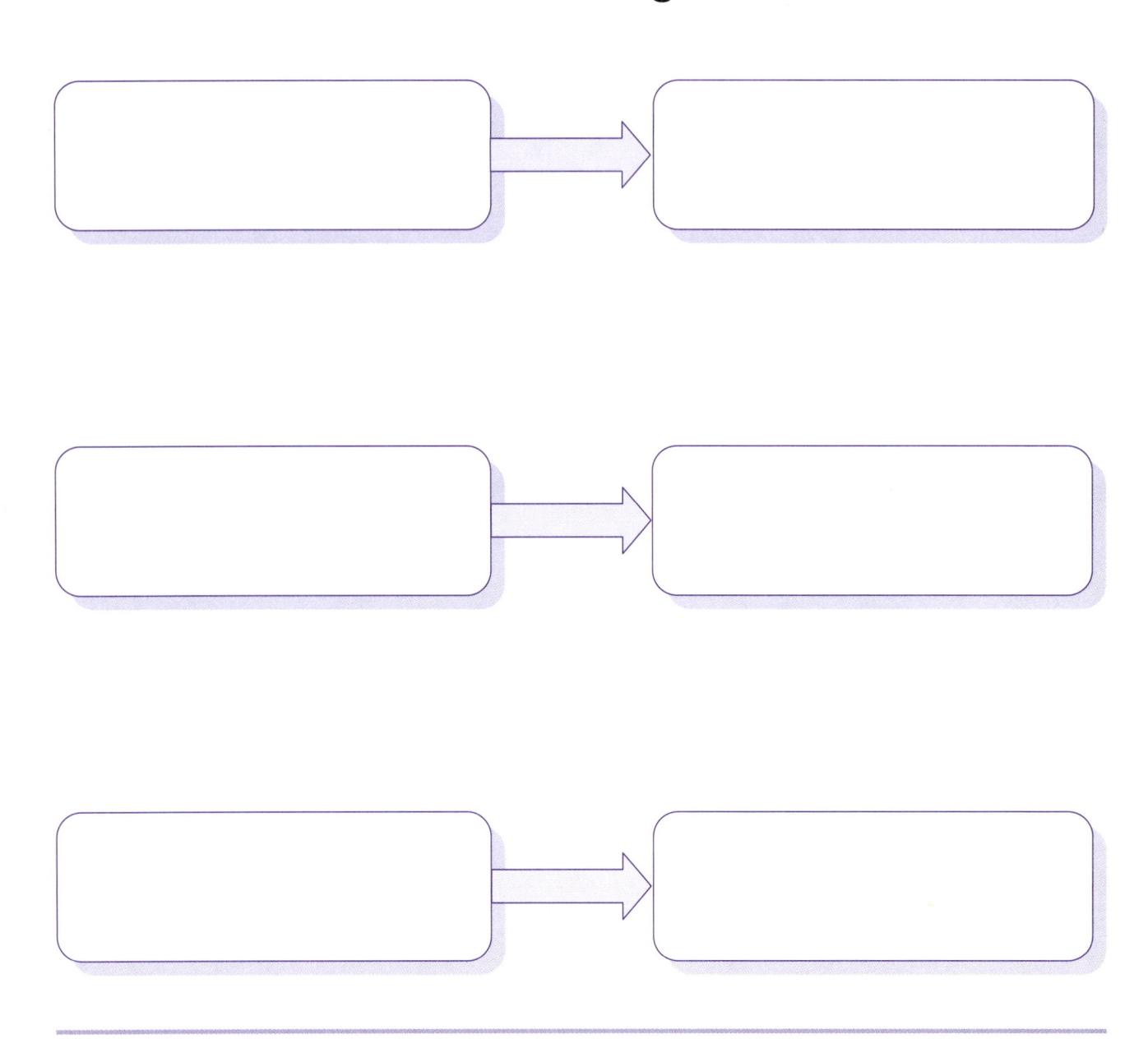

Comparison Organizer

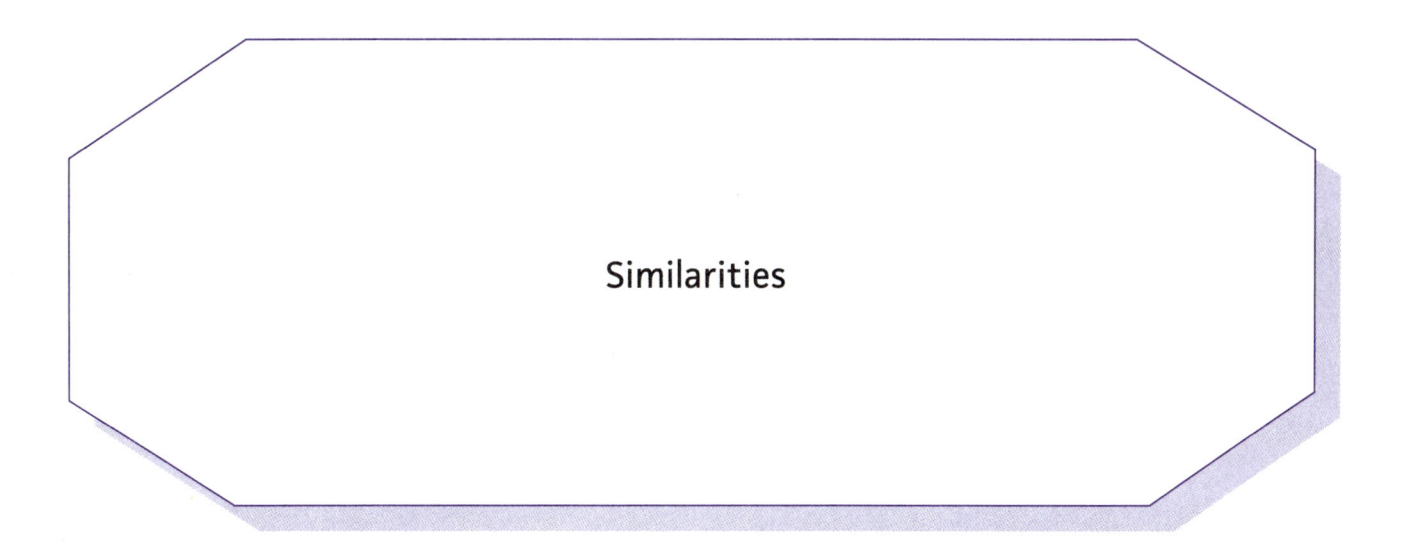

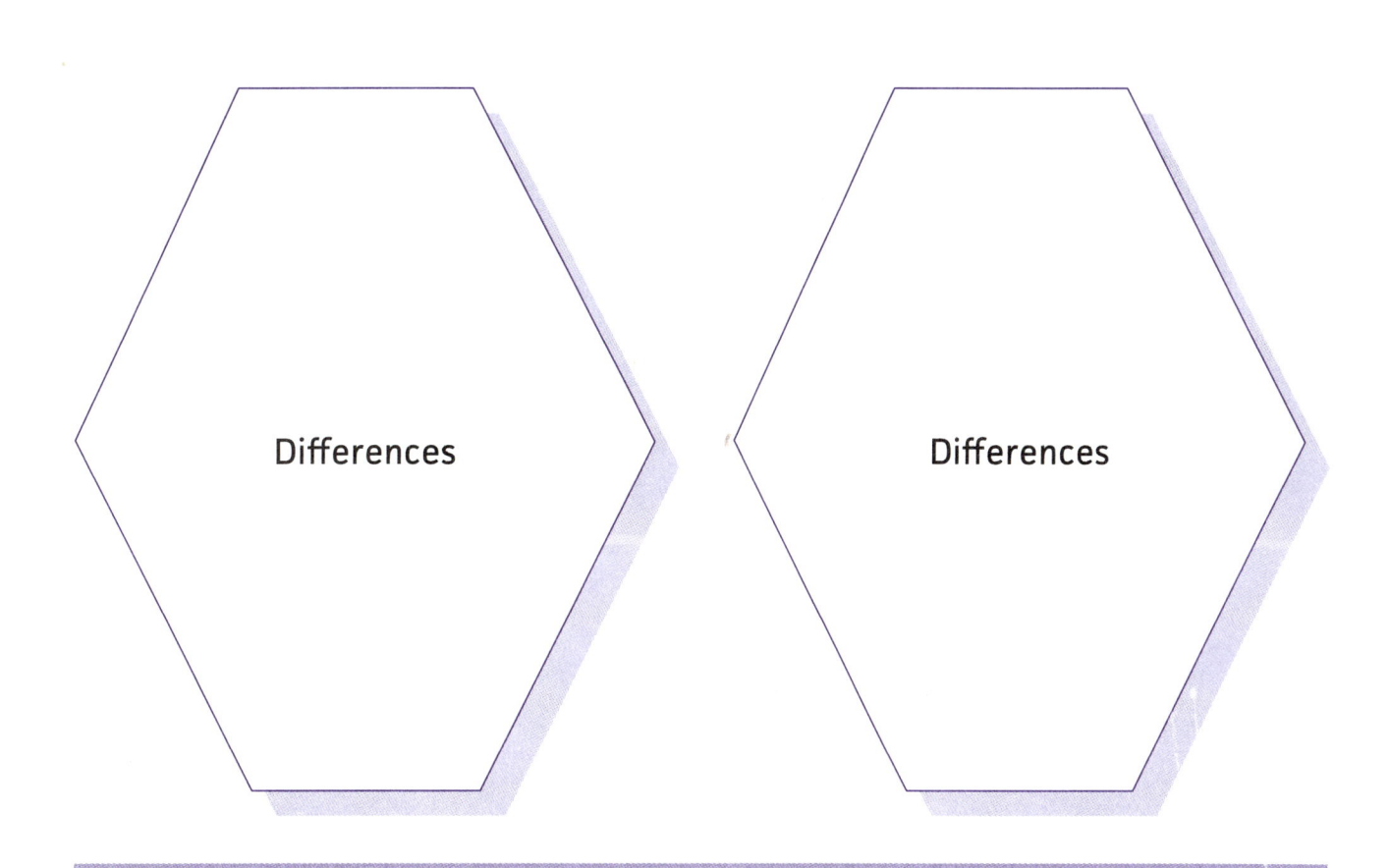

Similarities

Differences

Differences

Cycle Organizer

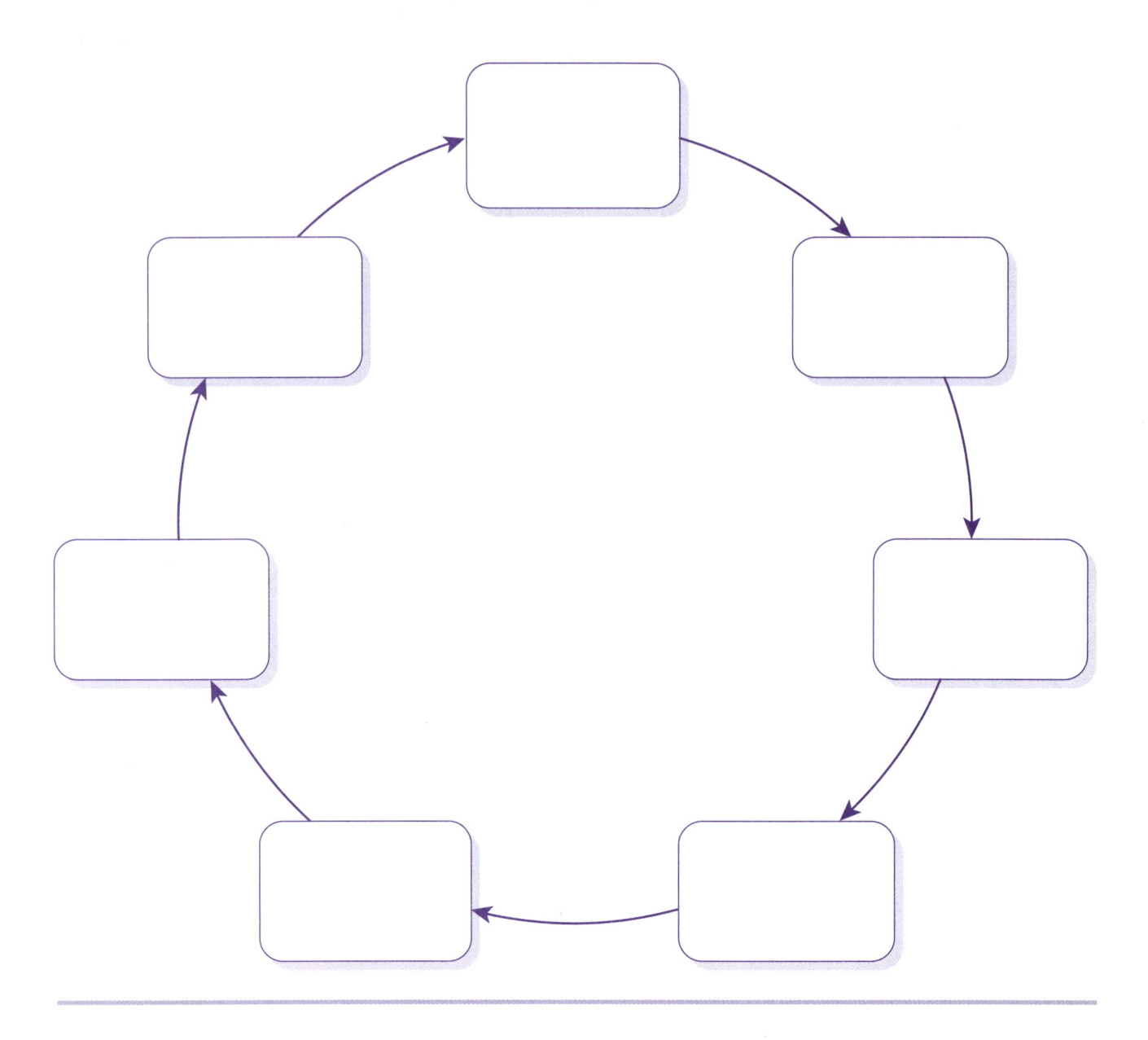

Sequence Organizer

- First
- Second
- Third
- Fourth
- Fifth
- Sixth

Topic Description Organizer

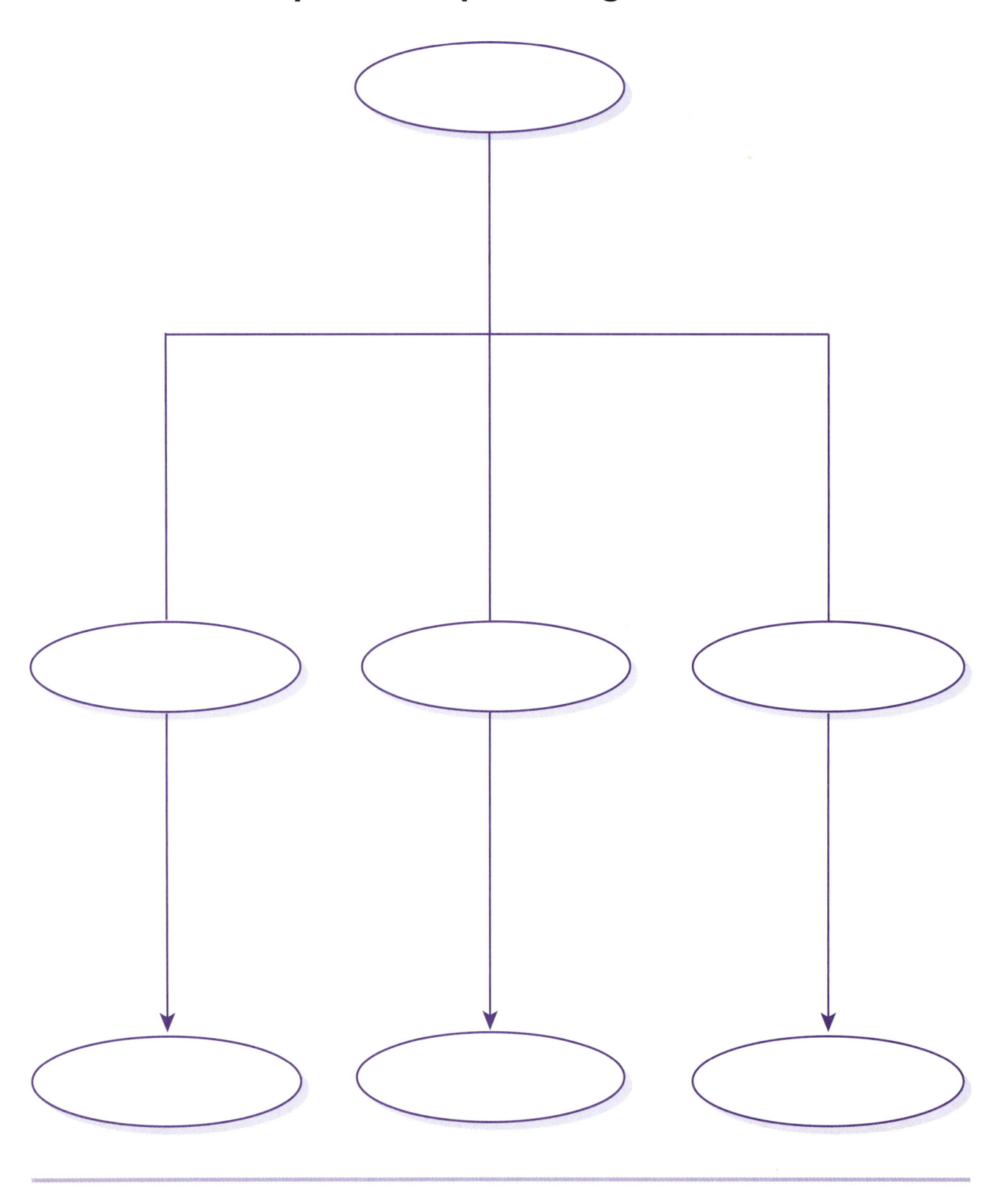

244 Engaging the Brain

Compare and Contrast Chart

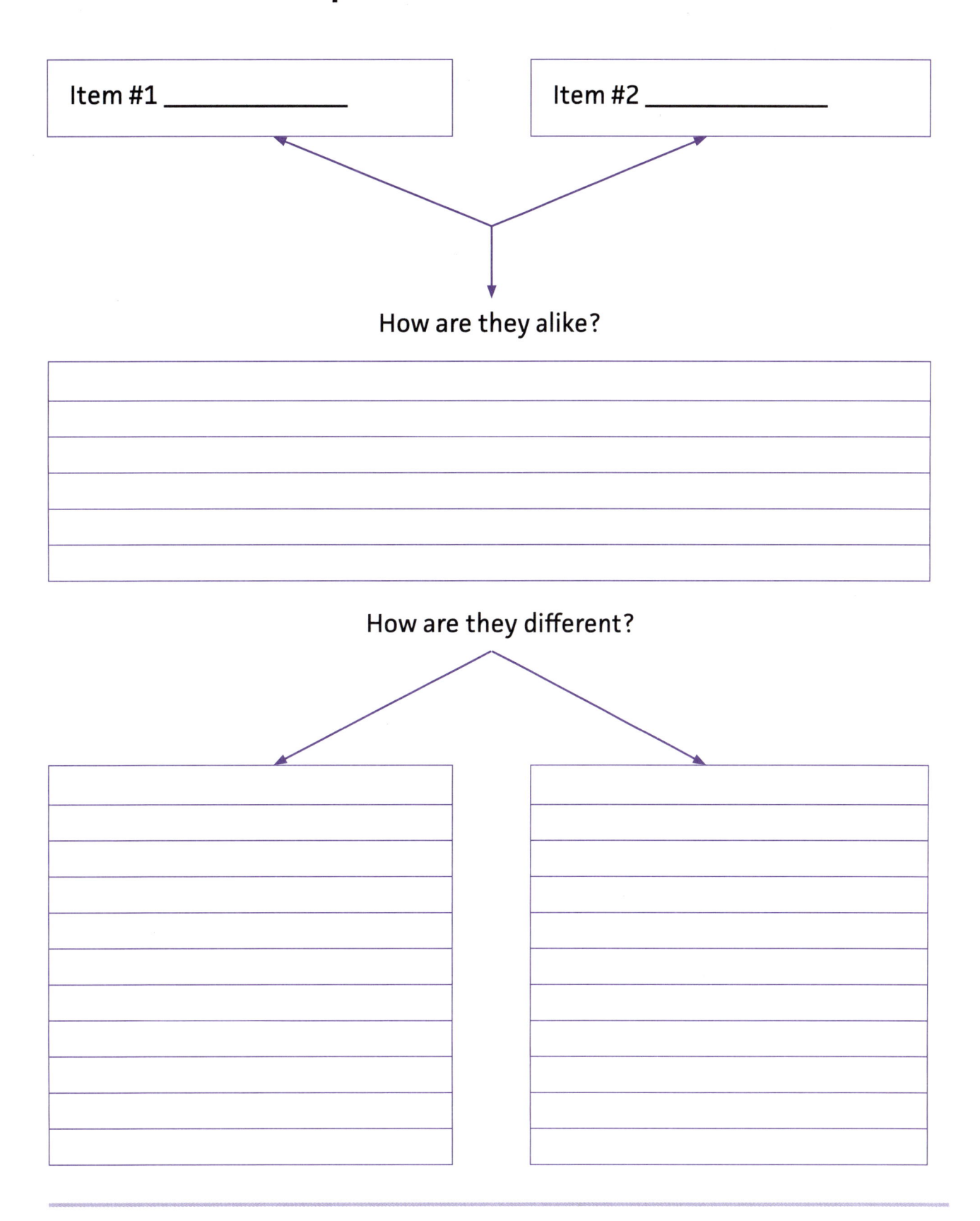

Item #1 _____

Item #2 _____

How are they alike?

How are they different?

Resource B • Graphic Organizers   245

Mind Map

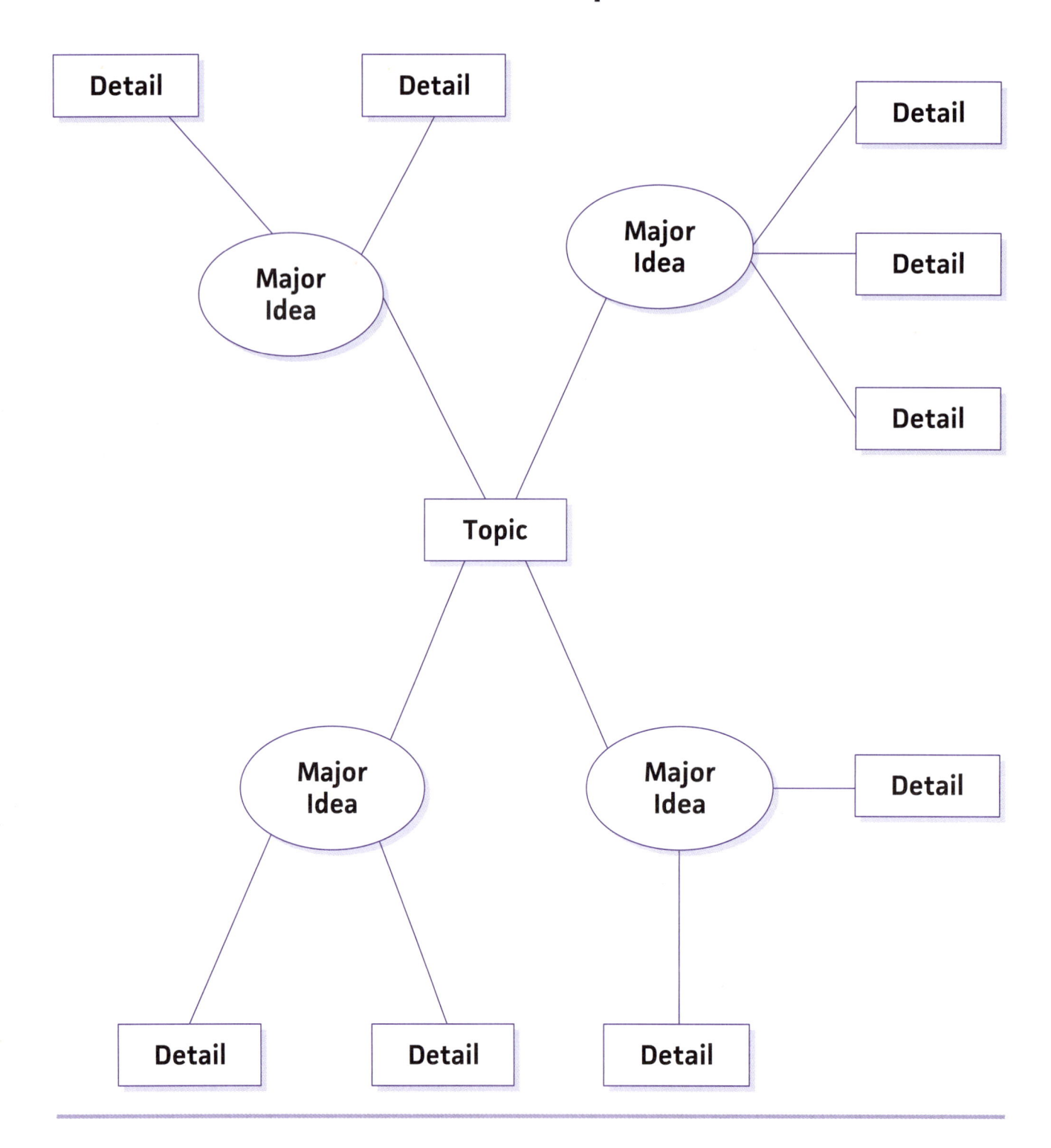

- Detail
- Detail
- Major Idea
- Major Idea
- Detail
- Detail
- Detail
- Topic
- Major Idea
- Major Idea
- Detail
- Detail
- Detail
- Detail

Bibliography

ACT Inc. (2009). *ACT national curriculum survey 2009*. www.act.org/research/policymakers/pdf/NationalCurriculumSurvey2009.pdf

Algozzine, B., Campbell, P., & Wang, J. A. (2009). *63 tactics for teaching diverse learners: Grades 6–12*. Corwin.

ALI Staff. (2023, August 11). *Bringing STEM to life: The role of hands-on learning*. Retrieved January 16, 2024, from https://blog.acceleratelearning.com/hands-on-learning

Allen, R. (2008). *Green light classrooms: Teaching techniques that accelerate learning*. Hawker Brownlow Education.

Allen, R., & Currie, J. (2012). *U-turn teaching: Strategies to accelerate learning and transform middle school achievement*. Corwin.

Allen, R., & Scozzi, N. (2012). *Sparking student synapses 9–12: Think critically and accelerate learning*. Corwin.

Allen, R., & Wood, W. W. (2013). *The rock 'n' roll classroom: Using music to manage mood, energy, and learning*. Corwin.

Anaya, E. M., Pisoni, D. B., & Kronenberger, W. G. (2017). Visual-spatial sequence learning and memory in trained musicians. *Psychology of Music, 45*(1), 5–21.

Anderson, M., Faverio, M., & Gottfried, J. (2023, December 11). *Teens, social media and technology 2023*. Pew Research. https://www.pewresearch.org/topic/internet-technology/user-demographics/age-generations-tech/teens-tech/

Angulo-Perkins, A., Aube, W., Peretz, I., Barrios, F. A., Armony, J. L., & Concha, L. (2014). Music listening engages specific cortical regions within the temporal lobes: Differences between musicians and non-musicians. *Cortex, 59*, 126–137.

Bailey, J. (2023, June 22). *Humor in the classroom: The serious benefits*. https://blogbrainpop.com/benefits-of-humor-in-the-classroom/

Balboa, N., & Glaser, R. D. (2019, May 16). *The neuroscience of conversations*. https://www.psychologytoday.com/us/blog/conversational-intelligence/201905/the-neuroscience-of-conversations

Basch, C. E. (2011). Physical activity and the achievement gap among urban minority youth. *Journal of School Health, 81*, 626–634.

Bellanca, J. A., Fogarty, R. J., & Pete, B. M. (2012). *How to teach thinking skills within the common core: 7 key student proficiencies of the new national standards*. Solution Tree Press.

Bender, W. N. (2005). *Differentiating math instruction: Strategies that work for K–8 classrooms!* Corwin.

Bender, W. N. (2012). *RTI in middle and high schools*. Solution Tree Press.

Bender, W. N. (2017). *20 strategies for increasing student engagement*. Learning Sciences International.

Bergee, M. J., & Weingarten, K. M. (2021). Multilevel models of the relationship between music achievement and reading and math achievement. *Journal of Research in Music Education, 68*(4), 398–418.

Berman, S. (2008). *Thinking strategies for science: Grades 5–12* (2nd ed.). Hawker Brownlow Education.

Berryman, S. E., & Bailey, T. R. (1992). *The double helix of education and the economy*. Institute on Education and the Economy, Columbia University Teachers College.

Better Help Editorial Team. (2023, December 20). *Visualization and how it can transform your life*. Retrieved January 22, 2024, from https://betterhelp.com>advice

Boris, V. (2017, December 20). *What makes storytelling so effective for learning?* https://www.harvardbusiness.org/what-makes-storytelling-so-effective-for-learning/

Boryga, A. (2023, April 28). *How to support and sustain rich classroom discussions*. https://www.edutopia.org/article/how-to-support-sustain-rich-classroom-conversations

Bouchrika, I. (2024, January 2). *The educational value of field trips in 2024: Advantages and disadvantages*. https://research.com/education/the-educational-value-of-field-trips

Boudreau, E. (2021, June 29). *Find fun: How to recognize video games that engage kids of all ages in learning*. https://www.gse.harvard.edu/ideas/usable-knowledge/21/06/find-fun

Bowman, J. D. (2018, June 20). *Making the most of visual aids*. https://www.edutopia.org/article/making-most-visual-aids

Brown, C. (2019, May 16). *12 pros and cons of technology in the classroom.* https:///www.hsredesign.org>blog.

Burgess, R. (2000). *Laughing lessons: 1492/3 ways to make teaching and learning fun.* Free Spirit

Bulla. D. (1996). *Think math! Interactive loops for groups.* Zephyr Press

Burke, K. (2009). *How to assess authentic learning* (5th ed.). Corwin.

Burkley, M. (2017, November 28). *Why metaphors are important.* https://www.psychologytoday.com/us/blog/the-social-thinker/201711/why-metaphors-are-important

Burns, M. (1996). *How to make the most of math manipulatives—A fresh look at getting students' heads and hands around math concepts.* https://marilynburnsmath.com/library/MathManipiulatives.pdf.

Busche, L. (2013). *Handsketching: Things you didn't know your doodles could accomplish.* https://www.smashingmagazine.com/2013/10/things-you-can-accomplish-with-hand-sketching-doodling/

Caine, R. N., Caine, G., McClintic, C., & Klimek, K. (2005). *12 brain/mind learning principles in action: The fieldbook for making connections, teaching, and the human brain.* Hawker Brownlow Education.

Catterall, J., Chapleau, R., & Iwanga, J. (1999, Fall). *Involvement in the arts and human development: Extending an analysis of general W and introducing the special cases of intense involvement in music and in theater arts* (CenteMonograph Series No. 11). Americas for the Arts.

Chanchal, M. (2023, May 1). *Why institutional learning matters: A neuroscience perspective.* https://www.linkedin.com/pulse/why-institutional-learning-matters-neuroscience-perspective-m-

Chatterjee, A. (2021, August 3). *Brains on metaphor. What is left to say?* https://www.psychologytoday.com/us/blog/brain-behavior-and-beauty/202108/brains-metaphor

Checkley, K. (1999). *Math in the early grades: Laying a foundation for later learning.* Association for Supervision and Curriculum Development.

Cherry, K. (2022, December 18). *How chunking pieces of information can improve memory.* https://www.verywellmind.com/chunking-how-can-this-technique-improve-your-memory-2794969

Coggins, D., Kravin, D., Coates, G. D., & Carrol, M. D. (2007). *English language learners in the Mathematics classroom.* Corwin.

Collier, C. (2010). *RTI for diverse learners: More than 200 instructional interventions.* Corwin.

Consilium Education. (2020). *Laughter: A contagion well worth catching* https://consiliumeducation.com/itm/2020/04/27/laughter/

Cooper, N., & Garner, B. K. (2012). *Developing a learning classroom: Moving beyond management through relationships, relevance, and rigor.* Corwin.

Costa, A. L. (2008). *The school as a home for the mind: Creating mindful curriculum, instruction, and dialogue* (2nd ed.). Hawker Brownlow Education.

Covey, S. R. (2020). *The 7 habits of highly effective people: Powerful lessons in personal change* (30th anniversary ed.). Covey Leadership Center.

Cox, J. (2020, September 16). *What is a graphic organizer and how to use if effectively.* https://www.teachhub.com/classroom-management/2020/09/what-is-a-graphic-organizer-and-how-to-use-it-effectively

Curlik, D. M., & Shors, T. J. (2013). Training your brain: Do mental and physical (MAP) training enhance cognition through the process of neurogenesis in the hippocampus? *Neuropharmacology, 64*(1), 506–14. doi: 10.1016/j.neuropharm.2012.07.027

Dalla, C., Bangasser, D., Edgecomb, C., & Shors, T. J. (2007). Neurogenesis and learning: Acquisition and asymptotic performance predict how many new cells survive in the hippocampus. *Neurobiology of Learning and Memory, 88*(1), 143–148.

Dean, C. B., Hubbell, E. R., Pitler, H., & Stone, B. J. (2012). *Classroom instruction that works: Research-based strategies for increasing student achievement* (2nd ed.). Association for Supervision and Curriculum Development.

Dewey, J. (1934). *Art as experience.* Minion Ballet.

Dewey, J. (1938). *Experience and education.* Macmillan.

Early Impact Learning. (n.d.). *17 benefits of storytelling (The full guide).* https://earlyimpactlearning.com/17-benefits-of-storytelling/

Ekwall, E. E., & Shanker, J. L. (1988). *Diagnosis and remediation of the disabled reader* (3rd ed.). Allyn and Bacon.

Ellis, B. (2023, May 8). *Proven classroom discussion strategies for deeper learning.* https://blog.tcea.ord/discussion-strategies/

Elmore, L. B. (2024). *Role play.* https://ablconnect.harvard.edu/role-play-research

Evagorou, M., Erduran, S., & Mäntylä, T. (2015). The role of visual representations in scientific practices: From conceptual understanding and knowledge generation to 'seeing' how science works. *International Journal of STEM Education, 2,* 1–13. https://stemeducationjournal.springeropen.com/articles/10.1186/s40594-015-0024-x

Explorable Places. (n.d.). *The benefits of field trips.* ExplorablePlaces.com

Feinstein, S. G. (2004). *Secrets of the teenage brain: Research-based strategies for reaching and teaching today's adolescents.* Corwin.

Feinstein, S. G. (2009). *Secrets of the teenage brain: Research-based strategies for reaching and teaching today's adolescents* (2nd ed.). Corwin.

Fernandes, M. A., Wammes, J. D., & Meade, M. E. (2018). *The surprisingly powerful influence of drawing on memory.* https://www.hsredesign.org

Fisher, M. (2013). *Digital learning strategies: How do I assign and assess 21st century work?* Association for Supervision and Curriculum Development.

Fogarty, R. J. (2009). *Brain-compatible classrooms* (3rd ed.). Hawker Brownlow Education.

Fraser, L. (2013). *The benefits of drawing.* https://www.thedrawingwebsite.com/2013/07/31/the-benefits-of-drawing-2/

Gagnon, R., & Nicoladis, E. (2020). Musicians show greater cross-modal integration, intermodal integration, and specialization in working memory than non-musicians. *Psychology of Music, 49*(4), 718–734. https://doi.org/10.1177/0305735619896088

Gardner, H. (1983). *Frames of mind: The theory of multiple intelligences.* Basic Books.

Gaviola, J. (2022, June 9). *10 science-backed benefits of drawing.* https://blog.skillsuccess.com/10-science-backed-benefits-of-drawing/

Gepp, K. (2022, March 31). *Memory and mnemonic devices.* https://psychcentral.com.lib/memory-and-mnemonic-devices

Glasser, W. (1999). *Choice theory: A new psychology of personal freedom.* HarperCollins.

Graham, S. (2020). An attributional theory of motivation. *Contemporary Educational Psychology, 61*, 101861.

Graham, S., & Perin, D. (2007). A meta-analysis of writing instruction for adolescent students. *Journal of Educational Psychology, 99*(3), 445–476.

Green, L. S., & Casale-Giannola, D. (2011). *40 active learning strategies for the block schedule.* Corwin.

Greene, J., & Kisida, B. (2013). *Research: School field trips give significant benefits.* https://news.uark.edu/articles/21975/research-school-field-trips-give-significant-benefits

Gregory, G. H., & Chapman, C. (2013). *Differentiated instructional strategies: One size doesn't fit all.* Corwin.

Gregory, G. H., & Herndon, L. E. (2010). *Differentiated instructional strategies for the block schedule.* Corwin.

Gregory, G. H., & Parry, T. (2006). *Designing brain-compatible learning* (3rd ed.). Corwin.

Hagoort, P. (2020). The meaning-making mechanism(s) behind the eyes and between the ears. *Philosophical Transactions of the Royal Society B. Biological Sciences, 375*(1791).

Hardy, C. (2022, November 23). *Combining movement and technology enhances learning.* https://edtechmagazine.com>article

Hattie, J. (2009). *Visible learning: A synthesis of over 800 meta-analyses relating to achievement.* Routledge.

Hattie, J. (2023). *Visible learning: The sequel: A synthesis of over 2,100 meta-analyses relating to achievement.* Routledge.

Hui, A. (2024, February 13). *Is there a "healthy" amount of time to spend on social media?* https://www.verywellhealth.com/social-media-timing-8573175

Indeed Editorial Team. (2022, June 24). *11 apprenticeship benefits.* https://www.indeed.com/career-advice/career-development/apprenticeships-benefits

Institute for the Advancement of Research in Education (IARE). (2003). *Graphic organizers: A review of scientifically based research.* Author.

Jacobs, M. (2022, June 3). *A pandemic practice to keep in science and math classes.* https://www.edutopia.org/article/pandemic-practice-keep-science-and-math-classes

Jandhyala, D. (2017, December 8). *Visual learning: 6 reasons why visuals are the most powerful aspect of elearning.* https://elearningindustry.com/visual-learning-6-reasons-visuals-powerful-aspect-elearning

Jensen, E. (1995). *Brain-based learning & teaching.* The Brain Store.

Jensen, E. (2001). *Arts with the brain in mind.* Association for Supervision and Curriculum Development.

Jensen, E. (2005). *Top tunes for teaching: 977 song titles and practical tools for choosing the right music every time.* Corwin.

Jensen, E. (2007). *Brain-compatible strategies* (2nd ed.). Hawker Brownlow Education.

Jensen, E. (2008). *Brain-based learning: The new paradigm of teaching.* Corwin.

Jensen, E. (2009). *Fierce teaching: Purpose, passion, and what matters most.* Corwin.

Jensen, E. (2022). *Teaching with poverty and equity in mind.* Association of Supervisors and Curriculum Directors.

Jensen, E., & Nickelsen, L. (2008). *Deeper learning: 7 powerful strategies for in-depth and longer-lasting learning.* Hawker Brownlow Education.

Johnson, D. W., Johnson, R. T., & Holubec, E. J. (1994). *The new circles of learning: Cooperation in the classroom and school.* Association for Supervision and Curriculum Development.

Karten, J. J. (2009). *Inclusion strategies that work for adolescent learners.* Corwin

Kavanagh, S. S., & Bernhard, T. (2023, January 9). *Managing tech integration in your classroom.* https://www.edutopia.org/article/managing-tech-integration-classroom

Kelly, M. (2019, September 14). Field trips: Pros and cons. *Thought Co.*

Kelly, M. (2020, March 14). *Mnemonic devices for students: Memory tools and strategies improve information retention.* https://www.thoughtco.com/memonic-devices-tools-7755

Kialo Edu. (2023, June 21). *The benefits of class discussion in the ESL classroom.* https://blog.kialo-edu.com/debate-argumentation/the-benefits-of-discussions-in-the-esl-classroom/

Konrad, M., Joseph, L. M., & Itoi, M. (2011, January). Using guided notes to enhance instruction for all students. *Intervention in School and Clinic, 46*(3), 131–140.

Kouyoumdjian, H. (2012). *Learning through visuals.* https://www.psychologytoday.com/us/blog/get-psyched/201207/learning-through-visuals

Krepel, W. J., & Duvall, C. R. (1981). *Field trips: A guide for planning and conducting educational experiences.* National Education Association.

Lane, S. (2023, February 10). *Importance of educational games for students.* https://eduedify.com/importance-of-educational-games-for-students/

Linkedin. (2023, November 23). *How can you use visualization to enhance your learning?* https://www.linkedin.com.advice

Lohr, J. (2015, May 1). *Can visualizing your body doing something help you learn it better?* https://www.scientificamerican.com

Longcamp, M., Boucard, C., Gilhodes, J. C., Anton, J. L., Roth, M., Nazarian, B., & Velay, J. L. (2008). Learning through hand-or typewriting influences visual recognition of new graphic shapes: Behavioral and functional imaging evidence. *Journal of Cognitive Neuroscience, 20*(5), 802–815.

Ma, H. H. (2009). The effect size of variables associated with creativity. *Creativity Research Journal, 21*(1), 30–42.

Manno, B. V. (2023, November 15. *Apprenticeships are the new learning campus.* https://fordhaminstitute.org/national/commentary/apprenticeships-are-new-learning-campus

Manohar, S. (2020, July). *Laughter clubs continue to be popular in India despite their being nothing to laugh about.* www.vice.com/en/article/xg84z3/laughter-clubs-comedy-india-pandemic

Maria. (2018, March 22). *Why learning how to draw is so important for youngsters.* https://superprof.com

Markowitz, K., & Jensen, E. (2007). *The great memory book.* Hawker Brownlow Education.

Marlett, D. (2019). *Facilitating learning with a graphic organizer instructional strategy.* https://learningfocused.com/graphic-organizer-instructional-strategy/

Marzano, R. J. (2007). *The art and science of teaching.* Association for Supervision and Curriculum Development.

Mayo Clinic Press Editors. (2023, October 16). *The intersection of art and health: How art can help promote well-being.* https://mcpress.mayoclinic.org/living-well/the-intersection-of-art-and-health-how-art-can-help-promote-well-being/

Mayo Clinic Staff. (2019, April 5). *Stress relief from laughter? It's no joke.* www.mayoclinic.org/healthy-lifestyle/stress-management/in-depth/stress-relief/art-20044456

McLaughlin, M., & Overturf, B. J. (2013). *The common core: Teaching K–5 students to meet the reading standards.* International Reading Association.

Melber, L. M., & Hunter, A. (2010). *Integrating language arts and social studies: 25 strategies for K–8 inquiry-based learning.* Sage.

Metsala, J. L., & Glynn, S. (1996). Teaching with analogies: Building on the science textbook. *The Reading Teacher, 49,* 490–492.

Ms. Miriam. (2021, August 26). *The importance of hands-on learning.* https://www.thethinkingkid.org>post

Mueller, P. A., & Oppenheimer, D. M. (2014). The pen is mightier than the keyboard: Advantages of longhand over laptop notetaking. *Psychological Science, 25,* 1159–1168.

National Council for the Social Studies. (2010). *National curriculum standards for social studies: A framework for teaching, learning, and assessment.*

National Science Teachers Association (NSTA). (2006). Picturing to learn makes science visual. *NSTA Reports, 18*(2), 20.

Nguyen, H. P. (2021, March 26). *How to use gameplay to enhance classroom learning.* https://www.edutopia.org/article/how-use-gameplay-enhance-classroom-learning

Okuha. (2023, April 19). *The importance of drawing— benefits explained.* https://okuha.com/why-drawing-is-important/

Palincsar, A. S., & Brown, A. L. (1984). Reciprocal teaching in comprehension-fostering comprehension-monitoring activities. *Cognition and Instruction, 1*(2), 117–175.

Pantuosco-Hensch, L. (2019, September 9). *Making movement a part of your classroom culture.* Retrieved January 28, 2024, from https://nea.org>nea-today

Park, M. H., Park, E. -J., Choi, J., Chai, S., Lee, J. -H., Lee, C., & Kim, D. -J. (2011). Preliminary study of internet addiction and cognitive function in adolescents based on IQ tests. *Psychiatry Research, 190,* 275–281.

Perez, K. (2008). *More than 100 brain-friendly tools and strategies for literacy instruction.* Corwin.

Pontifex, M. B., Gwizdala, K. L., Parks, A. C., Pfeiffer, K. A., & Fenn, K. M. (2016). The association between physical activity during the day and long-term stability. *Scientific Reports, 6,* 38148.

Popova, M. (2015, February 8). *The magic of metaphor: What children's minds reveal about the evolution of the imagination.* https://twitter.com/.../570760923763351

Posamentier, A. S., & Jaye, D. (2006). *What successful math teachers do, grades 6–12: 79 research-based strategies for the standards-based classroom.* Corwin.

Prensky, M. (2009). H. Sapiens digital: From digital immigrants and digital natives to digital wisdom. *Innovate: Journal of Online Education, 5*(3). https://nsuworks.nova.edu/cgi/viewcontent.cgi?article=1020&context=innovate

Previte, A. (2019, October 7). *The amazing benefits of laughter.* https://resilienteducator.com/classroom-resources/benefits-of-laughter/

Prystay, C. (2004, December 13). As math skills slip, U.S. schools seek answers from Asia. *The Wall Street Journal,* pp. A1–A8.

Renken, E. (2020, April 11). *How stories connect and persuade us: Unleashing the brain power of narrative.* https://www/npr.org/sections/health-shots/2020/04/11/815573198/

Rios, J. A., Guangming, L., & Bacall, A. (2020, January 21). *Identifying critical 21st century skills for workplace success: A content analysis of job advertisements.* https://journals.sagepub.com>doi

Rix, K. (2022, December 27). *The benefits of career and technical education programs for high-schoolers.* https://www.usnews.com/education/k12/articles/the-benefits-of-career-and-technical-education-programs-for-high-schoolers

Robinson, L., Smith, M., Segal, J., & Shubin, J. (2021). *The benefits of play for adults.* www.helpguide.org/articles/mental-health/benefits-of-play-for-adults.htm#

Schlaug, G. (2015). Musicians and music making as a model for the study of brain plasticity. *Progress in Brain Research, 217,* 270–280.

ScienceDaily. (2019, April 2). *How the brain finds meaning in metaphor.* Retrieved January 23, 2024, from https://www.sciencedaily.com>201...

Science World. (2016, December 30). *Metaphors and your brain.* https://www.scienceworld.ca>stories

Scott, D., & Marzano, R. J. (2014). *Awaken the learner: Finding the source of effective education.* Marzano Research Laboratory.

Sebesta, L. M., & Martin, S. R. M. (2004). Fractions: Building a foundation with concrete manipulatives. *Illinois Schools Journal, 83*(2), 3–23.

Secretary's Commission on Achieving Necessary Skills (SCANS). (1991). *What work requires of schools: A SCANS report for America 2000.* U.S. Department of Labor.

Sheriff, K. A., & Boon, R. T. (2014). Effects of computer-based graphic organizers to solve one-step word problems for middle school students with mild intellectual disability: A preliminary study. *Research in Developmental Disabilities, 35*(8), 1828–1837.

Singh, M. (2022, October 7). *Benefits of using manipulatives in math.* https://numberdyslexia.com/benefits-of-using-manipulatives-in-math/

Sousa, D. A. (2006). *How the brain learns* (3rd ed.). Corwin.

Sousa, D. A. (2007). *How the special needs brain learns* (2nd ed.). Corwin.

Sousa, D. A. (2011). *How the brain learns* (4th ed.). Corwin.

Sousa, D. A. (2012). *Brainwork: The neuroscience behind how we lead others.* Triple Nickel Press.

Sousa, D. A. (2016). *How the special needs brain learns* (3rd ed.). Corwin.

Sousa, D. A. (2017). *How the brain learns* (5th ed.). Corwin.

Sousa, D. A. (2022). *How the brain learns* (6th ed.). Corwin.

Sousa, D. A., & Pilecki, T. (2013). *From STEM to STEAM: Using brain-compatible strategies to integrate the arts.* Corwin.

Sousa, D. A., & Tomlinson, C. A. (2011). *Differentiation and the brain: How neuro-science supports the learner-friendly classroom.* Solution Tree Press.

Sprenger, M. (2007a). *Becoming a "wiz" at brain-based teaching: How to make every year your best year* (2nd ed.). Corwin.

Sprenger, M. (2007b). *Memory 101 for educators.* Corwin.

Sprenger, M. (2008). *The developing brain: Birth to age eight.* Corwin.

Sprenger, M. (2010). *Brain-based teaching in the digital age.* Association for Supervision and Curriculum Development.

Stauffer, R.G. (1975). *Directing the direct reading-thinking process.* Harper & Row.

Sternberg, R. J., & Grigorenko, E. L. (2000). *Teaching for successful intelligence: To increase student learning and achievement.* Skylight.

Strong, R. W., Silver, H. F., Perini, M. J., & Tuculescu, G. M. (2002). *Reading for academic success: Powerful strategies for struggling, average, and advanced readers, grades 7–12.* Corwin.

Summey, D. C. (2013). *Developing digital literacies: A framework for professional learning.* Corwin.

Suraj, S. (2018, December 14). *Is mnemonics for long-term memory or short-term memory? If I use mnemonics to study something, will I be able to retain it for many years?* https://www.quora.com>is-mnemo...

Tate, M. L. (2009). *Mathematics worksheets don't grow dendrites: 20 numeracy strategies that engage the brain.* Corwin.

Tate, M. L. (2012). *Social studies worksheets don't grow dendrites: 20 instructional strategies that engage the brain.* Corwin.

Tate, M. L. (2014a). *Reading and language arts worksheets don't grow dendrites: 20 literacy strategies that engage the brain.* Corwin.

Tate, M. L. (2014b). *Shouting won't grow dendrites: 20 techniques to detour around the danger zones* (2nd ed.). Corwin.

Tate, M. L. (2020a). *100 brain-friendly lessons for unforgettable teaching and learning (K-8).* Corwin.

Tate, M. L. (2020b). *100 brain-friendly lessons for unforgettable teaching and learning (9-12).* Corwin.

Tate, M. L. (2022). *Healthy teachers, happy classrooms.* Solution Tree Press.

Tate, M. L., & Phillips, W. G. (2011). *Science worksheets don't grow dendrites: 20 instructional strategies that engage the brain.* Corwin.

Taylor, A. C., & Dewhurst, S. A. (2017). Investigating the influence of music training on verbal memory. *Psychology of Music, 45*(6), 814–820.

Terada, Y. (2019, March 14). *The science of drawing and memory.* Retrieved January 17, 2024, from https://www.edutopia.org/article/science-drawing-and-memory

Tileston, D. W. (2011). *Closing the RTI gap: Why poverty and culture count.* Solution Tree Press.

Tileston, D. W., & Darling, S. K. (2009). *Why culture counts: Teaching children of poverty.* Solution Tree Press.

Turner, L. (2022, April 2). *The benefits of visual supports in the classroom.* https://www.twinkl.com/blog/the-benefits-of-visual-supports-in-the-classroom

Udvari-Solner, A., & Kluth, P. (2008). *Joyful learning: Active and collaborative learning in inclusive classrooms.* Corwin.

University of Arkansas. (2014, October 16). *Major benefits for students who attend live theater.* https://www.sciencedaily.com/releases/2014/10/141016165953.htm#google_vignette

Valid Education. (2022, December 19). *What is hands-on learning?* https://validedu.com/hands-on-learning/

Walsh, J. A., & Sattes, B. A. (2005). *Quality questioning: Research-based practice to engage every learner.* Corwin.

Warren, E. (2023). *Why visualization skills offer key benefits for students.* https://goodsensorylearning.com/blogs/news/student-visualization-skills

Wiggins, G., & McTighe, J. (2008). Put understanding first. *Educational Leadership, 65*(19), 36–41.

Williams, M. (2019, May 30). *Why you should use role-playing in the classroom.* Retrieved January 24, 2024, from https://www.classcraft.com>blog

Willis, J. (2006). *Research-based strategies to ignite student learning: Insights from a neurologist and classroom teacher.* Association for Supervision and Curriculum Development.

Willlis, J. (2007). *Brain-friendly strategies for the inclusion classroom.* Association for Supervision and Curriculum Development.

Willis, J. (2021, November 5). *How cooperative learning can benefit students this year.* https://www.edutopia.org/article/how-cooperative-learning-can-benefit-students-year

Wolfe, P., & Nevills, P. (2004). *Building the reading brain, PreK–3.* Corwin.

Wonacott, M. E. (1993). *Apprenticeship and the future of the workplace.* http://www.ericdigests.org/1992-3/future.htm

Yussif. (2023, March 24). *14 benefits of using humor in the classroom.* https://classroommanagementexpert.com/blog/14-benefits-of-using-humor-in-the-classroom/

Zhou, Y., Lin, F. -C., Du, Y. -S., Qin, L. -D., Zhao, Z. -M., Xu, J. -R., & Lei, H. (2011). Gray matter abnormalities in internet addiction: A voxel-based morphometry study. *European Journal of Radiology, 79,* 92–95.

Index

100 Brain-Friendly Lessons for Unforgettable Teaching and Learning (Tate), 165
3-Ps (page, paragraph, passing), 148
7 Habits of Highly Effective People, The (Covey), 217

Acronyms, 101–105
Acrostics, 101–106
Affirmations, 77
Alphabet books, 165, 210
Appointment clocks, 112–113
Aristotle, 36
Artists' greatest hits, 125
Assessments, 23, 172, 175–176, 214–15
Attention
   deficit disorder, 28
   enhancing, 121, 182, 189, 206
   paying, 2, 10, 12, 28, 81, 122, 145, 147, 161
   ways to gain/maintain, 72, 134, 145, 163, 174, 176, 184, 191, 215–18

Bingo, 49
Bloom's taxonomy, 21
Body spell, 156
Brain-derived neurotrophic factor (BDNF), 111

Candy Land, 45
Caracas, Gloria, 164
Career day, 200
Cartoons, 75–77
Cause and effect, 165
Challenge, 12, 18, 44, 134, 172, 215
Challenger space shuttle, 4, 217
Character traits, 61
Charades, 47, 155
Chinese proverb, 189
Chunking, 12–13, 120, 210, 214, 218
Cinquain, 127
Circumference conga, 115
Class clowns, 71, 74
Classical music, 122, 124
Clocks, 86, 112
Close reading, 20

Colonies story, 164
Competencies, 171, 199–200
"Conga" (Estefan), 115
Continent story, 163
Controversial issues, 24, 156
Cycle organizer, 64

Dendrites, 91
   growers, 6–8, 91
   growing, 11, 17, 55, 77, 165, 183, 202
Digital differentiation, 176
Directed Reading Thinking Activity (DR-TA), 19
Disc jockey, 126
DOVE guidelines, 19
Drill partner, 148

Emotions, 3–4, 18, 35, 154, 164, 174, 182, 209, 211, 215, 217–218
   connections, 4, 161–162
   developing, 28, 44, 121, 154
Engage the Brain (Tate), 67
Engage the Brain Games (Tate), 51
Estefan, Gloria, 115, 125
Ethnography, 39
Expectations, 10–11, 199, 214

Families, 32, 62, 114, 166, 177
   in class, 23, 146
Feedback, 18, 24, 44, 147, 148, 155, 172, 210
   positive, 77
Figurative language, 165
Foundational skills, 199–200
Four square writing, 207–208
Fractions, 31, 75, 84, 193
   cooking and, 136
   music and, 96, 121

Gardens, 38
Geometry, 38, 121, 133, 158, 173, 210

Have You Read Any Math Lately?, 165
Hippocampus, 110, 215

253

Hunter, Alyce, 36, 39, 134, 82
Hunter, Madeline, 214, 218
"Hustle, The" (McCoy), 116

I'm as Quick as a Cricket (Wood), 93
Instructional activities
    drawing and artwork, 27–28
    field trips, 37–39
    games, 45–51
    graphic organizers, semantic maps, and word webs, 57–67
    humor, 73–77
    manipulatives, experiments, labs, and models, 83–88
    metaphors, analogies, and similes, 93–97
    mnemonic devices, 103–106
    movement, 111–116
    music, rhythm, rhyme and rap, 122–127
    project-based and problem-based instruction, 135–139
    reciprocal teaching and cooperative learning, 145–149
    roleplays, drama, pantomimes, and charades, 155–158
    storytelling, 163–166
    technology, 173–177
    visualization and guided imagery, 183–186
    visuals, 191–193
    work study and apprenticeships, 199–202
    writing and journals, 207–211

Jeopardy, 47, 51
Jigsaw activity, 149
Jokes, 71, 73–76

Kinesthetic learning modality. *See* Learning modalities

Laughing clubs, 71, 73
Learning modalities, 6, 219
Lecturettes, 192, 208
Lesson objectives, 213
Lessons, relevant, 10
Logarithms, 95
Loop game, 48

Main idea with supporting details (table with legs), 60
MATH acronyms, 104
Math Curse (Scieszka), 165
Mathematics Worksheets Don't Grow Dendrites (Tate), 8, 165
McAuliffe, Christa, 4, 217. *See also Challenger* space shuttle

McCoy, Van, 116
Medicine
    laughter as, 71
    and visualization, 181
Melber, Leah M., 36, 39, 134, 182
Memory pathways, 2–3, 174
Momentum shift, 12, 185
Moore, Connie, 104
Multiple intelligences, 6, 13–14, 146
Muscle memory, 55, 109, 153, 158
Museums, 36, 38
My Stuff, Your Stuff, 145
My Turn, Your Turn, 145

Narrative chaining, 166
Needs, student, 145, 148, 157, 200, 215–216, 219
New age music, 122, 124
Nonlinguistic representation, 28, 57
Novelty, 145, 184, 216–217
Number line hustle, 116

Partner reading, 148
Password, 49, 51
Pearl Harbor, 35
Peer-to-peer tutoring, 144
Phillips, Warren, 86, 123, 126, 130, 131, 155, 164, 173, 201, 217
Physical education, 43, 51, 71, 185
Piano music, 3, 4, 109, 120, 124–125
Pictionary, 29, 50
PIE (persuade, inform, express, entertain), 209
Planetarium, 38
Point of view, 87, 156, 165
Positive energy stick, 77
Positive environment, 9
Positive feedback, 77
PowerPoint, 137, 174, 192
Price Is Right, The, 51, 109, 116
Procedural memory, 3, 4, 11, 55, 109, 111, 153, 156, 158, 174, 217. *See also* Muscle memory
Process observer, 147–48

Quick Writes, 210

Reader's Theater, 157
Reading, partner, 148
Reading and Language Arts Worksheets Don't Grow Dendrites (Tate), 8
Recess, 43
Richter Scale, 95
Riddles, 1, 71, 73–76
    riddle box, 75
Rock 'n' Roll Classroom, The (Allen & Wood), 124

SCANS Report, 171, 199
Scavenger hunt, 38, 174
School-to-Work Opportunities Act (1994), 202
Science Worksheets Don't Grow Dendrites (Tate), 8, 202
Seasonal appointment clock, 112–113
Sentence starters, 23, 139
Sequence of events, 165
Sequence organizer, 65
Service-learning project, 201
Seven, series of, 12, 218
Shouting Won't Grow Dendrites (Tate), 77
Singapore, teaching in, 28, 43, 183, 190
Sir Cumference (Neuschwander), 165
SMILE mnemonic, 73
Social skills, 144, 147–148, 172
Social Studies Worksheets Don't Grow Dendrites (Tate), 8
Socrates, 36
Solar system, 38, 83, 87
SOLO pyramid, 22
Sort and Report, 88
Speech, parts of, 101, 165, 192, 193
Sponge activity, 135
Sports, 11, 12, 37, 38, 185,
    and visualization, 181
"Story of the Algebraic Equation, The", 166–167
Story stool, 163
Stress, 12, 28, 44, 72, 73, 119, 214, 215
Survey technique SQ3R, 191
SWITCH game, 45–46
Synthesis, 127

Table with legs, 60
Tactile learning modality. *See* Learning modalities
Talent show, 127
Taxonomy, Bloom's, 21
T-charts, 147
TEGO, 122
Think, pair, share technique, 24, 149
Thinking proficiencies, 23
Tired words, 209
Top Tunes for Teaching (Jensen), 124
TWA (Teaching with Analogies), 95
Typing, 205–206

U.S.S. Arizona Memorial, 35

VAKT (visual, auditory, kinesthetic, tactile), 13–14, 219
Venn diagrams, 56–57, 97
Video games, 9, 12, 181, 189
Virtual field trips, 9, 35–36, 39
Visual learning modality. *See* VAKT

Warren, Erica, 181, 182
Wheel of Fortune, 47, 51
Who Am I? game, 49
Who Wants to Be a Millionaire?, 50
Willingham, Simone, 126, 129, 165
Wood, Audrey, 93
Word wall, 111, 193
Worksheets Don't Grow Dendrites (Tate), 8, 165, 183, 202
Writing process, 56, 207, 209–210

Helping educators make the greatest impact

CORWIN HAS ONE MISSION: to enhance education through intentional professional learning.

We build long-term relationships with our authors, educators, clients, and associations who partner with us to develop and continuously improve the best evidence-based practices that establish and support lifelong learning.